the **essential**
GUIDE TO
RECRUITMENT

the *essential*
GUIDE TO
RECRUITMENT

How to conduct great interviews and select the best employees

Margaret Dale

KOGAN
PAGE

London and Philadelphia

Publisher's note

Every possible effort has been made to ensure that the information contained in this book is accurate at the time of going to press, and the publishers and author cannot accept responsibility for any errors or omissions, however caused. No responsibility for loss or damage occasioned to any person acting, or refraining from action, as a result of the material in this publication can be accepted by the editor, the publisher or the author.

First published in Great Britain and the United States in 2006 by Kogan Page Limited

120 Pentonville Road	525 South 4th Street, #241
London N1 9JN	Philadelphia PA 19147
United Kingdom	USA
www.kogan-page.co.uk	

© Margaret Dale, 2006

The right of Margaret Dale to be identified as the author of this work has been asserted by her in accordance with the Copyright, Designs and Patents Act 1988.

ISBN 0 7494 4474 6

British Library Cataloguing-in-Publication Data

A CIP record for this book is available from the British Library.

Library of Congress Cataloging-in-Publication Data

Dale, Margaret.
    The essential guide to recruitment : how to conduct great interviews and select the best employees / Margaret Dale.
        p. cm.
    Includes index.
    ISBN 0-7494-4474-6
    1. Employees–Recruiting. 2. Employment interviewing. 3. Employee selection. I. Title.
HF5549.5.R44D287 2006
658.3'11–dc22

2006008961

Typeset by Digital Publishing Solutions
Printed and bound in the United States by Thomson-Shore, Inc

Contents

Introduction

A manager's success depends entirely on the quality of the people in the team. That is why it is essential that, new people have the skills and abilities needed to perform the job to the standard required when they are appointed. It is also essential that they fit in with the manager, the rest of the team and the organization. Being able to recruit, select and retain employees of quality can be the difference between an excellent and an ordinary manager.

For most managers new to recruitment, often there is very little practical help readily available. Generally, only the very large organizations provide training so, for most managers, the only guidance comes from their own previous experience, and from the stories heard from colleagues, friends and family. Often, these describe bad experiences, horror stories about the treatment handed out during an interview. Examples of good experiences are not that common, partly because they are not so good for the telling. For sure, it is possible to learn from bad examples but good practice is often obvious and easier to follow. It is just not spoken about so frequently.

If you are the manager of a team that has seen little turnover, filling a vacancy can be as daunting as if you were new to the task. Practice alters over time and the expectations of jobseekers change. You may be in the same position as a manager totally new to recruitment. The only help available will be your memory, advice from well-intentioned colleagues and the horror stories.

This book intends to fill this gap by providing practical guidance based on experience, good practice and theory. It will not, however, be theoretical.

Rather, each chapter contains examples and tips, and ends with a practical exercise to help you develop your own approach.

The starting point is being clear about the qualities you are seeking in your ideal candidate. If you miss this step, you will not know what you are looking for. Not knowing means that, when the candidates are in front of you, you will not be able to identify which is the best one to select. The other big danger is that you create an idealized image, based perhaps on the qualities of the person you are trying to replace. We all know now, from scientific research and headlines, that clones have some serious flaws. Alternatively, the image of your idealized candidate is one built from a stereotype. Stereotypes are generalized portraits of groups of people that tend to exaggerate their characteristics. For the unwitting manager, the use of such portraits could lead directly to unlawful discrimination. The law is becoming increasingly complex in this area as the negative effects of discrimination on the members of minority groups are being understood better. Rather than try to explain the law here, we will look at how you can avoid this minefield by describing the features you are seeking in ways that are directly related to the job the person will be doing. The time spent in producing an up-to-date job description and writing a good quality person specification will be an investment that will make the remaining stages of the recruitment and selection process easy.

The second stage of the recruitment process is when you actively seek the people who possess the qualities you are looking for. You need to tell the right people about your vacancy and make sure they know what the job is all about. You will also need to tell them something about the qualities you want. The contents of the job description and person specification will help you do this. The potential applicants will then know whether the job is the sort of thing they are looking for and whether they will stand any chance of being successful, if they decide to put themselves forward. You will want to fish in the largest possible pool to make sure that you reach as many of the people as possible who have the talents you seek. However, you will not want to be flooded out with applications from those who do not meet your minimum standards when, perhaps, the best person is sitting at the next desk. You, therefore, need to know what you are looking for and which pool is the one in which they are to be found.

Waiting until the applications have arrived is too late for you to start working out how you are going to choose between them. You need to get your act together as soon as you start the recruitment stage, if not before. The job description and person specification will help you again, this time by providing the criteria you need to distinguish between the applications and decide whom to interview. In Chapter 3, we will consider the other aspects of the process that need to be prepared before you start working on the design of the interview.

Good candidates do their homework – and are expected to do so. How many managers turn up five minutes before the first candidate arrives for an interview not having read the CVs or application forms? Is it likely they will have worked out what questions to ask and who will ask them? Poor preparation, for candidates and interviewers alike, is the route to poor performance. Good preparation by both parties leads to effective interviewing and excellent decisions – both are essential if you are to select the person who is going to be best for the job you are filling. We will therefore outline the steps you need to take so that you will be ready to greet your first interviewee.

An interview is the most common way most jobs are filled. It is a strange social ritual during which candidates are quizzed about their background, achievements and abilities. They are asked to account for themselves and justify previous events. Not many people would put themselves into this kind of situation if they had the choice! Moreover, research suggests that the most common forms of interview are not very good at predicting which candidate will perform best in the job. Why is it still used so extensively?

The answer is simple – we like meeting people and most of us believe we are good judges of others. We like the interview as it provides the opportunity for a social interaction. This provides the soft information that will tell us whether a particular candidate will fit with the organization and the existing team. It also tells us whether we will be able to form a productive working relationship with the person. This is crucially important, for how well the candidates and interviewers relate to each other and build a rapport are critical measures that indicate the nature of the future relationship. The importance of the social aspects of the interview should therefore not be underrated.

The interview is less good at assessing the candidates' ability to carry out the contents of the job. This is because it does not present the opportunities for the candidates to demonstrate any abilities other than those involved in building rapport and answering questions. Therefore, an interview is best when it is used alongside other selection methods.

Another reason why the interview is a poor predictor is that some managers mistakenly believe that, for an interview to be effective, it should contain hard questions and be an unpleasant experience. Thus the best candidate will be the one who can handle the situation and provide clever answers. This may be a valid conclusion if the job being filled requires these qualities. If not, the manager may inadvertently let the best candidate slip away simply because they did not do well in that environment.

The interview can be very effective, providing it is planned and run in a way that enables each candidate to be assessed according to the needs of the job. These will have been outlined in the job description and person specification. These documents, as well as informing the earlier stages of the process, will help the design and conduct of the interview. The interview can still be tough, in the eyes of the candidates. If they think the interview has been like this, it will probably mean that they will have been challenged and tested. This is what an interview should do. There is a difference, however, between testing the candidate's suitability against relevant criteria – which is fair enough – and testing a candidate's ability to withstand adversity – which is not.

If a candidate thinks the interview is easy, you will not have put them to the test or they are lying. Not many people go to interviews for fun. Nevertheless, we accept that if we want a particular job we will have to go through this somewhat gruelling experience. There is a lot an interviewer can do to make the interview more enjoyable but still keep it testing.

An enjoyable interview is one where candidates feel that they have been able to give a fair and full account of themselves. They will leave the interview room believing that they have been asked reasonable questions, relevant to the job for which they are applying. They will have been listened to, given the chance to finish their reply and ask their own questions. They will not have been cut off short, humiliated, or asked questions that are impossible to answer.

A good, tough interview should be demanding and hard work. It should also be thorough and probing. The purpose of an interview is to explore the candidates' abilities and experience against the criteria needed for effective performance in the job. It is up to the interviewer to make sure that the candidate chosen is the best person for the job, ie the one who will do the best job.

For you, the interviewer, this means making sure that the interview is fit for the purpose. Tough interviewing is not about setting traps for candidates. You do not have to put them under a lot of pressure to 'see if they can stand the pace' or ask them to jump impossibly high hurdles. Unless, of course, you are looking for someone who can stand up to difficult interviewers or is a champion steeplechaser. Many managers new to interviewing make this common mistake. They may think this is expected – perhaps because they have experienced this type of interview or because people talk about interviews in this way. Possibly, they see it as a way of getting even with all the bad interviewers they have met previously.

In reality, unreasonably tough interviews do little to enhance your chances of selecting the best candidate. Conducting an interview in a way that makes it hard for a candidate could have the exact opposite effect. The best candidate may decide that, even though the job has the best prospects and pays the most money, the way you treat people would not be worth it. So much for your reputation as the employer of choice!

On the other hand, conducting tough but well-constructed interviews that are searching, but still maintain the dignity of the candidates and are respectful, can do a lot for your reputation. As well as making sure you appoint the best candidate, you can create a positive impression on the person appointed *and* those who do not get the job. This may seem a little perverse but if people feel that they have been given a good chance to demonstrate what they are able to do and think that the process they have been put through is valid, appropriate and fair, they will accept the outcome, even if they are disappointed. If they feel they have been played with, tripped up and treated badly, they will leave with a bad taste in their mouths. They will have a memory of you as someone they would not want to work for, at any price. They will think poorly of your organization and could even lodge a formal complaint. None of this would do much good for your and your organization's reputation. It could cost a lot of money and even your job!

The employer is not always the one who makes the interview tough. Sometimes, candidates can turn the tables and put their potential employer through the mill. These individuals can throw even the most experienced interviewers. They are the job hunters who regard the interview as an opportunity to get the most they can from the situation, particularly when the salary on offer is negotiable. Some candidates will view the interview as an opportunity to polish their ego and see how much wool they can pull over the interviewers' eyes. They may be very professional in their approach: they will have read all the books and done their homework. They will know what you are looking for better than you and they will have had plenty of interview practice; possibly more than you. They will have met the interviewers who like to play games and think they are asking really hard, novel questions such as 'Why do you really want this job?'. They will know how to sidestep the searching questions they do not want to answer and they will know what you are going to ask next. They will have seen it all before.

You can beat professional interviewees at their own game and find out whether they have the qualities you seek without recourse to bad practice. This book will show how to conduct interviews that are searching and fair. The approach outlined will enable you to weed out those candidates whose real qualities are evading questions and leading interviewers astray. You will be able to construct interviews that leave candidates saying, 'Gosh, that was tough. They knew what they were looking for and found out what I could do. I would really like to work there', without browbeating them and asking them impossible to answer questions.

If you design the interview with the aim of leaving all the candidates with a good impression of you and your organization, you will go a long way towards ensuring that the person you select will accept the offer. It will also mean that those not offered the job will say good things about you to their friends and colleagues, thus helping to build your reputation as the employer of choice; an essential requirement when competition for good candidates and high calibre employees is fierce.

We have already agreed that questions should not be designed to trip up the candidates. However, they should be testing and challenging. You may want to find out if the candidates can think on their feet and withstand pressure, as most jobs need these abilities. A good interviewer explores candidates' abilities in these areas but in ways that create a good impression rather than leave the candidates seeing you in a poor light. You will also want to find out if the candidate has the other abilities, achievements and attainments, and where their weaknesses lie. Again, you can do this without stripping the candidates of their dignity and self-esteem. As it is unlikely that you will find the perfect person, there will be a good chance that the person appointed will have some training needs, so you will need to know what they are.

You will also need to find out if the candidate is telling the truth. It is a sad fact of life that candidates tell lies to get the job they want. Remember, job hunters are told that the CV is their sales document and they should present themselves in the best light, as if they were marketing a product. It is up to you as an interviewer to get behind the façade and well-constructed glossy CVs. This is where the tough questions come in: their role is to expose the gaps and weaknesses in the image the candidates want you to see and to expose the superficial interview performance.

In Chapter 4, we will discuss how you can construct an interview that will be both testing and fair. We will look at the different types of questions and the ways in which they can be asked. A question that works well in one situation may not be appropriate in another. You will be given a set of prepared questions and we will discuss how to construct questions so you can devise you own. Interviews are called tough because they are – and should be so. You will be able to draw from the example questions and amend them to help you design an interview that will explore all aspects of the candidates' background and abilities. Thus you will be able to assess the degree of their fit against your requirements in a way that will withstand challenge, should you be asked to justify your decision.

At the end of the interview you will have to consider each candidate's performance and decide which one best fits your criteria. We will look at how you can pull together all the information you have gathered and use it to make your decision. We will also look at the checks you need to carry out before making the offer. A fact often forgotten is that a verbal offer is part of the contract of employment and you can be held to it, even if you make a mistake in the negotiations with the candidate of your choice. You need to be sure of what you are doing before you ask the chosen candidate whether they want to accept the job.

We forget, at our peril, that the final decision is the candidate's. The worst outcome is the best candidate saying 'No thank you. I have a better offer elsewhere.' Oh, the waste and damage to your ego! You can avoid this dreadful situation by making sure the candidates have the information they need to make their choices early in the process, so if they are doubtful they can select themselves out sooner rather than later. The interview then becomes an exchange of information and a process of mutual assessment. Encourage the candidates to enter into a dialogue and, above all, treat them with respect. Make sure they have enough time to ask you questions. Encourage them to go beyond the normal 'How much will you pay me?' questions by providing this sort of background information before the interview.

Finally, we will discuss how to make sure the person appointed actually starts the job and stays with you. There is plenty of evidence to show that getting the first few weeks right influences how well the person will perform in the job. It also influences whether they are likely to stay beyond the first few months. The interview, if it has been well designed, will be one of the most rigorous and comprehensive assessments an employee will go through. It therefore makes sense to use it to create a good understanding between you and the person appointed. The assessment can inform their development plan, prepare the way for future appraisals, and be the foundations of a productive and fruitful working relationship.

The retention of high-calibre staff is the challenge facing most employers in the current labour market conditions. There is a climate where experienced and skilful employees can pick and choose jobs and employers are faced with the need to find ways of keeping hold of the people they value. Making sure that the employment contract is built on firm, well-negotiated foundations is a key plank in establishing a mutually satisfying and productive working relationship. Simple but effective recruitment, interviewing and selection are the essential firm steps you need to take to build the team you need for continued success. This book will guide you through the stages and give you examples and tips from which to develop your own practice.

1

Why you need the best person for the job

INTRODUCTION

Telling you that a manager's success depends on the abilities of his or her staff is such an obvious statement, you may wonder why it needs to be said at all. Some of the horror stories and mistakes often made suggest that not every manager shares this view. I wonder why this so when I reflect on the ways often used to recruit staff. We will therefore use this chapter to explore the obvious to make the case for taking more care when interviewing.

You are totally dependent on the performance of your people. If they do well, it will reflect on your abilities as a manager but if they are found wanting, you can hardly expect to be regarded very highly. It is therefore in your own best interests to recruit the best people. To do this, you need to be sure what it is you mean by best. There are plenty of examples where the most highly qualified, experienced candidate has been appointed but once in the job the person fails to fulfil the promise, perhaps because they are too well qualified. There are other cases where the manager defines the ideal person for the job and goes to considerable lengths to recruit and secure the person with this profile only to find in practice that the real job requires a different mix of skills. This tends to happen most when the manager is not that close to the job and its situation. We need to be clear about the difference between what we think we want and what we really need.

The recruitment process is peppered with pitfalls and the weakest stage is the one in which we place most faith: the final interview. Research into the reliability and validity of interviewing shows that the chances of an interview predicting which candidate will be most successful in the job are as low as 10 in 100. Other selection methods are better (for example, assessment centres can achieve a score of 60 in 100), but we still like to interview people. Understanding why we like interviews so much will help us appreciate their weaknesses.

One simple but effective way of improving the interview is to set out clearly what is required in the job. This statement has two parts: the description of the job's purpose and the specification of the knowledge and skills required by the job holder. We will look at how these statements can be produced and end the chapter with an exercise so you can try out the techniques on a job of your own. We will start, however, by questioning the statement of the obvious.

YOUR PERFORMANCE DEPENDS ON YOUR PEOPLE

A manager is only as good as the people who report to him or her. Is this a fair statement to make? Of course not. There are times when a very competent team is led by a poor manager and there are times when a good manager is let down by the performance of the team. In the first case, it is the responsibility of the manager's manager to recognize what is going on and take appropriate action to deal with the manager's poor performance. In the second case, it is the manager's responsibility to deal with the situation.

This can be difficult if the manager has inherited the whole team. The performance of individuals and the dynamics of the team can be hard to influence and change. This situation usually endures for a comparatively short time until at least one of the team members moves on. The manager will then have the opportunity to bring in new blood. This will allow the skills profile and the team's abilities to be balanced more closely to those needed to achieve the team's overall objectives. It also creates the chance of influencing the dynamics of the team by bringing in new people.

If these actions do not result in change and the team continues to return a poor performance, questions should rightly be asked about the manager's ability. We only have to look at what happens to managers of football teams slipping inexorably down the league tables to know who is held to account. Fortunately for us, most employers are not so uncompromising in their judgement of managers' performance and that of their teams. But the message is clear. A manager's success is dependent on the results achieved by the people reporting directly to her or him.

APPOINTING GOOD PEOPLE COSTS

Filling vacancies, organizing and running interviews and inducting new starters costs – and not just money. It takes up a lot of a manager's time. It makes enormous sense to get it right the first time round. This means attracting a pool of suitably qualified and experienced people so you can select the best from a good bunch. The state of the labour market means that this is far more easily said than done. At one time the problem was drawing up a shortlist from large numbers of people with similar backgrounds and abilities. The labour market is now tight. This means that employers are seeking employees, not the other way round, and the challenge in recruitment terms is attracting the candidates, any candidates. It is not unusual for a newspaper advertisement to cost several thousands of pounds. If no applications are generated or the applicants are not appointable, considerable sums of money can be wasted.

Having no candidates is bad enough. You may find yourself having to make a choice without being confident of the quality of the pool from which you are selecting. You may be faced with having to appoint someone who is not up to the job or may find that the person selected does not settle in and leaves quickly. In both scenarios, you may have to repeat the whole process again, at considerable expense in terms of your time and money. Advertising is not cheap and if you are using a recruitment consultant, the fees can mount up.

There is no easy way through this situation when there are difficulties in the labour market. The only way is to invest in the process and do your best to get it right the first time round to ensure that you obtain applications from the highest calibre of candidates, that the best person for the job is appointed and that the final decision is not open to debate. What is debatable is the meaning of 'highest calibre possible' and 'best for the job'. These phrases suggest that you should appoint the most highly qualified and experienced person who happens to apply to fill your vacancy. In some situations, however, offering the job to this person would be an absolute disaster, particularly if you wanted someone to join the team as a junior member. Yet many employers fall into this trap, with disastrous consequences. Such a person will probably receive a cold shoulder rather than the warm welcome they expect. Moreover, the person can become frustrated that his or her experience and ability are not valued. In either case the new starter can quickly become an early leaver or, worse still, stay to become a disgruntled employee.

It is easy to avoid these pitfalls. All that is needed is careful consideration of the sort of employee you are looking for to complement the abilities and experience of the existing team.

Do you know what you need?

How will you recognize the 'best candidate' when you see him or her? If you want to appoint a candidate who will perform well in the job, you do need to know what abilities and aptitudes, attainments and achievements that person needs to possess to enable them to do the job you want filling to the standard you expect. Again, these would appear to be obvious statements but so many employers merely place advertisements in the Situations Vacant columns in a newspaper and wait to see who applies. This can be a costly exercise that has little payback.

One reason for not attracting good applicants could be that you have failed to sell the job. The shift from the employer's to the employee's market means that people with skills and experience are in short supply. Some occupations and sectors are suffering more than others, but as a country the UK is close to achieving full employment. This means that there is not a pool of people seeking jobs; rather, people need to be tempted away from their current employer into a job that, to them, is more attractive. For those joining the labour market for the first time, this means looking for openings that offer the greatest rewards, in their terms, immediately and in the longer term. Thus employers need to sell the job in an attractive but realistic way.

Over-selling the job does not attract the same penalties as mis-selling a product or service but it can have similar negative consequences. These can include raising expectations to levels that are not attainable, such as promising career development opportunities you know will not arise, or target earnings that are not achievable or a working environment that does not exist. Being vague about the skills and experience required for the job can be equally misleading.

It is not difficult to develop a clear statement of the qualities required for the job and to devise an attractive but accurate picture of the work to be done. The following tips will help you draw the picture to describe the 'best' person for the job and define what you mean by 'high calibre'.

1 Focus on behaviour rather than personality

For example, it is common to see 'Wanted: good team player' in adverts. But what does this mean – do you want a winger, full back or centre? Each position requires different abilities as the holder makes a unique contribution to the performance of the whole.

If you work out in some detail the type and range of skills you need for effective performance now and for the foreseeable future, you have a far greater chance of finding someone with the required abilities. Remember the old adage: if you don't know what you are looking for, the chances of finding it are pretty slim.

2 Look for the type of personality needed to fit the team

It is true that, for some types of job, you will need a person with a particular type of personality. For most jobs, however, it does not really matter if someone is introverted or an extrovert. But this does matter if you need someone, for example, who can work alone for long periods of time or who will make a significant contribution to the life of your team.

Personality testing during recruitment and selection has grown considerably in recent years as its predictive validity is slightly above that of most types of interview. There is a danger of using tests for testing's sake and candidates can become weary of doing the same one over and over again. There is also the consequential danger of them learning how to manipulate the test. Nevertheless, if the dimensions making up the test complement the contents of the person specification, this selection tool can provide a useful source of information to help you make your decision.

3 Diversity brings richness but it can also bring conflict

Much is talked about the value of diversity and building a team made of people from different backgrounds. This can add richness but it can also create conflict. The main benefit of this richness is that the different backgrounds and experience give the team a greater ability to solve problems and address new situations. Team members will also have a broader perspective into the needs and interests of members of the different communities that make up our multicultural and diverse society. This factor can be particularly important in services industries, which now make up the bulk of our economy.

For you though as a manager, you may need to pay more attention to building your team, at least at the outset, to address potential conflict. Team members may need to learn how to respect views that are different from their own and value experiences and beliefs that at first sight may seem strange. Getting over these hurdles can be worthwhile as the understanding and insight created from the team-building efforts can lead to the creation of a highly effective group of people, able to work together to produce high quality outputs. Exactly what you need!

AVOIDING THE COMMON MISTAKES

Making mistakes when appointing people to jobs is easy. It doesn't require a great deal of work and you need very little preparation or professional help. Undoing the mistakes, on the other hand, can be very difficult. It can take considerable amounts of your time and potentially cost a lot of money. If you get it wrong, you may find that you need to engage the services of an expensive lawyer. Going to a tribunal is expensive and losing a case can incur considerable amounts of money. It can also damage the reputation of your organization, never mind yours. It makes a lot of sense therefore to invest the little bit of time and effort needed to get it right at the outset.

The starting point is defining the job that needs doing and identifying the skills, knowledge and experience needed to do the job to the standard required, now and for the foreseeable future. This sentence gives you the clues to success.

Using yesterday to design tomorrow

We study history to learn from past mistakes. The lessons learnt can be valuable and are ignored at one's peril. Sadly, we do not always learn from the mistakes made in recruitment and selection. Often managers come new to the task and have very little preparation save their own previous experience. Some of this may not have been particularly good practice but, unless a manager has been through a number of interviews personally, there is very little to compare against.

Being interviewed feels very different from conducting an interview, so forming your views about what has happened and what should happen from your own experience will be partial. As interviews are stressful, memory tends to distort what actually happened. This is especially true if the experience has been negative. Your brain will have found ways of rationalizing the outcome by attributing some of the blame for your lack of success to other parties. For example, you may believe the reason you did not get the job was not because you did not develop the skills the interviewers were seeking but because they did not ask you the questions needed for you to demonstrate fully the breadth of your experience.

Relying solely on your personal experience can lead you into some of the common traps. It is worth talking to your colleagues about their experience of both being interviewed and interviewing. Ask them what worked well as well as asking them what was not so good. It is possible to learn from good as well as poor experiences. The following guidance should help you avoid the most obvious mistakes.

1 Define the job

Your first task following the resignation of an employee is to get out the job description (if one exists). Is this a mistake, you may wonder. No, providing the job description is up to date and contains sufficient information to enable you to identify the skills, knowledge and experience required for effective performance of the job, now and for the foreseeable future. Most job descriptions do not provide this sort of information.

Traditionally, job descriptions contain a statement of key responsibilities and then go on to list a range of tasks. The modern approach is to create an outline, describing the part the job holder will play within the organization. This broad statement may also contain objectives. The biggest problem with the first approach is that the list of tasks may include a range of activities that demand widely differing skills. So wide, in fact, that no one person could possibly possess them all to the level needed. The biggest problem with the second approach is that the outline could be so broad that it becomes meaningless.

What is needed to help you fill the job is a statement that outlines:

▪ The **purpose** of the job – why it exists.

▪ The **key duties** – an up-to-date statement of the main components and areas of responsibility. Ideally, this will contain five or six main headings.

▪ The **main relationships** – this will include the post to which the job holder will report, any staff that report to the job holder and any other relationships that are critical to the performance of the job.

▪ The **main objectives** to be achieved – this will contain the current objectives and those to be attained over, say, the next year.

The aim is to create a document, at most two pages in length, that captures the essence of the job to be done. The person leaving may be able to make an important contribution to this document, as will colleagues. It is also worth asking for views from other people who will have to deal with the new person in post. Then, think forward, look at your business plan and ask yourself what will need to be done over the next year or so to enable you and your team to achieve your objectives. This may lead you to examine the make-up of the other jobs in your section so that any duplication, overlaps or gaps are sorted out. An example of a job description using this approach is given later in this chapter.

Once the job has been defined, you can go on to look at the skills, knowledge and experience required for its performance. At this stage it is worth remembering that the chances of finding someone who can 'hit the ground running' are low. Most people will need some time to settle in while they learn the ropes. You will be advised to think about the requirements you would expect immediately and those expected to be attained after some time.

2 Specify the person

A person specification describes the human qualities needed to perform the job as you have now defined it. Usually this specification is written in terms of behaviours (ie skills, the application of knowledge and the experience gained). It is possible to include personality types if these will have a direct impact and relevance to how the job is done. For example, there is little point in looking for someone who can act on their own initiative, if the job requires the application of tightly defined rules and regulations.

We do not like having to think hard or redo work, if we can possibly avoid it. If the existing job description and person specification look about right, why should we waste time rewriting them? The human brain, essentially, is lazy and likes to take shortcuts. It relies on its existing knowledge as a way of avoiding having to do any work, for thinking hard and creatively takes a lot of effort. The brain prefers to cruise along the surface. It tries to avoid having to access its deep memory banks if at all possible or transforming existing ideas. Even less does it like having to take on board new ideas. However, for effective recruitment, thinking hard and challenging existing models are critical. These will help you spot the most common pitfalls that need to be avoided.

Cloning

Placing undue reliance on the past to describe what you need from a new post holder in the future can lead you into all sorts of difficulty. Of course, information based on the previous job holder's performance is relevant and must be allowed to contribute to the creation of the person specification. However, if you try to replace the person who has left, you will probably be disappointed. You are taking the risk of looking for someone who does not exist: a clone.

A clone may contain the strengths of the original; it also contains the weaknesses. Trying to fill a job with someone like the previous holder denies you the chance to take stock and look for ways of filling gaps and remedying the weaknesses not only in the job but also in the team. You may also deny yourself the opportunity of obtaining other skills, experience and potential.

Inevitably a clone is rooted in the past. What may have worked well previously is not guaranteed to work again in the future. Situations alter and require fresh approaches. Demands change as problems take on a new hue. Normally, staff learn how to respond as they grow in experience. A clone, however, cannot do this as it is fixed in the point of time at which it was created.

Stereotyping

A stereotype is a similarly dangerous creature. It is a confection of characteristics assumed to be found in any example of the person found in a particular category. So for example, a graduate will, typically, be middle class, well educated and in debt. He or she will probably lack some of the basic skills needed by an employee but will be very competent when using mobile phones, the internet and DVDs.

It is very easy for stereotypes to creep in, for when you are compiling a person specification, you are asked to visualize what the best candidate will be like. This will draw you towards thinking about the sort of person you want; in other words, stereotypes. These are not real people so if you search for one, you are likely to be disappointed. There is nothing worse than finishing a selection interview feeling disappointed in the person you have decided to appoint. Even though you may be confident in their ability to do the job, the disappointment stems from the fact that they do not meet the person specification fully. The failure to fit is often seen as deficiencies of the person who has been offered the job; how often do we examine the person specification and conclude it was unrealistic?

You can avoid this trap by thinking of the things the person will need to achieve and the sorts of issues they will have to address in the job. This will lead you towards thinking about the skills and behaviours the post holder will need to demonstrate if they are to be effective. We will discuss this further when we look at ways of developing the person specification.

Someone like me

The other big danger is looking for a new person who is like you and/or the existing members of the team. Research into selection methods constantly shows that the typical interview is a very poor predictor of success in a job. Yet we continue to use interviews as the last stage in the process leading to the final decision – to offer the job to an individual. You may well ask why we continue to use the interview if it is such a poor predictor. The answer is that it provides the means of meeting the candidates in a formal setting. It provides the opportunity for the assessment of social fit and enables you to work out whether you think you will be able to work with the individual.

We place great store on first impressions. Generally we make up our minds within 30 seconds of meeting a new person and then seek evidence to confirm this view. We do this to assess the risks presented by the other person – will we like them or will they present a threat? This tendency is deep-seated and part of the human make-up. It was developed as a defence mechanism to protect ourselves from physical attack. The chances of a candidate leaping across the desk and biffing the interviewer on the nose are pretty small these days. Nevertheless, the brain is still hard-wired to work out whether we will like the new person or whether they are potentially dangerous.

There is a fundamental belief that someone with the same sort of background as the rest of the team will not pose a threat. They will have the same understandings and values as ourselves, because they have followed the same path and have had the same learning.

We also attribute the chances of success on the basis of very weak evidence. For example, if someone attended a school that currently is receiving good ratings in the target tables, it is reasonable to assume the person received a good education. It is even better if they went to the same school as someone we know and rate as being a good performer. We naturally seek these similarities and shared experiences as they provide the building blocks of a relationship and start to establish the trust that is so essential.

Once first impressions are formed, we seek evidence to confirm our judgements and actively discount any information that may suggest they are inaccurate. This tendency lies at the root of the interview's main weakness. Many of the techniques intended to improve its predictive validity try to reduce the strength of our first impression. Even so, there remains a strong drive to assess how well we will be able to work with any one of the candidates. It is not unusual to find, in most person specifications, headings such as interpersonal skills, team-working abilities or influencing skills.

There is some merit in assessing whether the candidate will work well with existing team members and yourself. It does not follow that they should have the same characteristics, preferences, likes or dislikes or the same sort of background. In fact, an excess of strengths can be a weakness in a team. People who are alike can fall out simply because their views and opinions are too similar. They can focus on the minutiae of detail to bring some variety. High levels of agreement can create a degree of intolerance of people with different views. This can lead to a distortion of priorities and a lack of appreciation of the needs of others.

The value of difference

Difference does not necessarily lead to conflict. Research into the make-up of teams suggests that a mixture of abilities and approaches gives richness. Diversity provides a strength as team members from different backgrounds will have a better understanding of the needs of a wider range of customers and other people. Their different views enable a broader approach to be taken and any disagreement can be used to generate new and imaginative solutions to new problems.

You may be better off seeking someone who is not like you or who fills a gap in the team's profile. In the next section we will look at ways of creating a person specification, the portrait of the person you are seeking. Having prepared this document you will be able to begin your search for the best person for your job. The starting point is to look at what you already have, identify the gaps and then think about the sorts of things you will be looking for.

Anyone, so long as they are breathing

This is the solution of the really desperate manager. If you fall into this trap you may find yourself stuck with the person you appoint for ever, especially if they can just do the job. The long-term problems caused by taking the first person who appears or the best from a weak pool may be more severe and costly than having to live with a vacancy for several months.

Nevertheless, there will be considerable pressure to fill a gap. Living with a vacancy can cause considerable operational problems. Other staff will have to cover the work left by the previous post holder, jobs will go undone and customers start to complain about slow responses. If this situation goes on for a long time, your people will become tired, stressed and irritable. Their performance may start to suffer and you will start to feel the heat. This situation can be even worse if the previous person was a high-level performer. Even if you are appointing to meet a new area of demand, you can still come under pressure to proceed to fill the post with haste.

There is a world of difference between moving forward speedily and rushing ahead like a steam train out of control. In the first instance the whole process will be planned, you will anticipate how long each stage will take and build in contingencies. Based on a realistic time frame, you will be able to discuss with your remaining staff how to deal with the situation. Options may include appointing someone on a temporary contract, finding cover from another part of the organization, or identifying other areas of work that can be postponed until the post is filled.

Going over the top

You may find yourself facing a star on the other side of your desk during the interviews. It is easy to fall into the trap of appointing someone too good for the job.

The over-qualified candidate may at first sight be very attractive. Appointing this person, you may think, will enable untold heights of performance to be attained and spur on the rest of the team. How realistic is this dream? Before selecting the all-round star, think through the effects appointing someone at the top of the tree will have – on you, your other people and the person you are about to appoint. Consider the following:

▌ Why has someone so good applied for your vacancy?

▌ What is their motive and what rewards are they seeking?

▌ Will you, your organization and the job be able to meet those needs?

▌ How long will the job remain interesting and challenging?

▌ What will start to happen when they have exhausted the job's potential?

▌ How will existing staff react to someone new who is regarded so highly – will they be able to accept such a star into the team?

▌ Will you feel challenged by someone so capable?

The consequences of over-appointing can be as bad as appointing someone who is only just able to do the job to the bare minimum. So again, consider the implications and balance these with the merits and difficulties caused. The person who appears to be the best may not be the best for your job.

If you are clear from the outset about the features of the best candidate, in your context, you will considerably reduce the chances of falling into the above traps.

DRAWING A PORTRAIT OF THE BEST

The person specification is as important as the job description and the two documents go hand in hand.

Identifying the skills and personality type required to do the job you need doing is not a daunting task, even though it may seem so at first sight. There is an exercise at the end of this chapter to help you create a person specification but before asking you to complete it we will have a look at some easy techniques.

Start with where you are at

We have already discussed the dangers you may meet if you only look backwards when starting to define what you are seeking from the new person. By all means use the past to inform your thinking but please remember, we always look backward through misted spectacles. Some of our memories are clouded; others stand out in sharp but often exaggerated focus. In all cases memories are partial and distorted by the passage of time. There is no choice, therefore, but to look to the present.

Filling a vacancy gives you the opportunity to look at the job that needs doing now; you can also use it as a chance to update or change ways of working. You can reallocate tasks between other members of the team, scrap activities that no longer add value and include new ones that are crying out to be done.

It is also an opportunity to take stock of how your team is organized and look at their skills profile. This may be uncomfortable to some, but if you carry out regular appraisals, you should have a fairly good idea of where your team members' strengths and weaknesses lie. But do you know their aspirations? The vacancy and the potential reorganization may present the opportunities an individual has been quietly waiting for. Now is the time for you to explore aspirations as well as carry out a skills audit.

Skills audit

Carrying out an audit of your team's existing strengths and weaknesses will help you identify the gaps that need filling, if you are to construct a balanced team that is geared up to doing the job and achieving your objectives. The audit will also enable you to look at who is doing what and whether that person is the best one to continue to do that particular aspect of the work. Having to fill a vacancy presents you with the very wonderful opportunity of making changes. The gap created by someone leaving provides the flexibility you need to move things about.

A skills audit starts with your objectives – what you need to achieve, say over the next year. You may find it useful to define the team's objectives using the

SMART approach. This acronym is intended to remind you to write in terms that are:

▌ Specific

▌ Measurable

▌ Achievable

▌ Resourced

▌ Time limited.

The number of objectives should be limited, but they should be reviewed regularly. Having a small number may seem a soft option but regular review should ensure that adequate progress is being made to achieve them. It is always possible to add in others if everything has been achieved before time. The danger of having too many is that people become overloaded and take a scatter gun approach, not knowing which objective should receive attention first. Achievers focus; losers spray.

Imagine you are the leader of a team whose function is to supply customers with office supplies and equipment. There are seven people in your team, one of whom has just resigned. Your collective objectives are to maintain your existing customer base and increase it by 5 per cent. In practice this means making sure that you do not lose any of your existing customers. This will probably involve:

▌ making sure that orders are filled promptly and accurately;

▌ responding efficiently and effectively to queries;

▌ making sure that any complaints are resolved quickly and to the customers' satisfaction;

▌ checking with customers to ensure they are receiving the sort of service they require;

▌ finding out what standards of service are expected;

▌ asking customers what other goods and services they might want and finding ways of providing them;

▌ anticipating what customers might be looking for in nine months' time, checking that your forecasts are accurate and working up plans to deliver the new services when they will be wanted.

Your objective will also mean seeking out new customers and tempting them to buy your services. This could involve market research to find out who your competitors are and what they are offering and to explore gaps in the marketplace. Do you and your team have all the skills needed to carry out these tasks?

If you make use of 360° feedback, in addition to the annual review of your team, you should have information about your own skills profile. The information you have from these sources will build a good basis for completing the skills audit. If you do not use these techniques, perhaps you should think about doing so.

Having clarified your objectives, the next stage in the audit is to draw up a grid into which you can profile your team members' skills and development needs. Such a grid could look like the one shown in Figure 1.1.

Using three levels for assessing helps to highlight areas of excess as well as potential weaknesses. It also indicates any aspects of work where you may be potentially vulnerable if key skills are vested only in one person. Rather than call the gaps weaknesses, the term 'development needs' is used as a more positive description. Rather than focusing on the negative, the column can be used to draw attention to areas that can and should be acted upon rather than as criticisms of the person.

You can complete the grid alone or you can ask the individuals to think about their own skills profile. Alternatively, you could use it as a development exercise. This is done by asking the team members to identify what to insert in each cell of the grid, for themselves and for each of their colleagues. This demands a degree of honesty and openness. It also needs to be approached in a positive way. Feedback about each others' skills and development needs has to be done in a constructive way otherwise the whole experience can descend into a mutual beating-up that will be counter-productive. However, if the team is mature enough to handle this approach, the outcome can be a very rich picture of the current team's development needs (individually and collectively) and what gaps and areas of vulnerability need to be covered.

The example given in Figure 1.1 draws a picture of a team that is administratively sound. There is some need to strengthen the use of computers and record keeping and possibly enhance the team's ability to respond to customers' issues. The biggest need, however, is about changing the ways of working. The profile suggests that the wish to build and maintain a harmonious team could get in the way of altering things. Also, the strength of the team focuses inwards. Perhaps it would benefit from exploring what is going on elsewhere. The skills audit thus informs the development of the person specification. It draws your attention to the skills and experience you need to recruit to strengthen your existing team, not by adding to the existing skills base but by plugging the gaps.

Team member	Strengths			Development needs
	Advanced	Competent	Foundation	
Benji	Compiling questionnaires	Responding to unusual requests	Computer use	Enhance computer skills
Nikki	Using spreadsheets	Creating databases	Responding to customers	Dealing with complaints
Philip	Sorting out delivery problems	Dealing with angry customers	Keeping records	Use of computers
Raj	Keeping up to date with developments	Finding ways of resolving customers' problems	Computer use	Enhance computer skills
Stuart	Keeping records and information sources up to date	Using databases and finding answers to questions	Responding to customers	Seeing other ways of doing things
Tasmin	Having bright ideas on how to make changes	Responding to customer queries	Computer use	Making ideas practical
Manager	Developing an effective team	Ensuring operational efficiency	Understanding what is happening outside your team	Anticipating and implementing changes

Figure 1.1   Skills audit grid for office supplies team

Deciding who is going to do what

Now you are ready to start dividing up the work that needs to be done. This should include both the development work needed to achieve your objectives and the day-to-day routine work that is needed to run your operations. Again, you may wish to involve your team in this process. They will have differing views which will enrich and round out your picture. Having done the work on the skills audit your team will probably have ideas on how the work can best be divided between them. They will have views on how the work could be done to fill their personal development needs, preferences and aspirations. It is your job to balance the needs and interests of individual team members and the overall requirement of collective efficiency. You will also want to make sure that the work left to be done by the new person is capable of being done by one human being. The work should also be interesting and provide satisfaction to the job holder.

Building jobs gathers together tasks often with no regard to the combination of skills and experience needed to complete those tasks to the standard required. For example, it is not uncommon to find tasks that require a meticulous approach and high levels of concentration to be coupled with responding to customer queries. Clearly these cannot be done at the same time. To build satisfying and achievable jobs you need to give some attention to the balance of tasks, the way they fit together and the overall shape of the job you are designing.

Exploring the work that needs to be done by the team and the new member in this way can be productive as it will help you identify any areas of work that are not adding value or helping you achieve your objectives. The above example indicates that perhaps too much time is being spent on record keeping and too little time devoted to looking at what is happening around the team. The questions to be asked of each area of work are:

▌ Does this help achieve the team's objective?

▌ If so, could the work be done simpler, faster, easier?

▌ Is the standard of work high enough or too high?

▌ Does the work make a difference to the customer?

▌ What else is needed to achieve our objectives?

The answers should be enlightening and informative.

Thus the new person for the customer service team will need to contribute to the day-to-day delivery of excellent service to existing customers and to carry out the market research needed to identify potential customers and to find out what is going on elsewhere.

Drawing the picture of the person you need

Avoid becoming too detailed. All you need is a thumb-nail sketch, or a broad-brush portrait. If you go down to the fine detail you could easily be misled into looking for narrow aspects rather than considering the whole person. The following set of headings will help you focus on the areas critical for effective performance of the job you need doing.

Think in terms of the expected standard of performance but remember any new starter will have some learning needs. Try to avoid being seduced into drawing a picture of an outstanding performer. Some people find it helpful to distinguish between aspects that are essential for effective performance and those that are desirable. To keep the task simple, we will think about the essential features at first. It is always possible to make the picture more complex as you gain experience of drawing up person specifications.

Ability   This heading covers the skills needed to carry out the tasks included in the job description. A skill can be learnt or the application of an area of knowledge. An example of such a skill would be the ability to communicate clearly and concisely. Another would be the ability to resolve complex problems.

Attainment   This heading looks for the learning required for effective performance. This could include the acquisition of qualifications or formal learning. Alternatively, it could include the completion of certain milestones, for example being regarded by colleagues as a source of expertise in the creation and use of databases and websites.

Achievement This heading looks at the track record and experience needed for the job. An example would include experience of conducting customer satisfaction surveys.

Aptitude   This covers the personal abilities and preferences. These need to be grounded in the needs of the job. So, for example, to enable the office supply team to move forward and introduce the changes to working practice, someone with the willingness to explore alternative ways of working and experiment would complement the team's existing profile.

Gazing into the crystal ball

Once you have defined the job you wish to fill and have drawn up the specification of the person needed to do it, you will need to carry out one last check. This check is to provide some future-proofing. As much as we may wish, none of us can forecast with absolute certainty. There is always an element of guesswork that introduces risk. This can be reduced, but never eliminated, if you make your predictions on the best information available to you.

Forward looking when filling a post is important. There is no point in appointing a new member of staff to do a job that will change as soon as they start. There is even less point in looking for someone with the skills to solve yesterday's problems. You need to look forward, possibly across the next year, to make sure that your definition of the job will endure and the specification will remain relevant.

If you have followed the guidance given above, grounded the definition of the job on your business and operating plans and involved your team in identifying gaps in the current services, there will be a good chance that you have already done some future-proofing. However, if you have simply dusted off the job description used last time the job was filled, not only will you have missed the chance to review the distribution of work but you may be building obsolescence into your team.

Before moving to the next stage, project yourself forward a year and ask, 'What will I expect the job holder to be doing?' This will help you check the specification to make sure it adequately reflects the abilities, achievements, attainments and aptitudes needed for effective performance. If your image and the specification match, go ahead and start to recruit. If you are not so sure, have another look. You may find it useful to involve the other members of the team. It will encourage them to think about the longer term as well as providing you with some reality checks. Doing this may slow you down a little. In the fullness of time, however, you will find that this checking will be worthwhile, even if it only removes the need to redefine the job a few months after the occupant has been appointed.

WHAT DOES THE DESCRIPTION OF THE JOB AND SPECIFICATION OF THE PERSON LOOK LIKE?

If we draw from the office supply team example given above, we can illustrate what a job description and person specification would look like for a vacancy for a *Customer Supporter*.

Purpose	To provide prompt and accurate support to customers, ensuring prompt delivery and responses to queries.
Key duties	Develop strong working relationships with customers. Identify customer needs and investigate their future requirements. Respond to queries; resolve any difficulties, disruptions to supply and complaints promptly and positively. Maintain records and databases. Act as a member of the team, providing support and cover as required.
Principle objectives	Maintain customer list at its current level.

Examine current working practices within the team and make recommendations on areas of possible improvement.
Explore ways of increasing total customer list.

Main relationships   Customers, team members and line manager, finance and marketing sections.

The specification for the person needed to fill this job could include:

Abilities	Customer service skills
	Communication and interpersonal skills
	Organizational skills
Attainments	Achieved formal qualifications at post-16 level
	Conducted customer surveys and investigations into their needs and wants
Achievements	Experience of customer service and complaints handling
	Use of common office IT applications to an advanced level
	Introduction of new ways of working
Aptitude	Strong team worker
	Able to challenge others tactfully and influence their approaches.

The importance of these two documents cannot be stressed enough. Together they are the lynch pins, essential for effective recruitment and selection. They will form the basis for your interview questions and give you the criteria for assessment and decision making. We will refer to them many times.

EXERCISE

It is now the time for you to create a job description and person specification for yourself:

1. Think of a job you know well.

2. Gather together any relevant existing documents (eg job description, appraisal reports, business plan).

3. Write down why the job exists:

> **PURPOSE**

4. Add the 4–6 key duties the job holder will have to perform:

KEY DUTIES

1.
2.
3.
4.
5.
6.

---

5. Write down what you want the job holder to achieve over the next year in the form of SMART objectives. Include aspects of the work that are:

- routine, such as the maintenance of operations, systems or services;
- developmental, which build or improve on existing routines and services;
- innovative, such as the introduction of new products, services or ways of working.

PRINCIPAL OBJECTIVES

1.
2.
3.

---

6. Identify any key relationships needed for the job holder to be successful:

KEY RELATIONSHIPS

---

7. Think of what the job holder will be doing so that after a year or so you will be able to say that he or she has been successful in the job. For example, think of the knowledge and skills they will be applying or the problems they will have resolved.

```
┌─────────────────────────────────────────────┐
│                                             │
│                 ABILITIES                   │
│                                             │
│                                             │
│                                             │
└─────────────────────────────────────────────┘
```

8. Think of the learning needed to attain the knowledge and skills required.

```
┌─────────────────────────────────────────────┐
│                                             │
│                ATTAINMENTS                  │
│                                             │
│                                             │
│                                             │
│                                             │
└─────────────────────────────────────────────┘
```

9. Think about the experiences needed to equip the job holder to perform at the level required.

```
┌─────────────────────────────────────────────┐
│                                             │
│               ACHIEVEMENTS                  │
│                                             │
│                                             │
│                                             │
│                                             │
└─────────────────────────────────────────────┘
```

10. Finally, think about any particular characteristics that are absolutely essential for success in the post. For example, if you are looking for an external sales person, you may need someone able to continue to motivate themselves in the face of adversity and setback. If you are recruiting a software designer, you may want someone who is methodical and thorough in their approach to their work.

```
┌─────────────────────────────────────────────┐
│                                             │
│                 APTITUDES                   │
│                                             │
│                                             │
│                                             │
│                                             │
└─────────────────────────────────────────────┘
```

2

Fishing in the biggest pond

INTRODUCTION

In the first chapter, we discussed some of the dangers often met when building up a picture of the best person for the job. By now, you should have a fairly good idea what the ideal candidate will be like, what they are able to do, what they know and what sort of track record will be required. All you have to do now is to find that person so you can ask them questions in an interview.

This sounds easy. There are well-established recruitment practices but the problem with them is that they assume there are sufficient people out there waiting just for your vacancy and they will appear in sufficient numbers to give you the choice of the best. This scenario is true when there is a pool of unemployed people. As this is not always the case, we will use this chapter to explore how you can use the job description and person specification to target your recruitment activity. This should ensure you tell the right people about your vacancy, encourage them to apply and ensure you get sufficient applications from suitable people. In other words, that you will get best value for your time and money.

You will want to fish in the largest possible pond to make sure that you reach as many people as possible with the talents and experience you want. This will assure you that you have tested the field, but the expense has to be balanced with cost and feasibility. There is no point in flooding yourself with hundreds of applications when the best person is sitting at the next desk. On the other hand, you do need to see beyond the end of your nose. This is particularly important if you want to make changes to working methods and to shift the dynamics of your team. This is why you need to be clear about the work to be done and the sort of person best able to do it. Once you know what you are looking for, you will be able to work out where you are most likely to find them.

WHY YOU SHOULD TEST THE FIELD

The British economy has moved closer towards full employment. Many of the lost manufacturing jobs have been replaced by part-time, often lowly paid jobs. There has been a significant growth in the number of people moving on to Incapacity Benefit from Unemployment Benefit and many people have chosen to retire early. Meanwhile the population is getting older.

This means that there are not lots of people waiting around for your vacancy. Many of the people you are trying to attract may not even be looking for another job. Even if they are, it is possible that their reason for wanting to move is due to dissatisfaction with their current position or employer rather than wanting to work for you.

If you are looking for someone in an occupation with known skill shortage you may need to think again about the recruitment methods you intend to use. Before we look at the merits and difficulties of each, we need to look at the factors that may limit your thinking.

Myopia

You could find yourself under pressure to limit your search to current employees and your choice will then be limited. It is possible that a suitable person is already employed somewhere else in the organization. In fact, transferring them could be an advantage as the person will bring knowledge of how the organization works and the perspectives gained from working in other sections. On the other hand, it could be a weakness, particularly if you are seeking someone with wider experience and able to challenge current practice. If you limit your search you will never be sure that you have tested the market fully. If you do appoint someone from outside, you may find they are set up to fail. It can be made more difficult if the person they are replacing was a high performer. There will be an implicit expectation that the outsider will be as good if not better – a hard thing to achieve, and even if you are supportive it can be difficult to reduce other people's expectations.

Over-familiarity

The opposite view can also be found. There may be a belief that everyone who works for your organization, particularly those in other or certain sections, are rubbish. People employed elsewhere, especially by your competitors, are far better, more able and know so much more. This may be true but is unlikely. If your staff are so poor, how come you have done nothing about it before? And how come your organization is still in business?

The biggest danger caused by this attitude is that you can blind yourself to the really good application from a current employee. This person could have exactly the qualities you are seeking but they may have been 'contaminated' by working in other sections (there is always one that is hated by everyone else – often finance or HR); nevertheless, their previous experience plus their inside knowledge may combine to make that person irresistible. You need to make sure before you rush towards bringing in 'new blood'.

You may be accurate in your analysis of the need to bring in fresh ideas and approaches but before you reject internal candidates, you should make sure that your team and the rest of the organization are ready to accept a new person. You will have heard of the adage 'a new broom always sweeps clean'. This is a truism; not necessarily the truth. There are many cases of people appointed to bring about change finding themselves rejected by their new colleagues, who resent the dismissal of existing ways of working and become fed up of hearing 'We did it like this in my previous organization.' The end result can be rapid turnover or a demotivated employee whose bristles have fallen out of their broom-head.

Market testing

You can avoid both of these traps by engaging in some testing of the market. This will help you find out what is going on elsewhere and explore the strength of the field. Conducting a test of the market need not require you to embark on a full-blown recruitment campaign. This can be a costly and time-wasting exercise. It could also be embarrassing.

There are a number of ways in which you can test the market without going public. As soon as you receive a letter of resignation, you can start scanning the places that are most likely to carry adverts for similar posts. This will give you a feel for the demand for such posts and the sorts of things other employers are seeking and offering. There is no reason why you should not obtain further details of similar posts, anonymously as a prospective candidate (this is often done) or by approaching the other employer directly. You never know, you may be able to pool resources. If you are both trying to fill a very similar vacancy, you may find you can work together rather than act in competition by exchanging information about the best medium and level of response.

Is open competition always a good thing?

Some people believe that all vacant posts should be filled only as a result of open competition. This will test the market properly and make sure, it is claimed, that everyone suitably qualified, experienced and able will have a fair opportunity to be considered. This may be true for entry posts but, as we have already discussed, there may be people already employed in your organization able to do the job. Putting them through a full-blown selection process in competition with outsiders may run against other organizational policies such as career development.

If in the end the internal candidate is appointed, you may find they and their colleagues have been demoralized by being put through the process. The end result could undermine your employees' belief in your willingness to invest in your people.

The idea that open competition leads to equality of opportunity simplifies the issue. The reasons why certain groups are disadvantaged in the labour market are complex. The belief that public advertisements are essential to remedy inequality has been around for about 30 years but the barriers are still firmly in place for some groups in some occupations and sectors. This is not to say that all posts can therefore be filled by internal candidates and there is no need to open up the opportunities to people from different backgrounds. To the contrary, we have already discussed why widening the pool of candidates can bring considerable benefits to your organization. We could take a whole book to debate ways of developing a diverse workforce. Suffice it to say here that the decision on whether to test the market or restrict the field to internal applicants only should always be made with the need to promote opportunities and remove unnecessary barriers firmly in mind.

How will your ideal candidate find out about your job?

Once you have decided whether to go to the market to seek candidates, you need to put yourself firmly in the shoes of those people you are trying to attract. Most recruitment activity takes the form of advertising. Usually this is in the Situations Vacant columns of newspapers. The recruitment industry is big business. A survey carried out by Monster Worldwide in 2005 suggested that annual expenditure in newspapers and magazines was running at around $4 billion in the United States with a further $1 billion being spent on internet recruitment. The UK position is also buoyant. The Advertising Association figures for 2004 showed that £1.3 billion was spent.

There appears to be no indication of this changing in the foreseeable future. Fifty per cent of employers surveyed by the Chartered Institution of Personnel and Development (CIPD) indicated that about half of them intend to recruit additional staff – at a time when unemployment levels are at a record low. This means that those looking to move jobs are able to pick and choose, providing they have the qualities being sought by employers.

Employers face the real prospect of not being able to fill jobs, particularly at the lower end of the spectrum, in the ways they have always done. Other changes are also affecting the labour market. For example, the decline in manufacturing and growth in the service sector has reduced the demand for certain skills and increased the demand for others. More and more young people have been encouraged to obtain a degree. Having more people with degrees has resulted in a redefinition of the traditional graduate jobs. The results of the Higher Education Statistics Agency survey in 2004 showed that 38 per cent of students entering the labour market that year were employed in non-graduate jobs. The increase in the graduate population has happened at a time when the shape of the population profile is changing. The ageing of the population means that the pool of new entrants is shrinking. Employers are having to rethink how they fill entry-level and training posts.

The changes to the labour market influence the level of competition between employers. This is evident in recruitment advertising as organizations become more intent on refining the way they attract and treat candidates. When there are plenty of candidates for jobs, recruitment advertising tends to be boring. Employers do not need to make much effort to attract the attention of candidates. However, when there is a shortage of candidates, advertisements become larger, more colourful and far more interesting. Competition between recruitment agencies also becomes fierce and the services they offer employers expand and become more sophisticated.

Competition in the media is also strong, but recruitment advertising has well-established traditions. Most jobseekers and employers know which newspaper carries advertisements for certain types of occupations on which days. Doing something different risks the advertisement not being seen by the people being sought. This could suggest that nothing alters or can alter in the recruitment business. This is not so, as the trends of the past 10 years clearly demonstrate. Not only does the industry have to keep pace with changes in the labour market; it also needs to keep up to date with changes in behaviour.

How the industry has evolved and developed can be seen in the growth of advertising on websites. In 2004, the Interactive Advertising Bureau showed that 11 per cent of recruitment expenditure in the UK was spent on online recruitment. It is now estimated that over 50 per cent of the population has access to the internet. This makes web-based advertising a very real prospect.

Newspaper advertising is chancy. The whole purpose of placing an advertisement is to tell the person with the qualities you are seeking about the wonderful opportunity waiting for them in your organization, but you can only hope that that person will see your advertisement. You only need to look at the circulation figures of the leading national newspapers to estimate the size of the chance. You are also totally dependent on the person you are looking for deciding to buy the newspaper on the day your advertisement appears. They then have to look through the Situations Vacant pages to see your ad.

Many employers have learnt to hedge their bets by using several media to gain maximum coverage. The comparative cheapness of internet advertising makes this financially possible and online advertising has other benefits that we will discuss later.

Many national newspapers now publish advertisements on paper and electronically (*The Guardian* is a prime example). Even local newspapers have their job sites, run for example by companies such as Fish4Jobs and Monster, and a lot of large employers have their own recruitment pages on their websites. Even the JobCentre Plus lists the vacancies notified to the Employment Service on its website.

This medium is definitely expanding apace. Internet advertising is low cost and fast. As access is possible 24/7 the recruitment process is speeded up considerably. It also has other associated benefits not provided by other media, such as the electronic submission of applications leading to online testing and even remote interviewing.

Most of the people who look at Situations Vacant pages or websites are seeking a job. They will know where to look and will be purposeful in their search. They will be seeking a particular type of job, possibly in a specific area, and have some idea of the salary range they want. Others will be looking, in general, just to see what is going and some will read the pages because they are interested in recruitment. Those most unlikely to be looking are those who are happy in their current jobs and have no wish to change. These could be the very people you are seeking.

This is why you have to think very carefully about your target population as there are a number of methods in the recruitment tool kit in addition to traditional advertising. These include targeting of individuals with the qualities sought or using recruitment agencies. Even if you are not able to afford the services of a professional agency, you can use the same techniques but to do so you will need to answer the following questions.

Where do the people you want to attract look for jobs?

Although recruitment advertising tends to be traditional, this has not prevented some very innovative and imaginative approaches. Some public sector services trying to recruit to hard-to-fill vacancies have been highly creative. Examples include advertising in magazines aimed at young women and men, encouraging them to consider careers in nursing, teaching and the police, and army recruitment which can be seen in cinemas. The downside is cost; both in terms of the amount of money needed for their production and the time it takes to prepare and plan such a high profile campaign.

For most employers, this type of advertising is beyond consideration but the approaches have some key learning points that will help you work out how to get to the people you are seeking. The key is the person specification explained in Chapter 1, and as discussed there, you may need to step outside your pre-conceived ideas about the sort of person most likely to possess the skills and experiences you are seeking, particularly if you are looking for applicants in one of the occupations known to be hard to fill. Then you can start to think about how and where to find them:

▌ Are they retraining? If so, perhaps the training provider or local college's career service can help.

▌ Are they likely to be a member of a support group? For example, those suffering from mental health problems may be in membership of a self-help group or parents with young children may take part in toddler group activities. Those having taken early retirement but seeking part-time employment could be active in community groups. Lists of such organizations can be found in local libraries and can be accessed easily through mail shots.

▌ Are they still at school or at college or university? Most have specialist services responsible for providing careers advice. If you are looking for a graduate, there are a number of services provided to employers by the various university careers services.

▌ Are they involved with the JobCentre Plus? The rules applying to those claiming Incapacity Allowance as well as those receiving Jobseeker Allowance require the individuals to engage actively with the JobCentre Plus staff.

▌ Are they already employed? Levels of unemployment are at record low levels. This means that a high proportion of the country is economically active and in work. So there is not a large pool of candidates waiting for your vacancy. Moreover, employers, concerned about losing key workers, are making considerable efforts to discourage them from leaving. Retention strategies now sit alongside recruitment policies. Golden handcuffs are as common as golden handshakes.

Some organizations accept that staff move jobs and see people advancing their careers as a testimony to their investment in development. This is particularly true when an individual moves to another organization with close links to the person's current employer. Such linked organizations include local authorities, health service providers and voluntary sector employers, research bodies and universities, and those with close client/supplier relationships.

If you are in such a relationship, you may be able to advertise your vacancy within your partner organizations. Doing so openly is less likely to attract the accusation of poaching. (This happens when candidates are attracted through clandestine contact.)

How do you get the attention of those able to do your job but not actively looking?

Before beginning a recruitment campaign and investing considerable sums of money and effort it is worth understanding why people move jobs. The most common reason, you may think, is for money. This conclusion has led many employers to invest large sums of money into retention schemes (golden hand-cuffs), hoping this will keep staff with sought-after skills and experience. Employees with specialist and organizational knowledge may thus attract quite high payments from their employer. However, this solution may not be the right one as it assumes that employees are motivated primarily by money and may cause the organization other problems. The most potentially damaging of these could be an equal pay for work of equal value claim. Anyone taking a case will need to demonstrate that the payments made to one person or group were based on gender rather than organizational need. If the reasons for making additional payments can clearly be linked to organizational need and real market pressures, there should be no case. However, you will have a real problem if the payments are given to a favoured few who happen to be men. Other problems can include a pervasive sense of unfairness and injustice. Unequal treatment does not have to be gender based to cause resentment and encourage those subject to less favourable treatment to start job hunting. Then you could really have a turnover problem!

Surveys show that the reason given by the majority of leavers is to secure promotion and career enhancement. Whilst this may be true, and is often the reason given on application forms, does it fully explain why people start looking for another job in the first place? Ninety per cent of employers responding to the 2005 CIPD recruitment and retention survey carried out exit interviews to explore the reasons why people were leaving their present position. Fifty-three per cent said it was for promotion outside the organization but 42 per cent said it was because there was a lack of development or career opportunities with their current employer. These are very laudable reasons but may conceal other motives that are less easy to articulate.

A survey of employees also carried out by the CIPD found that 40 per cent felt that they had little control at work. Twenty per cent said their jobs were very or extremely stressful, 25 per cent felt they had little if no support and more than one-third said their workload was too heavy. Other commonly known sources of discontent include poor internal communication, personality problems and frustration with the work and internal organization. People find these less easy to discuss, especially if they were among the 60 per cent plus who were unwilling to trust their managers. It is reasonable to conclude that people who are happy, well informed, believing they have a future and knowing there are development opportunities ahead are not very likely to be surfing the web pages or scanning newspapers and professional press for a new job. Those not wishing to move need to be contacted in other ways.

Of course, this does not apply to those seeking employment for the first time or possibly returning to work following an absence. Those new to the labour market may not know what they are looking for. The careers and advisory services do an excellent job in providing information about the content of jobs but unless the individual has been fortunate enough to have benefited from a work experience, they will not know what it is like in practice. Those returning after a break may be relying on their previous experience, not realizing just how much has changed in the interim.

What are jobseekers looking for in a new job?

Monster's survey of young professionals found that most were seeking career opportunities, flexible working conditions and a conducive work environment. The compensation package was included but only by 25 per cent. Other factors sought included responsibility, inspiring colleagues and challenging tasks. How often are these found in a job advertisement?

Advertising the vacancy in essence is exactly the same as advertising products and services. Generally, only large organizations with high turnover can afford to take such an approach. They can work with recruitment agencies as the cost of turnover justifies the investment in highly professional recruitment campaigns. These are the organizations that win the prizes in the recruitment industry's equivalent to the Oscars. But the motive for doing what they do is not to win the prize; it is to ensure that sufficient numbers of high calibre candidates are attracted to the vacancy. We can learn from their success and replicate what works, without necessarily spending the same amounts of money.

The first step is to consider the likely applicants, what they are looking for and what they want to know to encourage them to submit an application. We already know from the survey what young graduates are seeking. Another good way to find out is by asking those people recently recruited to your own organization. Has anyone asked them what attracted them, what was appealing and what they wanted to know? These very simple questions will give you some insight into the needs of applicants. The common things applicants will need to be told are listed next.

What do jobseekers want to know?

Traditionally job ads contain information the employer wants to give; they do not necessarily contain the information potential applicants want to know.

While a tight labour market encourages innovation and creativity, it does not necessarily mean that the right information is given. In fact, some of the information, intending to attract, could end up painting a picture that does not reflect reality. Job adverts are not covered by the same legal requirements that ensure that adverts for products and services are accurate and truthful. The only penalty facing an employer who over-sells a job is receiving a number of applications from people who are not appointable.

Key details that should be in any advertisement include the following.

Job title

This should be a reasonably accurate 'label' describing the purpose of the job. For example, 'Sales Representative' tells us that the job holder will be expected to represent their employer and sell things or services. Some job titles do exactly the opposite. What does 'Experienced Temporary Controller' tell us about the job's key responsibilities and duties?

You need to find a word or set of words that transmit the essence of the job you are seeking to fill. Our example used in Chapter 1 is 'Customer Supporter'. While not exciting, it does reflect the reason for the job's existence – to support customers. An example of a misleading job title is 'Teenage Pregnancy Co-ordinator'. What is this job all about?

The job title is usually given prominence in the advertisement. As it is sought by the eye of the jobseeker, it needs to be in the largest font. Some adverts highlight other phrases, for example 'Exciting Career Move', but how does that help the job stand out from the rest? Surely they are all exciting career moves!

Something about your organization

If you are a small organization, you cannot assume that your name is known in every household. Even large organizations find it beneficial to provide potential employees with a little bit of information stating what they do. This only needs to be a sentence or two but it does help applicants decide whether your area of work is one in which they are interested. This can be particularly important if your organization's name does not convey its business. The following example makes this point and shows how a few words can make the situation clear:

Magic Moments

We are a leading marketing/advertising agency looking for an exceptionally bright, efficient and outgoing assistant to support two demanding directors.

Main areas of responsibility

The amount of space depends on how much you are prepared to pay. Research shows that large adverts with lots of text are not necessarily the most attractive; white space matters. Therefore you need to be judicious with the amount of copy you put into your advertisement. This means every word needs to work.

This should be your guiding principle when drafting the description of the job; the main elements will ground the job title. The job description is the source of this information but you will only have the space to include the key components.

For the job of Customer Supporter the opening text could be:

Team member

To give high quality support to customers. As a leading provider of office supplies we pride ourselves on prompt delivery and responses to queries.

One way of building white space in the advert is to use bullets to highlight the main aspects of the job. Thus the Customer Supporter advertisement would continue:

Your main responsibilities will be to:

- Develop good relationships with customers

- Identify their needs and maintain records

- Respond to queries and resolve difficulties.

What you are wanting from the person appointed

This information comes from the person specification and should be sufficiently detailed to enable the person reading the advert to decide whether they are adequately qualified and experienced to do the job. Traditionally, phrases such as '10 years' relevant experience' were used but this does not say what kind of experience is needed. Are you looking for someone with 10 years in the same job or 10 years doing a broad range of varied activities? There is a danger of being too specific; this could simply place unnecessarily restrictive limits on the field of applications by discouraging potential candidates. On the other hand, if it is too general you could get applications from a large number of people who fancy the job or working for your organization but who do not have the qualities you need.

If you spend the time and energy carrying out an analysis of the job requirements and identify the key skills, experiences and attainments needed for effective performance as we discussed in Chapter 1, you will avoid this trap and save time later on. We know the Customer Supporter needs customer service skills, communication, interpersonal and organizational skills. Applicants will also need to demonstrate that they have carried out customer surveys and can use common office IT systems. They will need to be team players but able to challenge others tactfully and suggest ways of changing working methods. Education at the post-16 level of attainment is also required.

Clearly, there is a limit to how much can be put into the advert, unless of course you have a large recruitment budget, and there are other ways of giving applicants additional information. But judicious and skilful use of words will enable you to wrap the key points into a small amount of space, as the following example shows:

> Well organized and IT competent,
> you will be a strong team player who has investigated
> and introduced improvements to customer services.

What you are offering

Salary is a main factor influencing jobseekers' choice yet it is surprising how many job adverts do not given any indication of what is on offer. There may also be other pay-related benefits of interest to potential applicants. Some of these may be taken for granted and are not seen as being of significant interest to those outside the organization. For example, if you work for an organization with a well-established pension scheme, it may not occur to you that this would be a major selling point. Similarly, sickness and other employee assistance schemes may seem mundane to those who are used to them, especially if you have never used them. But, for those who have not had the benefit of such facilities, having them available may be a big pull and they tell applicants what type of employer you are.

The lack of opportunities for career development, advancement and not being able to use acquired skills and knowledge are known to be the main reasons why people leave their jobs. It should follow that offering these very features (providing they are really available) will be a draw.

Working out what the benefits of working for your organization are can be difficult for you. You may be too close. Many organizations use employee surveys to explore which aspects of work give employees most satisfaction and which are in need of improvement. If your survey contains questions like 'What do you enjoy most about your work' and 'What do you like most about working here?', you will have the information you need to go in the advert. If not, you could ask these questions of members of your team.

If they are a cynical bunch and say 'Nothing', you may need to do a little work with them to find out why they stay. You may find the reasons include good team atmosphere, close to good shops, interesting work, the organization is a good employer (but you will need to explore what they mean by this) and so on. You may also find out what is causing them difficulty, but if you ask, be prepared to act on the answers.

Where the post is to be based

Increasingly, with the growing use of web-based recruitment, employers are omitting to say where the job is located. The working population is far more mobile now but you should not assume that place of work does not matter.

People have commitments that limit where they can work; they also have preferences and prejudices. If you are expecting the person appointed to move, you should say what you are prepared to do to help them, for example in a relocation package. You do not need to include this in the advert but some indication of the job's location will be helpful.

How to get in touch and find out more

Advertisements have been seen without any details of how to contact the employer. You should make it clear and easy for those interested to contact you. You should also tell them how you want them to submit their application.

Some applicants like to talk to someone before deciding whether to apply for the job. You may wish to include an informal discussion in the later stages of the selection process (more of this later) but at the outset, simply having someone's name, phone number and/or e-mail address gives a personal touch. If you do this, however, you need to ensure that the person whose name has been given has the necessary information to hand, has the time to talk to applicants and will be at the end of the phone or in front of their computer in the days after the ad has appeared. There is nothing more off-putting than not being able to get hold of the named contact or for that person not to reply to messages.

The more you tell candidates during the recruitment stage, the better they can decide whether the job is for them. This should mean that you will not receive hopeless applications and will avoid having to spend precious interview time giving out basic facts.

HOW DO YOU TEST THE FIELD?

The CIPD 2005 recruitment survey found that 85 per cent of organizations advertised their vacancies in local newspapers. Admittedly these organizations, by and large, were large employers. Their average level of turnover stood at around 16 per cent and most experienced some recruitment difficulties. Again, most had a policy of advertising all vacancies. Internal advertisements were mainly on organizational intranets and on notice boards. Very few organizations engaged in succession planning. If they did, it was on an ad hoc basis.

Newspapers and journals

These are the most familiar places to place advertisements and are where most jobseekers begin their search. Newspaper and journal advertisement is tremendously traditional. Generally, most innovation is in the appearance of the advertisements; the graphics and style used tend to reflect the state of the labour market. When there are plenty of applicants for each vacancy, the adverts tend to be bland, with little to distinguish one employer from another. When there is a shortage of applicants, employers compete. This is when the advertisements become interesting. There is greater use of colour and graphics and the techniques used to attract the eye become creative and imaginative. The aim is for the advertisement to stand out from the page, to capture the eye of the reader and to interest them in the job and the organization.

National newspapers and the Sundays each have their own market segments. For example, the *Sunday Times* carries advertisements for senior positions in private sector organizations. Some of the dailies have particular days for certain occupations. Local newspapers tend to carry lower-level posts or those advertised by local employers. Daily local papers usually run the Situations Vacant column on a regular day. This degree of predictability makes it easy for jobseekers to know where to look.

Most professional bodies publish advertisements in their magazines and increasingly their websites. For example, people looking for work in personnel and human resource management know to look in *People Management* (the journal of the professional body). There are other magazines, not published by the professional body, which specialize in certain occupations. For example, people looking for work in hotels or catering use *The Caterer* and anyone wanting to work as a butler would look in *The Lady*.

It is increasingly common to find advertisements referring those wanting more details or to submit an application to a website. Some websites have been set up by a consortium of newspapers. For example, Fish4Jobs has been set up by a number of regional and local newspaper groups. At the last count, it carried 40,000 jobs and was visited by 1.3 million jobseekers each month. It is no surprise to see the traditional medium being used as a gateway to the new one.

Internet

The shortage of suitably qualified applicants is forcing employers to be more creative about filling vacancies and some are seeking recruits abroad. The **World Wide Web** has opened up global opportunities, thus enabling employers to shop in a world market, and jobseekers can hunt jobs across boundaries. Widening employment opportunities and offering wide-ranging and diverse experiences may seem as if the local labour market is being opened up to international pressures. The reality is very different. Most recruitment is local. People are not that mobile and many employers are very suspicious about the risks of employing someone with an unfamiliar background. Moreover, many countries have entry restrictions limiting those allowed to work in that country.

Nevertheless, the web gives both applicants and employers many benefits. A survey carried out by the Association of Graduate Recruiters found it to be the second most effective medium for recruiting graduates. It allows interactive adverts, gives access to far more information than can be given in an advert and opens the door to the other stages of the selection process, such as online screening. Many employers now prefer applications and CVs to be submitted electronically.

If you do choose to use the World Wide Web you need to decide whether to use your own website or make use of an agency. Obviously the first option depends on whether you have your own public site. The use of intranets for internal communications is growing dramatically even in small organizations. Many have public websites to promote their products and services. Whether you decide to use it alone for external advertising will depend on how easy it is for prospective applicants to find your site and then the adverts placed on it. Have you checked search engines to find out how easy it is to find your organization?

There is no reason why you cannot place the advert on your own site as well as using an agent. Many organizations are taking this approach and, as internet advertising is comparatively low cost, are combining this with traditional newspaper advertising. This can give wide exposure as most newspapers, even local ones, have their classified advertising online.

Other papers, such as the *Guardian*, have developed offshoots (in this case *Guardian Unlimited*) which can give access to corporate career sites. Other websites are growing in importance in particular sectors. For example, jobs.ac.uk is a main source for vacancies in the UK higher education sector. *CW* (standing for *Computer Weekly*) complements the paper edition for jobs in the computer and IT industry. *Monster* and *Total* jobs are very well-known general websites, and employment agencies, such as Reid and Manpower, have their own websites. Even the Jobcentre Plus service posts its vacancy listing on its own and WorkTrain's web pages.

When considering web-based advertising the factors you will need to think about including the following.

Cost

Is the additional cost (which may include redrafting and designing the advert) worth the benefit? If you do not have the links into other stages of the selection process, this can be a real consideration. On the other hand, by not making use of this comparably low-cost medium you could be excluding many suitable applicants. Much will depend on the market in which you are seeking candidates but a survey by the British Market Research Bureau found that the internet is the favoured job-hunting method for one in four of the UK adult population. Ofcom estimated that in 2005 one-third of the UK population used broadband to access the internet. This suggests that actual usage is higher as broadband is not the only means of accessing the internet.

Speed

The use of online advertising can speed up the process considerably but candidates will still need time to decide whether to submit an application or not and prepare their application. If you are happy to accept CVs, perhaps with a covering e-mail, you could receive an adequate response within days of the advert's publication. However, you need to remember that if one in four uses the internet, three in four do not. Not everyone has access to a computer and despite the prevalence of internet cafés and the access provided by local libraries, colleges and the like, not everyone is comfortable or able to use IT. Using the internet alone may therefore restrict your pool.

Targeting

Employers fall into a trap by treating every vacancy in the same way. For sure, if the vacancies are all in the same occupational group, they most probably will be. But treating a vacancy for a financial manager in the same way as the customer supporter, the IT engineer and the sales rep is asking for trouble. Much will also depend on the level of expertise and experience you are seeking. They are very different occupations, with their own conventions and traditions. Even if you use the same media, the language of the advertisement should be chosen to appeal to the particular audience you are trying to target.

Problems of headings and search engines

This brings us on to the problems caused by the imprecision of the English language. One word has more than one meaning and we have several words that mean the same thing. Search engines are very literal and will do exactly as they are told. You therefore need to think carefully about the title and keywords you use in your advertisement. It is worth putting some of the common job titles into *Google* or *Ask Jeeves* to see what sort of nonsense, as well as real jobs, comes back.

Only seen by purposeful seekers – no serendipity

One of newspapers' biggest benefits is that the pages can be seen by those not intending to look. You must have seen people reading over someone's shoulder (on the bus or train). Even if it is only glancing through the pages at the breakfast table or flipping through the local rag as you wait at a supermarket checkout desk, there is a chance you might see a vacancy that is of interest to you. This form of serendipity does not happen online.

Types of jobs (and numbers) advertised

Because the internet is worldwide, it has infinite capacity to hold infinite numbers of advertisements (as well as every other conceivable and inconceivable piece of data). This means that, for commonly vacant jobs, the number of advertisements can be overwhelming. This can be off-putting. Too much choice leads to no choice as people find the task of discerning between all the possibilities just too big.

As the employer, unless you use careful wording to tell prospective candidates exactly what you are seeking, you could find yourself flooded with hundreds of hopeless applications from around the world. You would not be the first to have your e-mail system jammed as your servers are overwhelmed by the rush of CVs and enquiries.

Link to additional information and other stages of the selection process

Even if your advertisement is being handled by an agency or is placed on a newspaper's website, you can give your organization's web address, thus giving links to other sources of information. This can save you the cost of providing a recruitment pack as you can give applicants the information they need to help them decide whether to apply electronically.

You can also provide an e-mail address so that interested people can ask questions. If you do this you need to ensure that the mailbox is cleared regularly and that the requested information is supplied.

Organizations contacted by online recruiter reed.co.uk reported that they prefer applications submitted electronically over those sent in by post. Electronic applications make it easier to screen and distribute applications around selectors without having to worry about photocopying and the slowness of internal distribution systems.

However, there are some risks in relying on electronic transmission:

▌ The sender, unless the receipt check is used, has no way of knowing if the application has been received.

▌ Job applications contain personal and confidential information. It is very easy to send attachments to the wrong person, especially if automatic name checks and address lists are in use. Admittedly, it can be difficult to ensure that paper applications are kept confidential, but there is a greater risk of electronic copies going astray, unless the employing organization is mindful of the need for confidentiality and care is taken.

▌ Files can be corrupted and viruses attach themselves to files. An organization will be more concerned about the safety of its system than receiving an application. If there is any risk from an e-mail, the chances are that it will be deleted. It is unlikely that the recipient will go to the trouble of contacting the sender to check if the e-mail is valid. It will therefore be the applicant's responsibility to check whether their application has been received.

▎ There is so much rubbish around now that it is very easy for legitimate e-mails to be deleted in error. The chances of this are greater if an ambiguous or misleading subject line is used. Asking applicants to quote a reference is one way of avoiding this.

Recruitment websites have a number of add-ons. These include advice to job hunters on how to compile a CV and what to expect at the later stages of the selection process. They also provide services to job hunters that enable them to identify parameters so that jobs fitting their specification can be e-mailed to them directly. Similar services are offered to employers. Job hunters are encouraged to 'file' their CVs which can then be made available for employers who have set out their selection criteria.

Online applications enable electronic screening. Applications can be scanned for keywords and other checks. These can include validating qualifications and looking for gaps in employment. This need is a sad reflection on the large number of candidates known to lie or distort their CVs. It is estimated that as many as one in four applications contains inaccurate information.

Electronic applications also enable online testing as applicants can be asked to complete tests and other forms of assessment online. There has been a growth in the use of psychometric tests anyway and, on the face of it, this seems to be a very real way of speeding up the selection process and obtaining more good quality information about the applicants. The downside, however, is there is no guarantee that the test will be completed by the applicant, alone.

It will be possible to overcome this in the future, when web-based conferencing enables visual as well as verbal contact. This advance may mean that it will be possible to conduct the whole selection process remotely, without any need for personal contact. Whether this will take off extensively is debatable, but certainly the benefits can be seen when there are great distances between the applicant and organization.

Agencies

Employment or recruitment agencies can help find candidates for you, thus avoiding the need to advertise at all as they have lists of people looking for work. Some agencies specialize in particular occupations, others limit themselves to a locality. Many are national, if not international, and can source both temporary and permanent staff.

You will have to pay the agency a fee for its services. What can and cannot be charged is laid down by legislation to protect jobseekers. But fees to employers are open to negotiation between the agency and employer. The costs may seem high on first sight but you will need to take account of the cost of your time. You should also consider your degree of expertise in recruitment and selection. If you are new to appointing staff, you may find it worthwhile to make use of an agency's expertise.

This can include:

▮ Supplying applicants from its register.

▮ Running a recruitment campaign. This can be done openly, using your organization's name and existing reputation, or anonymously if you do not wish to publicize the existence of the vacancy. (Some employers believe that letting customers and competitors know of a vacancy may be damaging or give away competitive advantage.)

▮ Actively seeking applicants. This is a good way to find applicants without letting anyone else know you are filling a vacancy. It also helps you find the people who have the qualities you seek but who are not looking to change jobs.

The use of search consultants, or headhunters as they are most commonly known, can be expensive but the method is widely used, particularly for executive and other senior posts. It has the advantage of confidentiality and can be a very quick way of filling a vacancy. Good search consultants can carry out initial screening and can conduct confidential checks.

Applicants for senior management, director and professional posts also rate this method as being highly effective as it enables them to discuss the post and the employer with an impartial party. They are also able to obtain advice on their application and feedback from someone with considerable experience of recruitment and selection.

Job centres and government schemes

The Jobcentre Plus advertises vacancies, most often for entry-level posts, and those best described as low skilled and in low-paid occupations. They also advertise jobs that turn over frequently as the service is free. The service, however, does not limit itself exclusively to such posts and some employers make use of Job centres as a matter of course. According to the CIPD survey, these are mainly in the public sector and voluntary, community or not-for-profit organizations.

Vacancy cards, stuck on boards with queues of people waiting to scan them, are no longer seen. All vacancies are filed electronically on the Department of Work and Pensions' website and are freely available. Local Job centres have VDU screens for those visiting the centre in person (a requirement for those receiving Jobseeker's Allowance and other benefits).

The Department runs a number of schemes, including participation on training courses, to help those looking for work find suitable employers. It can also help employers find suitably qualified people. Again, if you are new to recruitment and selection it would be worth finding out what help your local Job centre can offer you. ·

Graduate recruitment

The number of graduates in the labour market is bound to increase as a result of the government's policy of widening participation in Higher Education. There is evidence that the nature of jobs requiring graduate-level ability is altering in response to the increased supply of people with degrees. Research carried out by the Institute of Employment Studies found that, for graduates recruited by smaller organizations, limited career tracking was carried out. This resulted in graduates being under-utilized, the effect of this being:

I frustrated employees (who are likely to leave early or put their talents to use in dysfunctional ways);

I increased recruitment costs as a result of high turnover;

I missed opportunities as the employer does not take full advantage of the intellectual capability of employees;

I cynicism from existing staff who may feel that their abilities are undervalued.

This being said, there are many compelling reasons for employing a graduate. The stereotypical image of a young person (male?), with dense glasses, having attended a traditional university, with a serious attitude to life and driving ambition, is well out of date. The so-called 'new' universities produce equally well-educated graduates as the 'old' ones. There are now as many female graduates as male, and many are what is euphemistically called mature. Not all graduates aspire to be 'leaders' or senior managers within the first five years of their working lives. Some want to apply the professional and technical skills they have learnt. Many of those seeking the fast track to senior management will seek employment with larger organizations running graduate training programmes. In fact, smaller organizations can offer a wider range of experience – providing they are prepared to make full use of the capabilities and potential of the people appointed. But this maxim should apply to all staff, not just those with a degree.

Graduate recruitment is very similar to the recruitment of staff without degrees. However, there are additional ways of being able to reach students as they tend to be a captive audience. The vast majority of universities have well-developed careers advisory services that organize:

▌ training in job-seeking skills;

▌ notice boards (intranet as well as physical) and bulletins that contain advertisements from employers, locally, nationally and globally, advertising specific jobs as well as employment opportunities;

▌ the milk-round. This is a euphemism for the employment fairs held each year at which employers exhibit the opportunities they offer. Staff (sometimes recent recruits) are present to describe what it is like to work for the particular organization and to answer questions about the work, the career opportunities and what it is like for real. Many employers carry out initial selection or at least some testing to identify potential recruits. It also allows the students to find out whether the area of work is what they are seeking.

This type of event is not restricted to universities. Many towns run similar events, often in conjunction with Connexions, the former local authorities' careers service, local colleges, the Job centre and local newspapers.

Work placements

Work experience

Most colleges and schools have careers services that are able to advertise vacancies and possibly put you into contact with individuals who may be interested in your area of work. This can lead to work trials or work experience placements. These are regarded as being the most reliable forms of selection as they give both parties – the potential employee and the employer – the opportunity to test out each other over a period of time.

For many employers, taking on young people can be seen as a way to obtain an extra pair of hands in what inevitably needs to be unskilled and undemanding work. This, however, is a misuse of the opportunity. Used properly, work experience is a valuable way of finding out more about a potential employee and providing them with real opportunities to explore the world of work.

Apprenticeships

It is a long time since the traditional approach of recruiting junior staff – apprenticeship schemes – generally died out. There have been some attempts to reintroduce this; the Modern Apprenticeship scheme is the latest. This combines college attendance with practical work experience and leads to formal qualifications. It has had some impact but the vast majority of under-18s remain in education; either at sixth form or in further education colleges, many on their way to university. The Apprenticeships Task Force, reporting in 2005, recommended that resources should be available to enable employers to offer apprenticeships to 35 per cent of young people annually by 2010, so it is possible that the use and acceptability of apprenticeship schemes will increase.

Internship

This is a trend, or perhaps a word, creeping in from the United States. It is a form of apprenticeship or work experience programme but usually unpaid with no guarantee of employment at its end. In the United States, most interns work voluntarily alongside politicians, doing whatever is required. This approach is increasing in the UK as it is seen as the way into a career in politics for graduates. Other forms of voluntary work can be used as an entry to employment. For example, it is not unusual for school leavers filling time before going to university, or graduates taking a break from studying before starting work or returning to complete a higher degree, to spend their 'gap year' on worthy activities.

Other people, such as those returning to work after a career break or changing careers, are recommended to try to find work experience opportunities on an unpaid basis. Some employers see this as a highly effective recruitment method. Work experience, placements, trials and internships only realize their potential if they are well planned and structured. In addition to training and supervision, volunteers need to be coached and given feedback on their progress. The very worst examples include placements where the participants have been used simply as an extra pair of hands, doing highly routine and mind-blowingly boring tasks such as envelope stuffing, photocopying, filing or replenishing stock for days on end.

The very best examples have a previously defined programme which includes a variety of work, meetings and shadowing sessions with key individuals. The participants are generally given a task to complete so they obtain a sense of achievement from having done a real job and making a recognized contribution to the host organization. In return, the employer has the opportunity to find out what an individual is capable of doing and can start to form a relationship. If the placement works out and a suitable vacancy arises, the need to run a recruitment campaign may be avoided, thus eliminating the cost and expenditure of time.

Outdoor advertising

Fierce competition for staff has seen the return of street advertisements. Billboards outside shops and garages as well as recruitment agencies are springing up. During the recessions of the 1980s and 90s, this form of advertising virtually disappeared. All that remained were the occasional postcards in post office and corner shop windows, usually for domestic cleaners, child minders and dog walkers. Now, particularly in cities, the billboards are blossoming again – like spring flowers – heralding nearly full employment.

Some organizations, for example the armed forces and the NHS, have used the sides of buses, roadside hoardings and displays in bus and railway stations to recruit staff to hard-to-fill vacancies. Some large employers are also using these media. One employer, the winner of a CIPD recruitment award, created an interactive booth for use at recruitment fairs, shows and exhibitions.

Clearly, the scale and cost of recruitment methods will be influenced by your recruitment need and budget. If you are opening a store or branch in a new town and need to recruit a lot of staff, it makes sense to use an outdoor method. This would combine your recruitment campaign with advertising the opening of your store or branch. If, however, you want to recruit a receptionist and are well known locally, a small lineage ad in the local paper will do.

Grow your own

We know from the research quoted above that a lot of people leave their current employer because of the lack of career development opportunities. If your aim is to reduce turnover, retain capable employees with organizational knowledge and avoid the cost of unnecessary recruitment activity, it makes sound economic sense, as well as being good human resource management, to invest in your own staff. This means building career paths and having succession plans. Very few employers do the latter, possibly because their business plans only extend until the end of the current financial year!

Even with the high level of uncertainty that every organization faces, some general idea of the sort of skills and abilities you will need in the foreseeable future can be formed. In Chapter 1, we discussed why it is important to look forward when compiling the job description and person specification. The same reasoning can be applied to every job in your organization. Reviewing job descriptions and work plan objectives, regardless of whether they are occupied or not, should be a key part of your annual business planning cycle. This can be linked to the appraisal of your staff's competencies, generally and individually. This opportunity can be taken to encourage your staff to look forward in organizational terms and to consider where their careers are going. The result of such a process will provide valuable inputs into your business plan and create individual development plans. In this way, growing your own workforce can be as much a part of your normal way of working as growing your own business.

Word-of-mouth recruitment

Many small organizations and those with limited experience rely on word-of-mouth recruitment. Existing staff are asked if they know of anyone interested in working for the organization. Some employers have even instigated incentive schemes to encourage staff to nominate potential recruits.

This, on the face of it, is an easy way of avoiding recruitment costs and a quick way of filling vacancies with people who will probably fit in well. However, it is fraught with dangers. Creating a workforce made up of family members and friends can result in the importing of external relationship difficulties and divided loyalties. Imagine the argument from the night before carrying over into the workplace the following morning. It can lead to suspicion of deals being done outside work when partners or close friends work together. Because of these possible tensions, some employers have policies which forbid close family members and those in lasting relationships from working together.

The other problem caused by this form of recruitment relates to unfair discrimination. Using existing staff to identify potential employees can restrict the pool in which you are recruiting. Thus the dominant groups retain and strengthen their position and the chances of you being able to diversify your workforce are reduced. When the Sex Discrimination and Race Relations Acts were passed in the 1970s, employers were warned against using word-of-mouth recruitment as it creates very real chances of committing indirect discrimination.

DISCRIMINATION

Since the fundamental legislation was enacted, the understanding of the different forms of discrimination has extended and become more sophisticated. The scandal of the Lawrence case had a profound effect as the enquiry highlighted how discrimination can be institutionalized even when an employer believes that the necessary policies are in place. Since then, the legal context has become complex as more minorities have been afforded legal protection. It is beyond the scope of this book to explain the many facets of the law, as case law is changing and new legislation added to existing provisions.

Anyone engaged in recruitment on a regular basis should ensure they are up to date and have a good understanding of the law. For the majority though, all that is needed is a general understanding of the basic principles and knowing where to obtain an up-to-date and simple picture. The Department of Trade and Industry, with lead government responsibility for employment policy matters, provides a summary and publishes guides to help small businesses. These provide simple and clear guidance which many large organizations also find useful.

Every stage of recruitment and selection is about discrimination. The word in its purest sense is defined as making choices between one item or person and another. The whole point of the recruitment and selection process is to identify the best person for the job, to decide between applicants. There is nothing wrong with this, providing the grounds on which those decisions are made relate to the job and the needs of the employer. It is wrong when:

▮ those decisions are made about the person on grounds relating to their background or situation;

▮ the criteria used are covert or are related to other factors, such as the personal preferences of those making the decision;

▮ the processes are clouded in secrecy;

▮ decisions are made unfairly.

Direct discrimination

This is the most straightforward form of unfair discrimination to understand as it is overt and intentional. It occurs when conditions which do not relate to the job or the needs of the organization are set and they serve to exclude certain groups. For example, an advertisement seeking a Girl Friday would exclude men and one for a young man to work on a building site would exclude women. Similar laws apply to other minority groups, such as race, marital status, sexual orientation, religion or belief, disability and age.

Indirect discrimination

This form of discrimination is disguised but is deliberate. It occurs when requirements, rules or conditions serve to exclude members of certain groups or place them at a disadvantage even though the rules may appear to apply equally to everyone. For example, an Indian restaurant is not allowed to advertise for a chef who can speak Bengali as it would exclude all those who could not speak this language. It would be allowable if the job involved working only with those who could speak that language or when required for authenticity purposes. Similarly, an advert for the post of marketing manager asking for a degree in engineering and 10 years' experience could unfairly discriminate, and advertising for a fit and energetic manager would discriminate against those with a disability.

Institutional discrimination

This form of discrimination was identified in 1999 by the Macpherson Inquiry into the investigation of Stephen Lawrence's murder. The enquiry highlighted how systemic discrimination can occur even when those involved were trying to be fair. It may be unintended but the organization's practices will have an adverse impact on members of minority groups. An example is failing to have literature in a form that can be read by those with visual impairments. The need to tackle this form of unfairness was legislated for in the Race Relations (Amendment) Act of 2000. This requires all public bodies to mainstream the elimination of discrimination and the promotion of equality of opportunity and good race relations by making these integral to the way public functions are carried out.

The actions needed to comply with this Act suggest ways in which good practice can be developed to ensure that all minority groups receive fair and equal treatment. If you make sure that the following principles are applied, you will probably comply with all legal requirements:

1. Be clear about the job requirements.

2. Identify criteria for use when selecting the person to be appointed.

3. Use the criteria in the advertisement or other recruitment material.

4. Advertise the job openly, in places where those qualified have equal access to the advert.

5. Ask applicants to provide the information you need to assess their ability to do the job (this will be covered in the next chapter).

6. During the interview, ask questions that are related to the criteria (we will discuss this in Chapter 4).

7. Do not make assumptions about who will and will not fit in.

8. Be prepared to adapt to enable people with disabilities to apply, attend for interview and compete fairly.

9. Make sure that people acting on your behalf (eg agencies) comply with the law and best practice.

10. Treat people on their merits and use the criteria as the basis for your final decision (we will look at ways of doing this in Chapter 5).

DON'T MAKE A FOOL OF YOURSELF IN PUBLIC

Going public in an advertisement exposes you and your organization to scrutiny. Good recruitment advertising can do a lot to promote your image and complement your other marketing and promotion activities. It is, therefore, surprising how many employers fail to make the best use of this opportunity. Many advertisements, particularly in local papers, are boring and unimaginative. They fail to sell the job and they do not promote the organization. They simply state the obvious – that there is a vacant position to be filled. There is little information about the organization and, apart from pay, there is even less about the benefits to be provided to the successful applicant. Even worse, some advertisements make some very basic mistakes:

▌ No job title and only vague information about what the job entails.

▌ Silly job titles which are obviously being used for effect with little thought being given to the impression they will create.

▌ Silly graphics. Some have obtuse meaning, some make an attempt at humour but fall flat and some are simply silly. If you are considering using unusual graphics, it is advisable to check with a cynical colleague before giving the go-ahead.

▌ No address or other key information. The move to internet and electronic recruiting means it is common to see e-mail addresses and national phone numbers in the contact details but no location.

▌ Over-selling the job or organization. As employers compete for suitably qualified and able applicants, it is tempting to use marketing techniques. This can be commendable but as recruitment advertising is not governed by rules covering adverts for products and services, there is a temptation to over-egg the offering. Some advertisements promise untold opportunities for advancement, exceptionally high earnings potential and wonderful working conditions. The CIPD survey found that 13 per cent of recruits leave before they have completed six months and 27 per cent before the end of their second year. One of the reasons for early resignation is due to expectations being raised too high during the recruitment process.

The final word of advice is to be attractive but realistic. Before moving on to considering how to deal with the applications that have been generated by your advertisement and other recruitment activities, you are asked to work through the following short exercise.

EXERCISE

The examples given above for the Customer Supporter can be drawn together to form a brief advertisement. See what you think of it:

Team member
To give high quality support to customers. As a leading provider of office supplies we pride ourselves on prompt delivery and responses to queries.

Your main responsibilities will be to:

▌ *Develop good relationships with customers*
▌ *Identify their needs and maintain records*

> ▌ *Respond to queries and resolve difficulties.*
>
> *Well organized and IT competent, you will be a strong team player who has investigated and introduced improvements to customer services.*
>   *In return we offer a competitive salary and generous holidays with plenty of opportunities for you to develop your skills and progress.*
>   *Further details may be obtained from Melanie Peterson on 01234 567 8910 or e-mail at M.Peterson@knowitall.com.uk.*

Can you improve it?
   Have a critical look at:

▌ advertisements appearing in your local newspaper;

▌ a professional magazine;

▌ several leading nationals.

Then go surfing the net. Look at the pages of the leading providers of websites such as:

▌ Monster

▌ Total Jobs

▌ Fish4Jobs.

Can you find the sites of the leading agencies and publishers? Try:

▌ Reed

▌ Manpower

▌ Jobcentre Plus.

Then try looking for a job as an:

▌ IT engineer

▌ accountant

▌ building surveyor

▌ anything else you fancy.

Now write a job advertisement for a post in your organization and ask existing staff whether they would apply for it.

3

Preparing to interview

Now you have told the world of your vacancy, decisions about how the rest of the selection process is to be managed are needed. Ideally, you will have thought about these before going out to advertise. Avoiding these decisions or making shortcuts in the preparation can endanger the success of the whole exercise. They will certainly make the difference between a smooth and efficient interview and one that resembles chaos.

Preparation matters at every stage but it becomes even more important as you approach the final phases. Good applicants do their homework – and are expected to do so. But, how many interviewers turn up five minutes before the candidates, not having read the applications? How many will have worked out what questions need to be asked and who will ask them? No wonder interviews have the reputation of being poor predictors of performance in the job! If you are not prepared and have not sorted yourself out before the interview you may as well just pull someone in from the street.

This chapter will go through the steps you will need to take to ensure that the selection phase runs smoothly. These will give you the best chance of appointing the candidate who will do a good job for you. At its end, you will find an exercise that will help you create your own checklist to highlight the decisions and the actions required before you step into the interview room.

HOW WILL PEOPLE APPLY?

You will need to tell people in the advertisement how you want them to apply. There are five ways in which this can be done:

▎ application form;

▎ CV;

▎ letter or e-mail;

▎ telephone;

▎ in person.

We have already discussed how the internet is changing recruitment and selection practice and how it can speed up submission of applications. However, it has not fundamentally altered the application process. It will probably do so in future when it becomes possible to be more interactive. We will return to this after looking at the pros and cons of each of the application methods, both from yours and the applicants' perspectives.

Application form

Forms tend to be favoured by large organizations as they standardize the way in which the information is presented to the interviewers. For organizations with high turnover, having information in a standardized form makes life easier, interviewers know where to look for key information and they are able to learn how to process large numbers of forms quickly.

Most application forms gather personal information as well as asking for details about work and educational history as these provide the basis of the appointee's personnel record. However, asking candidates for information such as date of birth and home address may get in the way of fair decision making. Personal information of this nature can be a distraction, as research shows that it can lead interviewers to rely on their personal preferences rather than the selection criteria. For example, every town has areas with particular characteristics and it is easy to be drawn into forming stereotypes about the kind of people who live there. It is easy to conclude that someone living in the leafy glades will be well educated and from a middle class background whereas someone from the area with high crime rates and poverty will be from a large family with experience of periods of unemployment and probably poor health. These images are most likely to be wrong but drawing conclusions from applicants' home addresses could get in the way of assessing them against the qualities you are seeking.

Some organizations overcome this by separating personal information from that needed for assessment, thus allowing the interviewers to assess the merits of each application against the job-related criteria. This approach also helps to gather the information needed for equal opportunities monitoring.

Standardized application forms do not allow you to ask for any specific information you may need to help fill a particular vacancy. Generally, they contain sections for applicants to provide information about their education and training, previous employment, relevant experience and hobbies. They also often contain a section which asks the applicants for other information they want to include to support their application. Sometimes, guidance is given to applicants to help them structure the information. For example:

'Please list below your five most important achievements.'

This tells the applicants that you want a list of five, no more and no less, and that you want them to use the space you have provided. An alternative approach would be:

'Please summarize no more than five of your most important achievements. You may use additional sheets if you need more space.'

This invites applicants to write a narrative and to do so at some length. It also enables them to give only two examples if they so choose.

If you need particular information, for example in one or two areas that are very important, you can supplement the standard application form with a questionnaire. This approach is often found when a competencies framework is being used. Applicants are asked to provide evidence to demonstrate their abilities against each of the competencies. An example of a supplementary questionnaire that could be used for the post of Customer Supporter is given below:

Please provide examples from your experience that demonstrate that you possess the following competencies:

Competency	Examples
Ability to introduce sustainable changes to working practice	
Ability to relate to customers and respond positively to their needs	
Ability to work as a team member	
Ability to use a range of IT applications	

Using forms has a cost. They have to be designed, produced and dispatched to applicants, who then have to be allowed time to complete and return them. The normal turnaround time is around two weeks, but this does not give potential applicants a lot of time to do their research into your organization, think about their application and put it together.

They can take candidates a long time to fill in. At one time, it was expected that candidates would complete the forms in their own handwriting, as some interviewers believed they could detect personal characteristics from script. Very few now rely on handwriting, even though graphology is used in Europe.

Most people use word processors. They may complete the basic parts of an application by hand and attach additional typed pages. Interviewers then will have to sift through a lot of pages to find the information they want and often have to deal with forms that contain the words 'Please see attached CV.' Some organizations pre-empt this by telling applicants that CVs are not acceptable.

IT can be used to bring many benefits to both applicants and interviewers. Electronic production and distribution enables application forms to be customized so that they can obtain the information needed to fill a particular job. Sending out the form electronically means that applicants can complete their application in a standard format using pre-set boxes. They are thus able to think about the content rather than worrying about personalizing the form's presentation.

Standardization, moreover, can remove some of the factors that are known to distract interviewers and draw them to using their personal biases. We all have our own preferred fonts, type size and layout and using a predetermined form can remove some (but probably not all) of the other distractions such as spelling and typing mistakes that can simply get in the way of assessing candidates' real abilities.

London Jobs, as part of its online service, offers other services such as a component called Filtering Forms. An employer can ask as many questions as is necessary, including key questions that can be scored. The form is sent by e-mail to all those interested in the job. The returned forms are scanned and only those providing the correct answers to the key questions (ie those that satisfy the rules built into the form) will be sent on to the organization.

Electronic forms reduce distribution costs and can shorten time needed for candidates to complete and return the forms. It also simplifies internal distribution between the people involved in short-listing. However, it can be dangerous to rely on this as the sole means of application. As with only using the internet for advertising, it cuts out all of those who do not have access to computers and IT facilities. Using only electronic application could exclude the very person you are seeking, especially if you are not looking for someone who is computer literate or if these skills could be attained by on-the-job training. You still need to allow time for the candidates to do their research and complete the form.

CV

CVs are a frequently used and popular means of submitting an application for a job. For the applicant, they can be used repeatedly for most job applications. Only the covering letter needs to be customized for a particular job. The form enables the applicant to create the personal equivalent of a sales brochure.

Typically, a CV is limited to one, or at most, two pages. Yet it is meant to be a summary of the individual's working life. Some believe that this document should be a comprehensive and factual record. Others think it should bring out only the best bits: those that an employer would find most attractive. Some job coaches will work with jobseekers, helping them to develop their CV so it is attractive and as positive as possible. The brevity of the form allows applicants to conceal gaps in their work history and yet draw attention to the most telling aspects of their education and career history. Sometimes it can take a very experienced selector to recognize when this is happening and that it is the gaps between the lines that tell the real story.

Despite this potential pitfall, the CV does have much to commend it:

▌ There is less time lag between the advertisement appearing and the applications being received, as the applicant is not waiting for a form to be sent out and the employer is not waiting while the applicant completes and returns it.

▌ There are no production costs. All the costs are borne by the applicant.

▌ The fact that there is a widely accepted way of putting together a CV means that for the most part, all the necessary information will be provided. If extra information is required, this can always be obtained in the stage between long-listing and short-listing.

On the downside, the opportunity to send out further information about the job and organization is lost. This omission can be important, for, as we will discuss later, providing applicants with quality information early in the process can make a positive contribution to the long-term success of the appointment.

Having to read between the lines on a CV can be demanding. To avoid being wooed by one that conceals more than it reveals, you first need to regard the form as a sales brochure. The interviewers who see the CV as a factual statement are those most likely to be misled. If you approach the task of reviewing a pile of CVs with a degree of scepticism, you are less likely to be taken in by those wanting to hide something.

It is a sad fact that a significant proportion of applicants lie in their application. They falsify qualifications and claim the achievements of others. Even more, applicants exaggerate. They may, for example, increase their annual earnings or give acceptable reasons for leaving previous jobs rather than the truth. As very few interviewers make full checks, the risks of being found out are relatively low. Interviewers tend to accept and take what they are told on face value. Lying employees, however, have damaged some employers, and so increasing numbers are instigating rigorous checks. For the majority, the costs of this and time involved may seem high, especially as most of us think we are good judges of character and can read between the lines.

If you decide to ask applicants to send in their CVs you should make sure that you use your selection criteria diligently. You should look for gaps and be cynical about claims of achievements that seem a little grandiose. If you are doubtful, you should be prepared to approach previous employers and ask specific questions. Qualifications have undergone considerable changes over the years and it is not always easy to untangle abbreviations or equivalents. You may find it worthwhile to check qualifications. The internet is a good source but it tends to be better for current rather than historic information. Your local reference library may be able to help if you are unsure.

You can always ask candidates to supplement their CV by requesting them, in the advertisement, to provide a covering letter outlining why they think they should be appointed to the job.

Letter or e-mail

For letter, now read e-mail. At one time, an e-mail was considered to be the electronic equivalent of a memo. Now it is anything you want it to be. An e-mail can be anything from one word in length to a long discourse. Now the word e-mail mainly describes the mode of delivery rather than the content.

A covering letter, regardless of how it is sent to you, can be very revealing. As its presentation and content are not prescribed, the way applicants approach the task will tell you quite a lot about their communication skills, their thought processes and how they are able to structure a written document. If these qualities are part of the specification, the letter will be a useful adjunct to the other modes of assessment you can use in the selection process.

Relying on an application letter alone, however, is not necessarily advisable. Without an accompanying CV, you may find that critical pieces of information have been missed. In addition, the applicants will have their own individual ways of constructing their letters. This means that you will not find the usual consistency obtained in CVs or application forms.

A main benefit is that a letter or e-mail has no cost for the employer. The turnaround time from the appearance of the advertisement to the receipt of the application can be minutes, if electronic transmission is being used. The only real cost you will face is that incurred in assessing the merits of each application.

Telephone

Asking applicants to ring in is a method often used by recruitment consultants or employers with specialist recruitment teams. The CIPD survey found that telephone interviewing is now used by over a quarter of organizations. Its increased use reflects the growth in call centres and other types of service occupations that depend on telephone skills.

A structured telephone conversation allows a short and focused interview, which can be used to discount unsuitable applicants early in the process. The interviewer can gather basic information in a standard form and carry out some initial screening. However, the form is limited and the interviewer will need to set down questions so that each applicant is treated in exactly the same way as the others. Ideally, the interviewers should be trained, as this mode of interviewing requires its own set of skills.

The main limitation is the lack of face-to-face interaction. Non-verbal communications are known to be important when assessing a candidate's suitability for a post (we will discuss this in greater depth in Chapter 4). The other main limitation is the reliance on one interviewer. Unless the conversation is taped, or conference telephoning is used, only one interviewer will have direct experience of the applicants. Thus, there is the potential for discrimination to creep in. Certain dialects and accents may appeal to or switch off some interviewers, some may be hard to decipher and people with speech impediments may be disadvantaged.

The main benefit of the telephone interview is that it provides some interaction early in the process. This helps applicants, as much as an employer, find out whether they are likely to suit each other. The other main advantage is speed and the low cost. The main cost you will bear is the time needed to respond to applicants and deal with the assessment as well as answering their queries. Such phone calls could be expected to last as much as 30 to 45 minutes. The person dealing with the calls should make comprehensive records of each one so they can be used in the later stages of the selection process and withstand scrutiny if there are any challenges.

In person

You may think that the days when people walked into an employer's offices and said 'Gizz us a job, mate' are long gone, having disappeared with the high levels of unemployment and the last episode of *Auf Weidersehen Pet*. You are wrong. As organizations struggle for applicants, especially for customer service and entry-level jobs, they are returning to advertising billboards and posters. This method also heralds the return of the applicants turning up unannounced at the counter or the reception desk. The people staffing these points therefore need to be prepared so they are able to respond appropriately to the applicants.

Whether it is simply telling them how to apply or respond to the inevitable question 'What is it like to work here?', they need to be briefed. Failure to do this will result in your efforts to recruit being wasted. Poor applicant handling in the early stages can results in low numbers of applicants!

Confidentiality

Regardless of the method, you need to think about how you are going to handle the applications you have received. Ideally they should all be acknowledged. Nothing is worse for the jobseeker than receiving no response. It is discouraging and demoralizing. It is also discourteous. In the days when organizations were receiving large numbers of applications, it was acceptable, because of postage costs, to say that failure to hear within a certain number of weeks meant that an application was not successful. However, when organizations are competing for recruits, as now, this excuse does not hold good. It becomes even weaker if you are accepting applications electronically. There is no defence in the current labour market: you should acknowledge the receipt of the application.

You also need to think carefully about how applications are to be stored. Regardless of the mode of transmission or form of an application, they contain personal data and therefore they fall under the provisions of the Data Protection Act. This means that the information contained therein should only be used for the purposes for which it was gathered. You will also have to consider how and where the data is stored and who has access to it. This should be limited to those directly involved in the selection process.

If you intend to distribute the applications physically, you should ensure they are sent out in sealed envelopes marked confidential, therefore safeguarding privacy. This is less easy if you are distributing the documents electronically. In either case, how will you make sure that the other members of the selection process respect and safeguard confidentiality? It is not unknown for managers to show applications to other members of the team for their comments, and amusement. Applicants can make silly mistakes in the same way as students sitting exam papers. However, apart from the need to comply with the Act, imagine how the person appointed would feel if his or her new colleagues knew that in their previous job, they had been responsible for a large budgie!

It is your responsibility to make sure that all the other people involved in the process understand that they are dealing with sensitive information about real people's education and employment histories. They should be aware of the legal implications of misusing such information. More importantly, they should be aware of the impact their abuse of privilege could have on the people concerned.

HELPING APPLICANTS GET TO KNOW YOU

Research shows that the better the information you provide to the applicants, the more likely they are to participate as equal partners in the selection process. They are thus better placed to assess their fit with your job and your organization. If this means that an applicant decides that the job is not for them and they pull out of the process, this should not be seen as a failure; to the contrary, it is a positive decision that will save time and effort for both of you.

Research also indicates that the closer the applicants' expectations are to reality, the greater will be the chances of them settling into the job and your organization quickly. It also enhances their chances of success in the job. There are a number of ways in which you can provide applicants with the information they need about your organization. You will need to balance the costs of doing this with the benefits of having well-informed applicants and the value added to the process.

Informal discussions and visits

Some organizations find it is worthwhile to encourage applicants to make contact before they decide whether to submit an application. As well as providing them with information, you can use the opportunity to carry out initial screening. This can take two forms: you can make an assessment against your criteria and note potentially good and weaker applicants; you can also discourage those applicants who clearly do not have what it takes. If you do this, however, you need to ensure that it is the criteria contained in the person specification that is driving your judgement, not your personal preferences.

Informal visits also provide applicants with the opportunity to meet other members of the team and see the workplace. It gives team members the chance to say hello but this can be disruptive and can lead to the formation of wrong impressions. These can damage future working relationships if one applicant who shines in the selection process and is subsequently appointed made a poor impression during the informal visit.

The internet

The internet makes it very easy to provide applicants with good quality information about the job and your organization. It does not give you contact with the applicants but it can help them decide whether to apply or not. If this means that you are only receiving applications from those people who are really interested in your job and have the qualities you are seeking, surely this is to the good. A lot of the cost incurred in the recruitment and selection process is consumed by the work needed to screen out unsuitable applicants. If this is done by the applicants themselves, this will save you and them time and money.

The internet can provide directly relevant information as well as links to other parts of your website so candidates can be referred to information about your organization. How much investigation an applicant has carried out can be used as a measure of their interest in the job. However, it can also be a reflection of how much time they have. This may be dictated by the demands of their current job and thus be outside their control. It is also governed by their access to internet facilities. If this is not part of your selection criteria, you should consider the implications of what is in effect a restriction limiting the opportunities of those who do not have the equipment or access. You may be excluding really good candidates.

Recruitment packs

At one time, organizations, particularly those competing fiercely for recruits in specific markets, put a lot of effort into the design and production of recruitment packs. These contain additional information to help potential applicants decide whether or not to apply. Some packs contain guidance notes outlining how an application should be presented as well as giving background information about the job and the organization.

The format of these packs can vary considerably. Some comprise pages and pages of dense information that make one wonder if any but the most committed and determined applicant would be persuaded to apply. Others are highly imaginative, making full use of the graphic designer's skills. The quality of the information may be dubious but the artwork could be a candidate for an award. Rarely do organizations evaluate fully the effectiveness of their recruitment spend. There is a growing awareness of the need but evaluation techniques are not well developed. Moreover, the way the internet is replacing the traditional recruitment approaches introduces other considerations in addition to cost.

Nevertheless, it is worth thinking about the information applicants may need and how best to make it available. The easiest way to decide what to include is to put yourself in the applicant's chair and ask yourself what you would want to know about the job and the employing organization. Asking newly appointed colleagues what they found most useful and unhelpful when they were deciding what to do can also be revealing.

FINDING OUT MORE ABOUT THE APPLICANTS

The recruitment and selection process is all about making decisions on fit. You want to find an applicant who fits your specification, who will fit in with other team members and will fit with your organization's culture. The applicant will be looking for a job that provides the rewards, pay-offs and benefits that fit with their needs. They will also be seeking colleagues with whom they will be able to work productively as they will want to fit in. Both sides will need information so they can assess the degree of match. Good quality information makes this decision making easier and more reliable.

Providing and obtaining sufficient and accurate information is essential, as human decision making is fraught with problems. We use personal preferences, and our biases can skew decisions. We make errors in our judgements, for example assuming that the individual at the centre of our attention is solely responsible for events; we also assume that if we like one aspect of an application we will look favourably on all aspects. The reason for involving other people and obtaining information from a range of sources is that they serve to reduce the adverse effects of these errors and biases. They will improve the reliability of our predictions about likely performance on the job and will make our decision making more valid and robust.

However, you can go overboard by trying to obtain information from too many sources before the interview. This will increase the cost and time needed without improving the quality of your decisions. You will also have to consider whether the other sources of information you want to use are legitimate. Applicants do not like being asked to take part in selection activities if they see them as nothing more than games. They do not like being played with. Organizations were able to get away with some outlandish selection techniques, believing they would add value and tell them more about the applicants, when competition for jobs was high. Now organizations are competing for applicants, any selection method needs to have high face validity, ie it must be acceptable to the applicants as well as being closely related to the needs of the job and organization. If you approach external sources for information about applicants, you will need to consider the potential for breaching confidentiality and contravening the Data Protection Act.

Testing

The use of psychometric tests has exploded. The test agency Hogrefe surveyed the FTSE-100 companies and found that 81 per cent reported the use of psychometric tests and 76 per cent said they used both personality and ability tests. The CIPD surveyed a wider range of organizations in 2005 and found that 36 per cent used personality questionnaires, 39 per cent used numeracy and literacy tests and 40 per cent used general ability tests. One reason for this growth is to supplement the traditional interview, demonstrating the increased awareness of the need to improve the predictability of the interview. Another reason is as a result of the difficulty many employers faced during the years of high unemployment when trying to distinguish between applicants with similar qualifications and backgrounds. Other means of exploring potential had to be found.

The growth in demand for tests has been accompanied by an increased range of products. Tests available from a range of sources can be applied to most occupational groups. Reputable suppliers go to great lengths to assure the validity of the tests they sell and to ensure that they do not favour members of one group over others.

Despite court cases and the efforts of the main suppliers and the British Psychological Association to establish standards of best practice, there are some rogue practitioners operating in the marketplace. It is comparatively easy to get hold of tests on the internet that purport to have the same degree of validity as their legitimate cousins. One reason why this is comparatively easy to do is because most tests, particularly those assessing personality, are based on a few well-known theories that are relatively simple to replicate.

Tests can be broken down into three basic groups: personality, cognitive or thinking skills, and practical ability tests. These need not be mutually exclusive and it is possible to use the different forms of test in combination. Before deciding which type of test to use you need to be clear about why you want to use a test and which features of your applicants you want them to explore.

Personality tests

Sometimes called inventories, most take the form of a questionnaire based on well-known and thoroughly researched theories of personality and are designed to explore traits, personality characteristics and personal preferences. Examples can include introversion, anxiety, tolerance of change and stress, or preference for being alone or in groups.

The developers of the tests will have piloted them on different groups in the targeted population and will provide norm tables. They also train and accredit practitioners. The norm tables help to align the features being explored by the test to the criteria contained in your person specification and will help you distinguish between applicants. This is where the skill of the practitioner comes into play. They will interpret the results so that you and your fellow interviewers are able to combine the evidence produced by the test with that gathered from the other modes of assessment being used. The practitioner will also be able to provide feedback to the candidates.

Some of the tests are very well known and have been used extensively for a number of years. You may find that your applicants will have completed the test previously. Generally speaking, this mode of assessment is widely acceptable as applicants appreciate the need to have rigour in selection. They also welcome the feedback normally offered by organizations using tests, for even if they are not offered the job this means they will get something from the process that may help increase their chances of success in other applications.

Thinking abilities

This type of test can assess the cognitive or intellectual abilities of applicants by exploring performance, for example in problem solving, critical reasoning, learning abilities or analytical skills. They can also test basic thinking abilities, for example in areas such as literacy and numeracy. These are of considerable concern to employers as more become aware of the widespread difficulties some people have in these areas. In some parts of the community, difficulty with reading, spelling, writing and using numbers can be as high as 25 per cent of the population.

Practical abilities

There are a number of commercially produced tests that help you explore practical skills. The most well known include typing and computer usage as well as tests of manual dexterity. Most administrative, professional and managerial jobs require the application of practical skills, which can be assessed through the use of tests such as a case study or an in-tray exercise.

Interpersonal and communication skills can be assessed by a test that simulates certain aspects of the job. For example, it is possible to have someone role play a customer with a complaint and ask each applicant to demonstrate how they would respond. Great care is needed to ensure that each applicant is faced with exactly the same situation at the beginning but as it rolls out it will depend on how the 'customer' and applicant interact. Again, care is needed to ensure that no one applicant is treated any more or less favourably than the others.

It is also legitimate to assess your personal reaction to each applicant, if interpersonal skills are included in the person specification. If an applicant offends you or impresses you with their abilities to build rapport rapidly, your perception can be used as legitimate evidence to be included in the assessment. You will need to be able to say what made you react to the applicant in the way you did, and why, for there is a danger that you are relying on prejudices and personal biases. However, if you are able to articulate the aspects of the applicant's behaviour that caused you to react in a particular way, this will provide legitimate evidence to help you assess their fit against the criteria.

Testing in person

If applicants are going to be asked to complete a test, it is courteous to give them warning as they will need to know how much time to allow and to prepare themselves. You will need to arrange for them to be able to complete the test in a suitable environment. You must also find out if any have disabilities that require special assistance or accommodation. For example, someone with visual impairments may need a reader (either human or electronic) to enable them to complete the test. Others may need additional time.

You should ensure that each applicant has the same chance to demonstrate their abilities and is treated equitably. This does not mean treating everyone exactly the same; some flexibility is needed so you can respond to an individual's particular needs and answer their questions. The main factor is to ensure that no one is given an advantage that would enhance their chances. Test publishers provide guidance on how to achieve this. They have also published useful guidance on how to comply with the Disability Discrimination Act.

Testing online

Asking applicants to complete a test online appears to offer many benefits. Applicants can complete the test in their own time. You do not have to provide special facilities or arrange complex timetables. The results can be scored electronically and presented to you quickly.

The major disadvantage, however, is that you will never be sure that the applicant alone has completed the test. They may have had help or even had someone else do it for them. You will never know. This uncertainty begs questions about the value of online testing.

Some tests, mainly personality inventories, can be obtained freely or at low cost on the internet. They may be based on the same theories of personality as the tests available from the major suppliers. However, it is unlikely they have the same level of validity, as it is unlikely they have been tested with the same degree of rigour. This means that the results are questionable and can lead one to wonder if they have any more value than the questionnaires that appear in popular magazines.

The main benefit of using tests to supplement an interview and to augment an application is that they provide you with evidence you would not necessarily be able to obtain easily elsewhere. This evidence can be tremendously helpful when it relates to the factors that will contribute to the success or failure of the person appointed to the job.

The main argument against their use is cost. You will need to buy them and probably secure the services of an appropriately trained and qualified practitioner. You will also have to insert another stage into the selection process, which will increase the time needed to fill the vacancy. More importantly, you should resist the temptation of introducing a test into your selection process simply because you think it is the right thing to do. You should be clear about the reasons why you want to test your candidates and know what value it will add.

Assessment centres

Assessment centres have also increased in popularity as employers seek ways of improving the predictability of selection. An assessment centre is not a place; it is a collection of exercises and tests put together to explore the criteria drawn from the personal specification. The combination of assessment modes means that the applicants' abilities across the whole range of job demands can be explored. Several assessors carry out the assessments, thus giving breadth to the assessment of the applicants' abilities and providing a more rounded picture. This picture, being based on the criteria, means that the assessment is directly related to the needs of the job. It also means that all the applicants are assessed consistently.

Figure 3.1 shows how a matrix can be developed to ensure all the criteria are assessed by several different types of activity. The activities are designed to enable the demonstration of the skills across the range of tasks normally found in the job.

Post – Customer Supporter	Exercises			
Criteria	**In-tray**	**Presentation**	**Case study**	**Group exercise**
Customer service skills		/	/	/
Communication and interpersonal skills		/	/	/
Organizational skills	/	/	/	
Achieved formal qualifications at post-16 level	See application			
Conducted customer surveys and investigations into their needs and wants	See application			
Experience of customer service and complaints handling	/	/	/	/
Use of common office IT applications to an advanced level	Assess in separate test			
Introduction of new ways of working		/	/	/
Strong team worker		/	/	/
Able to challenge others tactfully and influence their approaches	/	/		/

Figure 3.1   Assessment centre matrix

The matrix also shows the need to use other sources of evidence to explore the full range of requirements. Ready-made assessment centres can be purchased from test producers but if you decide to do this, you will need to exercise some care to ensure the centre's activities assess the right criteria and reflect the nature and conditions of the job. Failure to do so may backfire as you could select someone who performs wonderfully in the assessment centre but cannot do your job. Choosing non-relevant activities may also result in applicants feeling as though they are being asked to play games. No one likes this form of treatment. If you fall into this trap, you could find yourself with no applicants.

Providing you do not make these fatal mistakes, assessment centres are generally well accepted as applicants feel that they are given opportunities to demonstrate their abilities. They also receive good quality feedback. The major disadvantage is that their design requires specialist skills. This has a cost. The assessors also need to be trained and the centre takes time to run. All of these factors add to the cost. So, as a result, the use of assessment centres tends to be confined to senior posts and larger organizations that have high levels of recruitment activity.

References

References provide evidence of applicants' previous experience. You should not, however, fall into the trap of asking referees to assess candidates' abilities to do the job you are seeking to fill. All they can tell you is how the applicant performed when the referee had contact with them. The fact that as many as one in four applicants falsify their applications has increased the reliance on references and some notable court cases have drawn attention to the need to carry out checks.

The major weakness with references, however, is your reliance on the abilities of the referee to provide you with the information you need, in a form you set. You will not know the nature of the relationship between the provider of the reference and the applicant. Some organizations have a policy of authorizing only named people to provide references. This is to safeguard the organization against claims for damages, if the reference is inaccurate or contains defamatory comments. In practice, it means that the person writing the reference may have little if any knowledge of the applicant apart from that given in their factual employment record.

Some employers seek further information by approaching referees in person or asking for a telephone reference, believing that being able to speak to the referee directly will enable them to be more revealing and thus able to disclose a more accurate picture of the applicant. However, this again leaves you prey to the referee's ability to describe performance dispassionately. Moreover, you are not aware of the nature of the relationship between the applicant and their previous employer. We know that many people seek to leave their current jobs because of the quality of this relationship, and who is to say that the referee is competent?

We will return to this subject in Chapter 5 as it is more common to obtain references later in the selection process. As many applicants do not want to tell their current employer that they are looking for another job, it may not be appropriate to seek a reference from this source before the interview. It may be possible to approach other referees but applicants will probably only name someone willing to give them a good reference. Mostly, the information from these more remote sources will provide confirmation rather than adding anything of real consequence.

SIFTING THE APPLICATIONS

This stage is alternatively called making the first cut or initial screening. This is when you decide which of the applications are from people you would like to interview and which are not acceptable. When carrying out the screening, you should rely exclusively on the predetermined criteria. You have entered the first stage of selection, where you discriminate between the applicants, reject some and turn the others into candidates.

What? Discriminate? Yes, selection is a matching process; what matters is that the discrimination (ie the exercise of your judgement) is made fairly, on grounds that are relevant and related to required features of the job. The processes you use to make these decisions should be open and capable of being scrutinized. You developed the selection criteria to support this process. Now you must put them to use.

You can do this in two stages. In the first, when you draw up a long list, you go through the applications looking for those that do not meet the basic, essential requirements. Having reduced the numbers, the second stage allows you to focus on the areas that need more detailed consideration. The resultant shortlist will contain the names of those individuals you have decided to interview: your candidates.

You can make this task easier by involving other people. It is always advisable to have at least two people involved in selection decisions to balance your personal preferences with those of another. You can either short-list together or do so separately. In this case, comparing your conclusions can be very revealing. It will show whether you have the same or different understanding of the criteria and whether your personal preferences have come into play. Discussing these will give you insight into your own thought processes and how your biases can affect your decisions.

If you decide to involve more than one other person, you will need a mechanism to draw together your respective views. A short-listing meeting is the most common way of doing this, but if there is a difference of view between those involved, you may have to use your role as the line manager of the post to assert your right to make the final decision.

Accepting applications electronically facilitates the use of advanced technology to screen applications by scanning for key words or certain terms. Care must be exercised initially to ensure that the words or terms chosen relate to the criteria laid down in the person specification, and that synonyms and acceptable alternatives are included in the scanning rules. You will have to monitor the system to watch for any signs of unfair discrimination. You also need to remember that, under the Freedom of Information Act, applicants have the right to know how decisions made about them by computers have been reached.

For most recruiters, this approach is still in its early days. So, for the meantime, most of us will have to rely on the more traditional ways of short-listing candidates. However, technology is developing rapidly so it will not be long before short-listing will be done automatically.

Who can help you make your decisions?

Even when artificial decision making becomes widespread, the key selection decisions will be made by humans. This brings us to considering who to involve. You may think it is easier to interview on your own but if you do so you could make yourself vulnerable to charges of unfairness and discriminatory practice. Involving other people acts as a safeguard as well as providing support and assistance during the interview. This can be far more beneficial than just acting as an insurance policy, as fellow interviewers can listen, watch and make notes while you are asking your questions (and you can do the same for them). When it comes to making the decision, you will each remember different parts of the interview, so your collective memory will be more complete. Your more rounded picture of the candidates will help you be confident in your decision. You will also have added transparency to the process, as the reasons for your judgement will have been discussed. This allows them to be recorded and used to justify the outcome of the interview, should you be challenged. But who do you involve?

You may find it helpful to have the assistance of a colleague from a section with which the job holder will be working closely. It will also give the person appointed an initial contact with whom they can start to build their new working relationship. If your organization has an HR department, it makes sense to draw in the HR manager responsible for your area, and, if the post is a specialist one, requiring technical knowledge you do not have, you may find involving someone from that field useful.

Should you involve someone from your existing team? This can be a tricky decision. The strongest argument for so doing is that the person appointed needs to be acceptable and fit into the team. How do you decide which team member to involve and what happens to the opinions of those not included? What happens if the candidate not selected by the team member is appointed? Will you have to overrule their view? On balance, it may be better to find other ways to make the existing team feel part of the process. For example, by inviting them to meet candidates in informal settings, perhaps during a tour round the workplace or by joining them for lunch.

What about your boss? This decision depends on how much delegated authority you have and the nature of the relationship between the two of you. If you work well together and your boss trusts your judgement, working together to appoint a new member of staff can be beneficial. You can benefit from your boss's advice and working together can provide an opportunity for your boss to coach you and add to your development. However, if the relationship between you is strained, it may be better to argue against your boss's participation. If you do not win the argument, however, you will just have to manage the situation by negotiating your respective roles.

Ideally, you and your boss will have agreed who will make the final decision and what will happen if you have different views. Don't forget, it will be you who will be responsible for managing the new appointment and will, to a certain extent, determine whether the new job holder will be successful or not. If you are not committed to the decision and appoint someone who, in your mind, is second best, the chances of that person being successful will probably be less than if your first choice was appointed. Discussing this and the possible impact on the performance of your team may help you and your boss work out your respective roles in the selection process.

The use of a simple decision-making technique, the matrix, will help you manage the involvement of several people. A matrix provides a means of analysing applications in a way that can help reduce subjective judgements. It also provides a rigour to the assessment that will help you withstand pressure to short-list applications that do not meet the criteria. Moreover, the use of a matrix creates a record that can be used to demonstrate equity and transparency if your decisions are ever challenged.

SHORT-LISTING MATRIX

Building the matrix is easy. You start with the criteria you developed in the early stages of the process when you were writing the person specification. You then simply add the names or identifiers for each application. All those involved in the short-listing will have their own copy to assess each application against the criteria. You can develop a scoring scheme, if you wish, so the applications with the highest scores are from those to be invited for interview. Alternatively, you can use indicators so the final decision is qualitative in nature. You will be able to see the difference in the two examples given in Figures 3.2 and 3.3. They both use criteria taken from the person specification we created in Chapter 2 for the post of Customer Supporter.

If you prefer to use a scoring scheme, you will need to make sure that, as well as having the same understanding of the criteria, the other short-listers develop a common meaning for the numbers. It is not unusual to find that people using rating scales or scoring schemes use the numbers in different ways. You can overcome this to some extent by providing descriptors, as we have done in Figure 3.3.

Post – Customer Supporter	Short-lister				
	Applicants				
Abilities	**A**	**B**	**C**	**D**	**E**
Customer service skills					
Communication and interpersonal skills					
Organizational skills					
Attainments					
Achieved formal qualifications at post-16 level					
Conducted customer surveys and investigations into their needs and wants					
Achievements					
Experience of customer service and complaints handling					
Use of common office IT applications to an advanced level					
Introduction of new ways of working					
Aptitude					
Strong team worker					
Able to challenge others tactfully and influence their approaches					
Short-list?					

Please use the following indicators to record your assessment of each application against the criteria laid out in the person specification.

✓   Meets criteria   X   Does not meet criteria
?   Further information needed   O   no evidence

You should use your assessment to indicate which applicants should be interviewed.

Figure 3.2   Short-listing matrix with indicators

You will notice that there are six levels. This is to avoid the centralist tendency. Research has shown that no matter how many numbers are provided we tend to use them in a bell-shaped pattern. This means we use the highest and lowest numbers the least and the ones in the middle the most, the normal distribution curve. If there is only one number at the middle (3 if we use 1–5 for the rating scale) we will use it the most. Thus, according to this we can get away with sitting on the fence most of the time. This is not helpful when we have to make choices.

Post – Customer Supporter	Short-lister				
	....				
	Applicants				
Abilities	**A**	**B**	**C**	**D**	**E**
Customer service skills					
Communication and interpersonal skills					
Organizational skills					
Attainments					
Achieved formal qualifications at post-16 level					
Conducted customer surveys and investigations into their needs and wants					
Achievements					
Experience of customer service and complaints handling					
Use of common office IT applications to an advanced level					
Introduction of new ways of working					
Aptitude					
Strong team worker					
Able to challenge others tactfully and influence their approaches					
Short-list?					

Please use the following scoring scheme to assess each application against the criteria:

6   Meets criteria fully
5   Meets the criteria but has some inconsequential gaps
4   Meets the criteria but has some gaps that require further assessment
3   It is not clear whether the criteria are met. More information required.
2   Significant gaps
1   Does not meet criteria
0   No evidence

The applicants with the highest scores will be interviewed.

Figure 3.3   Short-listing matrix with descriptors

Using a scale with an even number forces us to make a decision one way or the other.

The matrix assumes that all the criteria are of equal worth. If some are more important than others, you can introduce a weighting system. Figure 3.4 illustrates how you can distinguish between the criteria, making those you deem to be more critical to performance more valuable than the others. Multipliers are then applied to the score given to each criterion. It requires the short-listers to use some simple maths and makes the matrix seem a little more complicated but it does give greater fineness to the use of a scoring scheme.

For example, if you assess the application as meeting the customer service skills criterion but there are some gaps which need clarifying, you will place a score of 4 in the S column for that application. You will multiply this by 15 and put 60 in the T column.

Then add up all the numbers in the T column. The applicants with the highest scores will be interviewed.

On first sight, this approach may seem complicated but, in practice, it provides for greater differentiation between applications and stimulates purposeful discussion between short-listers. This can prove valuable, particularly if you are considering applications that appear to be very similar. It is also valuable in situations where some of the short-listers have strong views but it is important that all are able to contribute to the final decision.

It is critical to ensure that all involved in the process are trained. This need not involve sending people on expensive, time-consuming external courses, which may or may not be relevant. You can organize your own training as, in essence, it needs to be practical and focused on your own system.

GETTING THE CANDIDATES TO THE INTERVIEW

Once you have sifted the applications and decided whom you want to interview, they have to be asked to attend. Do not be surprised if some choose to pull out at this stage. Some may be dissuaded if you intend to put them through a battery of tests or ask them to make a presentation on an obtuse subject. Others may decide that the job or your organization is not right for them. Others may simply not be able to attend at the time or on the day you suggest and, believing there is no alternative, simply withdraw. If applicants withdraw at this stage, there is no reason why you should not ask for their reasons for doing so. If they decide to answer, their responses will provide you with useful feedback about your practices from people who have nothing to lose.

It is normal practice to send candidates a formal letter, giving them details of the selection process, especially if it is to include anything more than an interview. You will also need to tell them where to report and at what time. Some organizations tell applicants who will be interviewing them, and they also need to know what else is expected of them. For example, if you want them to join the other candidates for lunch or visit the place of work, let them know. You will also need to tell the candidates to bring with them any documents you will need to inspect. These may include:

Criteria	Weights	Applicants											
		A		B		C		D		E		F	
		S	T	S	T	S	T	S	T	S	T	S	T
Abilities													
Customer service skills	15												
Communication and interpersonal skills	15												
Organizational skills	10												
Attainments													
Achieved formal qualifications at post-16 level	5												
Conducted customer surveys and investigations into their needs and wants	10												
Achievements													
Experience of customer service and complaints handling	15												
Use of common office IT applications to an advanced level	10												
Introduction of new ways of working	5												
Aptitude													
Strong team worker	10												
Able to challenge others tactfully and influence their approaches	5												

Please allocate a score, using the following scoring scheme to assess each application against the criteria laid out in the person specification:

6   Meets criteria fully
5   Meets the criteria but has some inconsequential gaps
4   Meets the criteria but has some gaps that require further assessment
3   It is not clear whether the criteria are met. More information required
2   Significant gaps
1   Does not meet criteria
0   No evidence

Then multiply your score by the criterion's weight.

Figure 3.4 Short-listing matrix with weightings

▌ qualification certificates;

▌ proof of residence or work permit;

▌ evidence of achievement, such as testimonials or samples of output;

▌ examples of work, such as a portfolio of artwork or photographs.

Some organizations expect candidates to wait until the last interview has been completed and the final decision has been made. This enables the successful person to be told there and then. Those not to be offered the job can also be informed as quickly as possible, in person. Whether it is reasonable to do this depends largely on how many people are being interviewed. If you are spending all day seeing candidates, it may not be reasonable to expect the first person you interviewed to wait until the end. There are other ways of telling candidates. These can be less time-consuming for them and are a little more sensitive. After all, candidates invest their hopes in applying for the job so they deserve consideration. Unless they were really turned off during the interview, they are likely to be a little bit disappointed when they do not succeed.

How much notice do candidates need?

Most people will have diary commitments they will need to rearrange so they can attend the interview. Telling candidates right at the beginning of the process on which day the interviews are to be held will help them keep the date free, in anticipation of being called. Most of us do not mind having a free day if an expected event fails to materialize. This is better than having to rush around trying to rearrange several appointments.

If you have not told the candidates in advance, it is reasonable to give two weeks' notice. Most people can free themselves up within this timescale. Less than this is pushing it a little and, unless you are able to be flexible, you may find that some candidates are not able to attend. If you are really struggling to give more than a week or so's notice, it may be better to contact candidates in person rather than rely on the post.

Doing so, however, demands sensitivity. If the candidates have given you a mobile or work phone number or work e-mail address, you will need to remember that other people may see the e-mail heading or overhear your phone call. The same applies if you leave messages for candidates to ring you back. Not all candidates tell their current employer or work colleagues of their application, so insensitive messages or inappropriately timed phone calls may create considerable difficulties.

What happens if a candidate can't attend?

Most organizations like to get the selection process over in one day and certainly within a week. Where the process comprises activities in addition to an interview, it is not unreasonable to spread them over two days or so. However, this time demand may make it difficult for some candidates to attend for no fault of their own. For example, the holiday season now extends from Easter until the end of September. Anyone recruiting during the summer needs to make allowance for candidates being on pre-booked holidays. Others may have inescapable work commitments.

When planning your schedule, you should consider what to do if candidates tell you they are very interested in the job but simply are not able to attend on the day you suggest. You have several possible responses:

I Tell the candidate that you are very sorry but you are not able to make other arrangements.

I Try to rearrange all the interviews to suit the one who can't attend so you can interview all the candidates on the same day.

I Find out when the candidate can attend and arrange to see them separately on a convenient date, without altering the other candidates' interviews.

Each option has its own advantages and difficulties. If you do see one candidate before or after the others, you will need to take account of the way memory decays with the passage of time. It is wise to make good quality notes during and after each interview so that you have contemporary records to help you and the other interviewers recall all the candidates when you are making your assessments.

Special needs and the Disability Discrimination Act

The Disability Discrimination Act was passed in 1995 and now applies to all employers. The Act requires you to make reasonable adjustments to enable candidates with disabilities to compete with able-bodied candidates without suffering any disadvantage because of their disability.

The Act is not prescriptive in its expectations as the needs of one person with a particular condition can differ from those of another even with the same condition. You are expected to be flexible and the best way of being sure you are doing the right thing is to discuss the individual's needs with them directly. The Act only expects you to make reasonable adjustments. Prohibitive costs can be one reason why the provision of an aid or alteration is not reasonable. However, cost cannot be used as an easy excuse. Many adjustments are not expensive; they simply demand flexibility, tolerance and understanding. The Disabilities Rights

Commission has an informative website that will help you think through what you can do to enable all candidates to demonstrate their abilities and how they can match your criteria.

PREPARING THE SPACE

The location of the interview and the physical arrangements merit consideration and planning.

Room

Finding a room of the right size can be a challenge. You will need a room that is neither cupboard-sized nor the size of a ballroom. Candidates do not want to be eyeballed by the interviewers; they need some defensible space but being huddled in the corner of a massive room can be intimidating and may result in a stilted conversation and probably monosyllabic answers to your questions.

The room should be close to the waiting area and private. You do not want interruptions. It should also have adequate heating and lighting. You should have sufficient space around the furniture, so that those with mobility difficulties have adequate room to manoeuvre. You must also consider your needs so the cloakrooms and refreshments should be nearby.

The chairs should provide good support. After all, you and your other interviewers will be sitting in them for some time. You will also have to think about the table you will use. You will need some kind of surface on which to place your papers and, unless you use a clipboard, palmtop or laptop, you will need to be able to write your notes.

You will also have to think about where to seat the candidates. Some organizations like to place them in the middle of the room so there is no hiding place for nervous foot-tapping or finger-twiddling. Candidates do not like to be so exposed so may prefer to have a desk in front of them. In any case, they may also wish to refer to their documents. Candidates draw conclusions from the way they are treated during the interview, so being considerate of their needs can score you some brownie points in their eyes.

Interviews can therefore be conducted around a desk or table, with the candidate on one side and the interviewers on the other. There are variations on this theme, for example having the interviewers in a semi-circle and the candidate in the middle. Seating arrangements will depend on the number of interviewers just as much as on the furniture available to you. When planning the layout, it is advisable to place yourself in the candidate's shoes and see how it feels.

Timing

How long should an interview last? It is a well-known fact that we make our minds up about other people within the first minute of meeting each other. So why should you spend any longer than this and go to all the bother of conducting a formal interview? The reason is very simple: we know that first impressions are frequently wrong. They are based on personal preferences and biases and are distorted by the errors of judgement we all make about each other, especially on first meeting.

The general rule of thumb is to allow between 30 and 60 minutes. Anything less than the minimum will barely give you the chance to say hello. Thirty-minute interviews should be used only when you have a lot of information about the candidates and the job is a basic, entry-level one.

If you go beyond 60 minutes, unless you have a lot of ground to cover and the interview is going into technical detail, there is a good chance of you repeating yourself. It will be difficult for you, your fellow interviewers and your candidate to concentrate for longer than one hour. It is also debatable how much more information you will glean towards the end. If you do need to go into a lot of detail in specific areas, a case can be made for running two interviews.

Allowing 45 minutes for the interview should allow you sufficient time to fill any gaps of information identified in the candidate's application, assess their fit against your specification and answer their questions. This later stage is difficult to gauge as some candidates will have a lot of questions and some perhaps none. If you build in 15 minutes between interviews, you will give yourself time in case the interview overruns. It will also give you chance to write up your notes, discuss your assessment with the other interviewers and have a short break.

Breaks are important, particularly if you are interviewing many candidates. You will start to get tired; asking questions and concentrating on what the candidate is saying and doing is hard work. There is a danger of the candidates merging one into another as your memory of them starts to blur. You may remember the first person well and the last one, but what about those in the middle?

In practice, you will probably be able to interview no more than five or six people in a day. Trying to do more will be pushing it, especially if you want to make your decision that day. After you have finished interviewing you will need time to consider each candidate, weight his or her respective merits against the criteria and decide who will be the best person for the job. This stage, as we will discuss later in Chapter 5, cannot be rushed and you will need to be able to concentrate on your assessment and those of your fellow interviewers. After all the hard work expended in the earlier stages, it would be a shame to spoil the process by shortcutting the last one.

Refreshments

You and your fellow interviewers will need something to drink during the day and, if you are going on all day, some lunch.

Your candidates will probably appreciate the offer of some water during the interview. If the candidates are being asked to take part in other selection exercises as well as the interview, you will probably need to make other refreshments available during the day.

If you are offering them lunch, you will need to check whether any of the candidates have any special dietary requirements and make available meat and non-meat choices. You will also have to consider whether the candidates should eat alone, together, be joined by the interviewers or meet other members of the team.

If the interviewers join the candidates for lunch you will have to decide whether their assessment should continue during the meal; if you decide the lunch is to be informal, you will need to remember that. It will be difficult for the interviewers to suspend judgement, as impressions formed over lunch about the candidates will inevitably meld with those created during the interview. The biggest problem is that, without the structure provided by the criteria you are using for the formal assessment, there is a chance of your personal preferences creeping in. Even if you tell the candidates they are not being assessed, are they likely to believe you? Probably not, so the idea of them being able to relax is most likely to be a false one. On balance, it is probably best to let the candidates eat either with members of the team or in private and for the interviewers to eat alone. This way you can all have a break from the formalities. Unless, of course, you want to assess candidates' social and feeding skills!

Waiting space — before and after

Most candidates arrive before the given time. You should therefore think about where they will wait. Will they be expected to sit in the general reception area, or are you able to provide them with some private space so they can calm their pre-interview nerves, gather their thoughts and prepare their papers?

Access to a cloakroom and toilet facilities will also demonstrate your understanding and concern about your candidates' (and employees') comfort and well-being. Provision of refreshments in the waiting room and perhaps the provision of some relevant reading material may also be appreciated.

Try not to run behind schedule and keep candidates waiting, if you can help it. Failing to keep to time does not help your reputation! It demonstrates poor time-management, a lack of planning and is discourteous. No matter how well provisioned and comfortable the waiting room, your candidates will not appreciate being kept hanging about.

If you are asking candidates to take part in other activities, they will need somewhere to wait in between. This will probably mean that the candidates will meet each other. If they have more than a few minutes together, they will inevitably start to talk about the only things they have in common: you, your job and your organization. They will compare notes! If you are treating the candidates differently, you will surely be found out – and deserve to be.

If candidates have to wait more than 30 minutes, you should think about organizing something to keep them entertained. This may include meeting members of the team, visiting the workplace or looking through some material that will be of interest to them. This should not, however, be too demanding as you can hardly expect them to concentrate on something when most of their attention will be on the interview, the job and what outcome is likely to occur.

GETTING READY TO INTERVIEW

While the candidates are doing their homework and freeing up their diaries you need to be completing the final stages of your preparation. This will include:

1. Deciding whether to interview alone or involve other people. If you want to involve other people, you will need to decide whom to include and whom to leave out.

2. Holding a pre-meeting with your fellow interviewers; this is to brief them so they have a good understanding of:

    - The job and its component demands. If you are using external assessors, you will need to ensure they have a good insight into how your organization works and where the job fits into the structure.
    - The meaning of the person specification and the selection criteria. It is easy and dangerous to assume that they share your understanding of terms such as good interpersonal skills and leadership. They may not. You all need to be clear about the terms otherwise you could find yourselves assessing different things and drawing very different conclusions. If you are using a matrix with a scoring scheme, you will need to ensure that all the interviewers understand how it works.

3. Discussing roles in the interview:

    - Who is going to chair the interview?
    - Who is going to start the questioning, who is going to ask which question, who is going to answer the candidates' questions and who is going to close the interview?

You may also need to arrange some training in interview technique, particularly if you or your fellow interviewers are new to this task. This training could include:

- question technique;
- listening skills;
- observation;
- note taking;
- awareness of personal preferences, the dangers of using assumptions, prejudgements and stereotypes and the errors made when assessing other people's behaviour.

4. You may also need to clarify how the final decision will be made:

- Are you going to make the decision alone but with the advice and guidance of the other interviewers?
- Are you all going to contribute to the decision and strive to achieve consensus?
- What are you going to do if it is not possible to agree – go on a majority decision or decide not to appoint?

It is worth discussing possibilities in advance, pre-thought can be given to them. All sorts of surprising things can happen during interviews. You do not have to make cast-iron decisions about what to do if certain events occur but it is wise to consider what options will be open to you just in case.

Now you are ready to start constructing the questions. How to do this is the subject of the next chapter. Before moving on you may like to complete the following exercise.

EXERCISE

Having read the above, your task now is to put together a checklist of the items you need to prepare. You should include:

- the decisions you need to make;
- the actions you need to complete to make the selection process run smoothly;
- what you need to tell other people;
- what you want other people to do.

4

Greatest questions

Now that the preliminary stages have been completed and you have decided how to conduct the interview, you can start thinking about the questions you and your fellow interviewers are going to put to the candidates.

These should not be designed to trip up the candidates but they should be testing and challenging. It may be important to find out whether the candidates can think on their feet and withstand pressure, if the job entails this. It is more important to gather evidence directly from the candidates that will tell you whether they will be able to do your job to the standard you are expecting. You need hard facts so you can make an assessment of their abilities and form a conclusion in a relatively short space of time.

The interview is perhaps the only time you will meet the candidates to assess the chances of them being able to do the job to the standard you require. It is unlikely that you will find the perfect person so the interview is the best opportunity you will have to find out if the person whom you think will be the best performer has any needs that can be addressed through early training or longer-term development

You will also need to find out if the candidate is telling the truth. It is a sad fact of life that as many as one in four candidates tells lies or misleads employers in their attempts to get the job they want. It is up to you as an interviewer to get behind the words contained in the CVs. You need to remember that jobseekers are told that the CV is their sales document; it should be used as a vehicle in which they present themselves in the best light, as if they were marketing a product. Some people have their CVs created professionally by agencies or advisers. Your questions should therefore be designed to expose any gaps and weaknesses in the picture the candidate wants you to see. Your job as an interviewer is to gather as much relevant and useful evidence as possible to enable you to assess each candidate's fit against the person specification and job requirements.

The early stages of the recruitment and selection process have been designed to form a fact-finding exercise during which you and the candidates can exchange information about each other. You should make sure that you continue this approach in your design of the interview. This will be the main chance for you and the candidates to ask questions directly to each other. It is surprising how many interview questions are asked with no thought being given to the likely or desired answers and how they will provide the interviewers with the evidence needed to assess the candidate's ability to do the job. Good answers to questions will allow both of you to make good decisions about how well you each think you will fit with the other. The candidates, therefore, should be allowed enough time to ask their questions. You can encourage them to go beyond the normal 'How much will you pay me?' type of question by providing this sort of obvious information in other ways.

It is also worth remembering that the final decision is that of the candidate. You will make an offer of employment but it is up to the individual to decide whether to take the job. The worst outcome of a recruitment exercise is the best candidate saying 'No, thank you. I have a better offer elsewhere.' Oh, the waste and damage to your ego! The chances of this happening will be much reduced if the early stages have been executed well; even so, you need to be mindful of the impression you create during the interview. Poor treatment of candidates, badly structured questions asked in a rude or aggressive manner, is a guaranteed way of getting them to reject your offer. Can you afford this when competition for high calibre employees is fierce? A lot can be done to prevent this happening by thinking carefully about the conduct and content of the interview.

We will examine each stage of the interview, work through what you need to know and what questions you need to ask. The pages will be peppered with examples you may like to try in practice. We will also look at the questions we should not use and think about other ways you might use to get the information you will need to make a fair and valid assessment of the candidate's suitability.

THE INTERVIEW

Purpose

Why do we interview candidates? We know from the research that an interview is a very poor predictor of performance in the job. The interview's reliability can be increased by improving its structure and involving several interviewers who have all been trained. Some organizations add other selection methods alongside the interview to provide additional evidence of candidates' abilities and improve the predictive power of the process. But most rely on an interview at the end to help them make the final decision.

Why do we do this? The simple answer is that the interview provides a superb opportunity for social interaction. Even if the candidate is technically outstanding, if you do not think the person will fit in with the team and you are not sure you will be able to form a productive working relationship with that individual, there is little point in offering him or her the job. After all, you are considering entering into a contract that is legally binding and will commit you both to spending a considerable amount of time in close proximity with each other. Your success will depend on the performance of the person you appoint and, more importantly, we all want to be surrounded by people we like. This is why assessing the quality of this future relationship from the interaction and the rapport developed during an interview is so important.

Structure

Research into the predictive power of interviews has shown repeatedly that, with a structure, the interview's ability to forecast who will perform best in the job can be improved. The criteria contained in the person specification will provide the structure for the main part of the interview by highlighting the areas to be explored. This needs to be surrounded by an opening and a closing stage. Time also needs to be allowed for the candidates to ask their questions.

It is well known that interviewers form an early impression of candidates within the first 30 seconds of meeting. Certainly, after the initial two minutes a strong and enduring image will have been created. This image will be based on:

▌ What you know already about the individual. This will have been gathered from their application, any other evidence gathered, for example from informal contacts, other selection assessment activities and references, if they have been seen before the interview.

▌ How the candidate enters the room. This includes how they carry themselves, the overall picture created by their dress and self-presentation, what they say to you and how they behave.

▌ The way in which they talk, including any accent or dialect they have, their tone and how long they speak for, just as much as the words they use.

Candidates also form impressions about you and your fellow interviewers in exactly the same way. They will assess how you greet them, how the room is set out and how your fellow interviewers behave towards them. Are they looking down, reading papers, completing the paperwork from the previous interview, drinking or, worst of all, talking to each other? All of these factors combine to give the candidate information about what it will be like to work for you. This will be coupled with the information they have gathered about you and your organization during the recruitment stage and may have been augmented by research they have conducted in preparation for the interview. Their view will also be informed by the way they have been treated from the moment they enter your doors, including the behaviour of reception staff, people they encounter in the corridors, members of your team, if they have been introduced, and what happens to them as they wait for the interview. From these pieces of data they will draw conclusions about how you treat your staff. These will influence their thinking during the interview and will have an impact on the final decision; will they accept the job if it is offered to them?

Once an initial impression has been formed it is very hard to alter. We all tend to seek information to confirm our early view. Most of us believe we are good judges of other people and actively strive to prove ourselves right. We also discount any information that might counter that first impression; we try to avoid being shown to be wrong. The ways in which we do this include generalizing aspects of behaviour we like. So, if a candidate did well in an aspect of their previous job of which we approve, we conclude that their performance was strong across all aspects of the job, thus creating an overall favourable impression. This is known as the halo effect. Likewise, if we do not like a candidate and we find a part of their previous experience was weak, we generalize this to apply to all aspects of their work history. This is known as the horns effect; we demonize them, condemning them forever. Nothing they say or do will alter this unfavourable picture.

We also tend to remember events that happened first and those that happened last. Our memory of what goes on in the middle tends to be weaker, unless something out of the ordinary happens. This tendency applies just as much to the people we meet as incidents that happen. If the candidate makes you laugh, or if they have a coughing fit, your memory of this event and the candidate will be strengthened. If everything goes smoothly and to plan, there is a chance that the interview will become a blur. You can improve your recollection of the candidate by taking notes, not just of what is said but how the candidate reacted and behaved. These need not be lengthy; just enough to trigger your memory.

These aspects of the human cognitive process are strong and hard-wired into our brains. They served a useful purpose in the earlier stages of our evolution as they were intended to trigger the fight or flight response. When humans lived in high-risk environments when the chances of attack were real, the accuracy of image formation and speed of reaction could mean the difference between life and death. Most of us now do not live under such conditions and the chances of something like this happening during the course of an interview are low. Nevertheless, we are programmed to form early impressions. Turning off this tendency is very difficult. All you can do is be aware of what is happening when you meet someone for the first time. You can then strive to delay the formation of your judgement and make sure you gather evidence from each stage of the interview. After all, what happens and is said in the middle of the interview can be just as important as that said or done at the opening or the end.

We will look next at how to break the interview into four distinct stages. This will help you balance the need to build rapport, gather information and answer the candidate's questions.

Opening the interview

The opening stage should be welcoming and aimed at getting the candidate ready to do the real business of the interview. How you greet the candidate is a matter for personal preference but, at the very least, you should introduce your-self and other interviewers. It may also be useful to tell the candidate what the other interviewers do and why they are involved in the interview.

You may also wish to ask the candidate about their journey and whether they had any difficulty in finding your premises. Intended as an icebreaker, this topic of conversation can open the way to a long description of problems with the buses, difficulties on the motorway, lack of signs on the ring road and problems with car parking. Generalized comments on the weather may be a safer way of acclimatizing the candidates.

Guiding the candidate to their chair is a sign of courtesy. Offering a drink is also polite and hospitable. If the candidate has a coat, offering to hang it up is another sign of consideration. You may also wish to check that the candidate is comfortable, can see and hear the interviewers and has everything they need before starting the interview.

The opening stage should be comparatively brief, perhaps taking 5 to 10 per cent of the available time.

Exploratory stage

The main body of the interview is when you explore the candidate's application and assess them against the person specification. The criteria you developed from the person specification will provide the structure. Using them in this way to underpin the interview will make sure you have gathered sufficient evidence to enable you to make your assessment of each candidate fairly and consistently.

This part of the interview is where the main business is done. It needs to be thorough and detailed. If this stage is skimped or cut short you will find that at the end of the interview you will not be able to make an easy decision. The human brain has a solution to this dilemma. It fills in the gaps by tempting you to make assumptions. These will be based on other evidence but will be influenced by cognitive processing errors such as the halo and horns effects and another known as causal attribution. This occurs because we believe that the person at the centre of our attention is directly responsible for events in which they are involved. We attribute responsibility for events and outcomes to that person assuming they were the cause, even if their real association was as an innocent bystander. So we conclude that if a project on which a candidate worked went wrong or was successful, the person to blame or congratulate is the one we are interviewing. Of course this may be totally wrong, but without the information we can only guess. There is only one thing certain about assumptions and guesswork: they are most likely to be wrong.

Good quality questioning and detailed probing will improve the effectiveness of the exploratory stage. This stage should take the bulk of the available time, perhaps between 60 and 70 per cent, depending on how long you spend on the opening and closing stages.

Responding

This is when the candidate is given the opportunity to ask you questions. It is very difficult to predict what these might be. If you have provided good quality information about the job and conditions of employment before the interview, questions such as 'How much holiday will I have?' should have been dealt with.

Some candidates may come armed with a list of things they want to go through. Candidates are encouraged to treat the interview as an opportunity to assess you as a boss and employer so they may want to be assured about matters that are important to them. These could include career development opportunities, training facilities, opportunities to expand the work or their brief. They may also want to know more about what it is like to work for your organization. This could include exploring your policies, for example, on work–life balance, employee assistance and supervision facilities (particularly if the job is stressful) or the organization's future development plans.

If candidates have no questions you may find it useful to suggest some. This will help equalize the power balance of the interview and make sure it does not end on a down. There are safe topics that you could introduce, such as your commitment to staff development, the provision of extra benefits such as membership of fitness clubs or policy on dealing with change. Discussions on topics such as these can be important as they will inform expectations. However, you need to be realistic and avoid the temptation to exaggerate. Expectations and reasonable anticipation that opportunities will or will not be available can be deemed to be part of the implicit terms of the contract of employment and will certainly form part of the psychological contract. In other words, you should take care not to make promises or raise hopes that cannot be honoured.

You should allow perhaps 20 per cent of the available time for candidates' questions. If the time is not taken up, you should not be tempted to fill it. Instead, finishing an interview a few minutes early will give you more time to make notes, have a drink, walk about and ensure you start the next interview on time.

Closing

The end of the interview is your last chance to make a good impression on the candidates. Certainly they should be thanked for coming and giving you their time. You should also tell them what is going to happen next. If possible, give the candidates some idea of when you will have made your decision. This should be realistic and have some time built in for slippage. You may find it harder to make your decision than you anticipated.

You should also check that you have the right contact details for the candidates and find out if there is any time you should not contact them, if you have agreed to telephone. If you intend to ring the day following the interview, they may have commitments in their current job or may not want to be phoned at work. Thus, you may have to contact them in the evening so they can take your call in private. Alternatively, you may find it necessary to leave a message. If so, you should respect the candidates' need for confidentiality. Imagine having to deal with the disappointment of not getting a job you really wanted and having to face the consequences of your employer finding out you are looking elsewhere. Some employers take a dim view of staff with itchy feet. Carelessly left messages can do considerable damage.

The closing stage should take about 5 to 10 per cent of the available time.

Choosing the right type of question

How a question is constructed will determine the sort of response it receives. When planning your questions, as well as thinking about the topic you want to cover, you should also think about the form a question should take so that you will obtain the sort of answer you are seeking. Asking a good question in the wrong way is a waste. For once a question is put to the candidate, it is virtually impossible to ask it again.

Having pre-scripted questions can make the interview seem forced and false. You should be aiming for a flow, a dialogue during which you are able to explore aspects and areas of the candidate's application. You can achieve this end by developing an outline of the interview structure and plan how you want it to flow. Understanding the importance of question form will enable you to select the types of question to ask at which stage of the interview. You will thus be able to plan the sorts of question you want to ask without having to write a script. Being able to phrase good questions that elicit the right sort of response is a key part of the interviewer's skill.

In this section we will look at the different types of question and some suggestions will be made about when they may be most useful. This is not to say they do not have value at other stages, depending on what is happening in the interview. As you develop your skills and gain experience of interviewing, you will find out which type of question to use when.

Closed questions

A closed question tends to result in a limited response. It tends to be most useful when you want to check facts or have a brief exchange before moving on to a topic you want to explore in greater depth. You will find a closed question helpful at the beginning of the interview, when you are settling the candidate into the process and getting him or her ready for the exploratory stage. By their nature, closed questions tend to be easy to answer.

For example:

Q   Were the directions useful in helping you to find your way here?

A   Yes, thank you, they were very clear.

Or

A   No, not really. There were no signs on the ring road and I took the wrong exit.

Q   You say in your CV that you obtained a second class degree from Bristol University but you do not give the subject. What was it?

A   It was in Ancient History with Greek and Latin.

Q   When answering the previous question, you said that when you worked for MT Telephones you were responsible for creating a customer database. I have understood you correctly?

A   Yes, it was a short-term project and once the database was in general use, I moved back to the call centre.

Closed questions are also useful when you want to close down a topic or if a candidate is going off on the wrong track.
   For example:

Q   So to summarize, when you worked as a sales representative you had experience of finding new customers and cold calling them. If a potential customer was interested you passed their details on to a technical sales representative. I have understood what you said correctly?

A   Yes, that was more or less how it worked.

Or

A   More or less but I also maintained a database so we didn't call the same prospect twice in the same year.

Q   This is getting very interesting but we really need to return to the time when you worked as a web designer. You said that you were doing this in 2003, is that right?

A   Yes, that was when I was working for the Glenside Housing Association.

Open questions

Open questions are intended to signal to the candidate that you want him or her to talk at some length. They are good, therefore, for topics you want to explore in some detail. For example, you may want the candidate to describe how they approached a particular project or to say what they learnt from an experience. Generally, the open questions are used in the main body of the interview. This is when the candidate should talk more than the interviewer.
   For example:

Q   On your CV you say that the time when you were working on the customer help desk was one of your main achievements. Tell me why.

A   Up to this time, I had been working on software design and had very little contact with end users. Moving on to the help desk gave me direct contact, usually when someone was struggling to use the system. Being able to sort them out and hear the relief in their voices when they found out how to make the system do what they wanted was really rewarding.

Q   We are looking for someone who has had experience of organizing events. Have you ever done anything like this?

A   Yes. When I was at university I was the match secretary for the football club. I had to arrange all the matches for the session. I also had to make sure the coaches were booked for away matches and the pitches were available for the home matches. That was really complicated as the park was used by eight other teams. I also had to keep a note of the results and make sure the captains sent the match cards to the league secretary.

Probing questions

If a candidate has not given you enough information in response to an open question, you may need to push them further:

Q   You have just told me you found that being able to help people was enjoyable. Surely, there were times when the customer wanted to complain. Did this ever happen?

A   Occasionally, people were angry when they rang up. Often this was caused by their frustration at not being able to get the system to work properly. Some wanted to rant a bit but once we were able to get into working out what was going wrong and identifying how to resolve their problem, they tended to calm down. I think I only had one formal complaint in the two years I was on the help desk.

Q   Were you ever not able to help a customer?

A   No.

Or

A   I can remember only a couple of occasions. One customer had a computer that was simply not up to running the software. If I remember correctly, he didn't like the answer. The other one, I think, was trying to do something the software was not designed to do and once this had been explained she understood.

Probing questions are also useful when you suspect you need to test a candidate in a particular area. You may think that they are being superficial, trying to cover up something or avoid answering the question. Using appropriate probing questions will allow you to put the candidate under some pressure and focus on the area you want to explore in more detail.

   For example:

Q   The sorts of events we organize are business conferences. Can you please outline how your experience as a football match secretary would help you if you were appointed to our job?

A   There were a lot of factors that had to be right. I had to make the original bookings but then I found it necessary to confirm with the other teams, the coach firm and the pitch staff to make sure that nothing had changed. I had to make sure the captains had remembered to organize their teams. I also had to remind them to make sure the kit was clean and to collect match fees. There were times when I had to rearrange matches. But most importantly, it was about communication and keeping people happy. I guess these apply to your job as well. People want to know what is happening, what they need to do and where they are to go, and when.

Q   Did you ever get any arrangements wrong?

A   I once sent a team to play an away fixture when it was a home match. The opposition turned up to play at our ground only to find that there was no one there. They were pretty fed up and our team was furious.

Q   What did you learn from that?

A   To check and double check that the arrangements are correct, myself. When it went wrong I had asked someone else to do it and have learnt that for anything important, I should do it myself.

Leading questions

This type of question enables you to take the candidate in the direction you want. You can also use it to obtain the sort of answer you seek, to gain clarity or confirm that the impression you are developing is correct.

For example:

Q   We now would like to ask you some questions about your time spent at university. It says on your CV that you studied Business Studies at Manchester. Can you tell me about your final project, please?

A   It was on the impact of the Working Time Directive on production costs.

Q   Was your degree an ordinary degree or with honours?

A   It was a 2:1; that means it was with honours.

Q   Can I check that I have understood what you have said, please? You have told us that you worked for a car sales company as an Administrative Assistant with responsibilities for keeping customer records. Is that right?

A   Yes, but I was also responsible for logging complaints and sending out mail shots.

Situational (hypothetical) questions

Some say that you should not ask the what-if type of question but posing hypothetical situations can be very useful as you can use them to project the candidate into the job. You can use them to create a scenario so you can ask the candidates to outline how they would react and the action they would take in that situation. You can then use open or probing questions to encourage the candidates to describe their thought processes and reasons for choosing one course of action in preference to another.

The argument against this type of question is that candidates can say anything they want and you will not have actual proof to show you that they would take the course of action they have outlined when faced with the situation. They can guess at the right answer and you have no evidence to demonstrate that they will actually do what they say they will do. On the other hand, seeing how the candidates approach a problem can be very revealing, especially if you follow up with some probes to explore their thinking in greater depth or to challenge their choice of approach. A lot will depend on how you phrase the question and how predictable it is. For example:

Q Imagine you have been appointed to the post of Service Engineer. Late on a Friday afternoon just before a Bank Holiday, you get a call from a valued client telling you that their system has crashed. Worse still, they had planned to work over the holiday on an urgent job. They need someone on site quickly to get it back up. Your manager has gone on leave, you were planning to finish early so you could get away for the weekend and you know that the only other person trained on their system has plans for the evening. To make matters worse, you know that the person who called has a reputation for calling you out when they could solve the problem in house. What would you do?

A Call my partner to say I may be late home and get over there as fast as possible.

Q Why would you do that?

A I wouldn't want to take the risk of it being a real problem. If I had spent time on the phone trying to get them to sort it out, they could actually make matters worse. So in the end it would take me longer to fix the problem. In any case, it is important to keep customers happy and if they are panicking because of their urgent job they will appreciate our help even more.

This is exactly the sort of answer any employer would hope to receive. The candidate has given no thought to pressurizing their colleague to take on the job and has put their responsibilities before personal commitments. But how can you be sure that, if the real situation arose, this is the response the candidate would make? You can't. This is precisely why an interview is all about predicting the likelihood of a candidate's future performance matching your requirements and expectations.

Many candidates for senior jobs will expect to be asked: *'What do you think is the greatest challenge facing this organization?'* The answer is fairly predictable, depending on the organization, and if the candidates have done a little bit of research they should be able to find out. Sources will include:

▌ the Chairman's annual report to shareholders;

▌ notes to the company's accounts;

▌ recent press reports;

▌ comments in databases such as Fame.

Often the preferred answers are given away anyway in the literature made available to applicants or by having it freely available on the organization's website. Some are highly predictable because they are likely to occur in any organization. For example, typical future challenges facing any organization would include:

▌ managing the pace of change;

▌ improving internal communications;

▌ maintaining and expanding the current customer base;

▌ developing new products;

▌ keeping costs down and managing the cash flow.

Do any of these sound familiar?

Problems can be specific to particular sectors. For example, the public sector's main problems are seen by some as the rate and extent of change driven by central government policies and the need to keep costs down. The voluntary sector's big problems can be attributed to the need to obtain a steady income flow and persuade volunteers to give up their time. The private sector faces problems from competition and the need to keep products and services up to date. Any candidate worth their salt could make a reasonable stab at working out what the main challenge facing your organization is.

A more revealing way to explore this topic is to ask the following:

Q   You will know from our website that we are concerned about our need to find new income streams. Supposing you were appointed to the post of Sales Manager, which market would you suggest we try to break into and how should we go about it?

A   That's a tough one for me as I don't have all the details about your current market share. But rather than rush into action, I suggest that we should first do some market research to find out where there are gaps. We could also work out what we would need to do to break into new markets, the strength of the competition and the barriers that would get in our way. Only then would I come to the board with recommendations.

Q   Would you do the market research yourself or consider commissioning an agency to do it for you?

A   That would depend on the other things I had to do and how much money is available. Market research agencies are expensive but if there were other jobs I had to do at the same time, it would be a case of balancing cost over priorities.

You can also use this type of question to explore very specific topics. This can be particularly useful if you need to assess the candidate's technical or professional expertise. For example:

Q   Imagine you have been appointed to the post of Personal Assistant and your boss asks you to organize a trip abroad. She tells you she has heard wonderful things about social housing in Portugal and wants to go to see for herself how housing associations organize themselves there. How would you approach this task?

A   I would first find out how many housing associations exist in Portugal. I would then ask my boss when she wants to go and how long she wants to spend away from the office. I would also ask whether she wants to visit only big or small housing associations or a range. I would then contact the housing associations to find out whether they would be prepared to meet her. Once I had a list of possible organizations, I would start to build a schedule to meet my boss's requirements.

Q   Can you think of any other ways in which you could help your boss make best use of her time in Portugal?

A   I would carry out some background research into social housing provision in Portugal and brief her as fully as possible. This would mean that she could concentrate on what she is really interested in rather than having to glean basic facts when she gets there. I would also get some population data so she would have some background information about the client base. There is no point in looking at provision that is aimed at people in situations very different from our own.

Multiple questions

This type of question can cause candidates considerable difficulty. If you ask a long string of questions all at once, the candidate might forget some parts of the question, not know which to answer first and generally get lost in the midst of it all. You would end up without any answers and a befuddled candidate who may struggle to clear their brain in enough time to answer your next question. For example, if you were a candidate, how would you deal with the following?

Q Please can you tell me what you enjoyed most about working for XYZ Ltd. Which aspects of the job were the most satisfying, which were the ones you found difficult and what did you learn from your time there? Did you have any particularly challenging experiences? How did you deal with them?

Multiple questions can be useful, however, if they are carefully phrased and intended to assess the candidate's abilities to deal with complex situations. The components of the question should be clearly related to each other and follow a sequence with a rationale transparent to the candidate. For example:

Q We are trying to put together a volunteers' programme. How do you think we should go about it? How should we publicize the programme? Are there any particular methods you think we should or should not use? What do you think we should allow in the budget?

This has a logic and flow that can be followed by the candidates when constructing their replies. They can see where you are going and they can build up their answer to ensure they have covered all the components.

Remember you do not have to ask everything all at once, as if you were emptying a bucket full of questions over the candidate. You can ask several linked questions by pursuing a theme and following up by using probing questions, in a steady flow.

Behavioural or competency-based questions

The use of questions designed to find out how the candidates have approached a particular task or event previously has increased in popularity as interviewers have become more aware of the need to improve the predictive power of the interview. The starting point for this type of question is the specification of the behaviours or competencies required for effective performance of the role.

As you have been encouraged to take this approach throughout this book, making use of this type of question should cause you no difficulty. In fact, it will follow on naturally from the development of the person specification. You will wonder why you had not thought about using it before. 'Competencies' are patterns of behaviour or collections of skills and abilities. In fact they can be used to describe any aspect of human behaviour that can be learnt. 'Behaviour' is the focused application of knowledge and skill that results in some outcome, frequently pre-planned and intended.

Thus, you can ask a candidate to outline the behaviours they used, for example, in a situation where they had responsibilities for leading others. Such behaviours could include:

▍ Running the project to achieve the Investors in People standard. This involved bringing together a team of people, making sure they understood what the standard meant in practice, drawing up a project plan, ensuring everyone had their own areas of responsibility and resources they needed, monitoring progress, helping those slipping behind and acknowledging achievement.

▍ Being the captain of the local football, darts team or secretary of the parents and toddlers group. The main responsibility was arranging meetings or fixtures. This meant making sure everyone knew when the meetings (matches) were taking place, at what time and where.

▍ Organizing the Christmas party. This involved finding out where everyone wanted to go and what they wanted to do, resolving conflicts, agreeing the date, getting the deposits from everyone, organizing transport and gathering in final payments.

In this example the sorts of leadership competencies you might be looking for could include:

▍ communication skills;

▍ planning and organizing;

▍ agreeing clear and achievable goals;

▍ delegation;

▍ monitoring achievement and praising performance;

▍ developing team members' abilities and their capacity to work together;

▍ resolving disputes.

The types of questions you will need to construct when taking the behavioural or competency-based approach are very similar to the ones outlined above. Open and probing questions are the ones you are most likely to use. Leading and closed questions would be rarely used as the aim is to encourage the candidate to talk so that the interviewers are able to discern the actions the individual took and the reasoning underpinning their behaviour. The main differences would lie in the way you phrased the question and the extent of the probing you carried out.

The use of behavioural or competency-based questions will allow you to take specific examples of previous experience drawn from what the candidates have already told you, in areas relevant to the job in hand. Thus, you can construct a sequence of questions that build one on another so you can explore one or two of the more important criteria in some detail. The following example is intended to gather evidence of leadership skills. The sequence of questions is based on the candidate's claim, included in their CV, for winning a product design award. The interview questions would take the following path:

Q   Let's talk about the award-winning design project you said you were responsible for. Tell me first about the nature of the project, please.

A   We were asked to put forward proposals for a new line of Christmas cards, wrapping paper and decorations. We first had to decide the colour scheme and general shapes. We did this by looking at the fashion parades, the mail order catalogues and winter holiday brochures and then coming up with some proposals. We submitted these to the Product Line Manager who decided which one we should go with. We then worked up more detailed designs and started discussions with the Production Manager to work out costs.

Q   Who is the 'we' you talk about?

A   The design team. There were four of us involved.

Q   Who was responsible for what?

A   Mick did the cards, Janie the wrapping paper, Freddi was responsible for table products and I did the decorations; wall hangings, tree decorations and things like that.

Q   What was the award given for and by whom?

A   It was a trade magazine award for new ideas. We won it for making use of recyclable material in all the lines.

Q   So it was an award for the team effort, is that right?

A   Yes, we were all delighted. Our manager paid for our Christmas party on the back of our success.

Q   What was your role in the team?

A   I was a designer the same as the rest.

Or

A   I was the team leader responsible for ensuring that we all worked to the same brief.

Using a structure such as the one outlined above enables you to check details without the need to ask a direct question which may seem somewhat confrontational. However, if you suspect the candidate is trying to cover something up or mislead you, you cannot beat a closed question such as the one used in the example above to get to the root of the matter.

Using this approach enables you to go into greater depth. In addition to exploring the extent of an individual's involvement and asking about the actions actually taken, you are able to explore the reasoning behind the choice of actions. For example:

Q   You said that you decided the colour sequence and shapes. Tell me more about how this was done.

A   We looked at what was happening in the fashion shows.

Q   Tell me what you did, personally.

A   I was in charge of finding out what was driving children's fashions. It was the year Harry Potter came out, so everyone was into wizards. This suggested that we should use black and silver, and star shapes.

Q   Stars? What led you to this conclusion?

A   It was the association with magic and mystery.

Q   Why not moons and strange letters?

A   Because it is easier to use stars on the sort of merchandising we produce.

Q   Are you saying this is a major factor when making your decisions?

A   Yes. If we did not take account of cost and practicalities of production our ideas would be unfeasible.

Another main benefit of the behavioural or competency-based interview question is its ability to give a measure of choice to the candidate. If we need to explore the candidates' abilities to act on their initiative, instead of asking *'Can you use your own initiative?'* (it is unlikely anyone would say no), you could ask:

Q   Think of a time when you had to use your own initiative to solve a problem. Tell us about the experience.

Most people will have something to tell you and their choice of example would be revealing in itself. Even if they have not had the opportunity in their work experience to use their initiative, there will be some other part of their life when they have had to sort themselves out, when there was no one else available to help them. You could receive replies as diverse as the following:

▌ Our car broke down as we were driving to France for the first time. It was before the days of mobile phones and I was not a member of the AA. As we thought we had plenty of time before the ferry we had taken a side road to see the Kent countryside. We were about two miles away from the nearest town when the engine died. It was about 6.00 at night. I had to find a phone and then get a number of a garage (and so on).

| I was asked to help out with the children's school sports day by the PTA. The person responsible for organizing the publicity had fallen ill and nothing had been done. I had to start from scratch, only it was not from scratch. She had been doing it for years and I was given a huge file which, I was assured, contained all the names of people who would display posters and get out fliers. It took me days just to sort out the old paperwork.

| When I was working in the print shop, I was asked to sort out the stores cupboard. It was a right mess. I was left to decide what to throw away and what to keep. There was a box in the back corner which looked as if it contained a load of old font slugs. It nearly went in the skip but something about it stopped me. I took a sample to the local museum. It turned out that they were originals of a very famous typeface. They were sold at auction for quite a lot of money. My boss was over the moon and I received a very nice cheque.

You can relate a competency-based question to an aspect of the person specification. This will enable you to obtain evidence that can be directly related to the criteria you are using to aid your decision making. The following exchange illustrates how this type of question can be used to good effect:

Q   Can you give me an example of a time when you thought you had given a customer good service?

A   It was when I was working for the recruitment consultancy. We were expected to ring our customers every month to find out whether they had any vacancies they wanted us to fill. One of our most regular clients found this really irritating. By pure chance we always managed to ring when he was really busy. The last time I rang he blew his top at me. I let him say his piece and then said I would see what we could do to make things easier for him. I thought about what we could change and then asked my manager if, for this one client, we could stop ringing and send him a proforma each month so he could fill it in himself when he had the time. So in effect we would leave him alone. My manager agreed so I rang the customer back. He was delighted with the suggestion.

You can follow up this type of question by asking what the candidate thought made this an example of good customer service. The sorts of components you could expect the candidate to identify could include:

▌ I let him talk. I didn't try to stop his anger. I listened to what he had to say.

▌ I tried to be flexible and alter the service to suit an individual customer's needs.

▌ I got back to him quickly.

The choice of example as well as the behaviours described will tell you a lot about the candidate and the nature of their experience. Sometimes, people have hidden talents that are not given the opportunity to be used and shine at work. Questions of this nature provide the candidates with the chance to tell you about their other experiences of which they are particularly proud.

Taking this approach can be helpful when you are faced with candidates returning to work after a career break or who are new to the labour market. They may not have the traditional work histories from which to draw to demonstrate their abilities, but there may be other aspects of their life that can be used to show what they are able to do. Interviewing candidates with limited recent experience can be particularly challenging, as they can only draw on their achievement in situations that may no longer exist. Certainly working conditions and the pressures of the workplace will have changed even if the career break has only been a year or so. Those who have been out of the workplace for longer may struggle to find evidence to illustrate, for example, their initiative to improve services to customers. But if you ask an open question about times when they used their initiative, as the example above shows, you may find a wealth of evidence from non-work-related areas. If the candidate is not able to give you any examples, well – you will still have the answer to your question.

The use of behaviour or competency-based questions is based on the premise that past performance is a reliable means of predicting future actions. Using past performance to predict future behaviour is the main reliable measure available to us. This source of evidence is well accepted by those who need to predict the behaviour of those who may present a risk to others, for example those with a history of offending or severe mental illness. It should therefore be a comparatively safe and valid approach to use in selection.

Working with other interviewers

Traditionally each interviewer takes responsibility for exploring a particular area during the interview. For example, in the case of the Customer Supporter, one interviewer would ask questions about, say, experience of and approaches to customer service, another would question the extent of IT usage and a third would ask about any change project the candidate has introduced. The topic areas and sequence of questioning should be worked out in advance during the preparation stage.

This can be effective as it provides each interviewer with a valid role and ensures that all important areas are covered. For the candidates, if you have told them in the opening stage who is going to ask about what, they will know what is happening and what to expect next.

However, it can lead to the interview seeming stilted and require the candidate to change topic rapidly. This can give a disjointed feel to the interview rather than it being a cohesive whole, a flow, a discussion with a purpose. Providing some links between the interviewers can help to overcome this in part. The linking can be done by each interviewer saying something like 'I will now pass over to Jasmina who is going to ask you about your experience with IT.'

Working as an interviewing team means that you are able to support each other. While one interviewer asks questions the others can watch, listen carefully and make notes. This enables the interviewer asking the question to focus on what is being said and think about what follow-up questions may need to be asked. The other interviewers can also spot gaps in what is being said and either ask the supplementary question or pass a note to the lead interviewer so they can do so.

Listening

We often miss what is being said to us because our brain is too busy thinking about what we are going to say next. Active listening is a skill and it is hard work. You need to concentrate on what the candidate is saying. You also need to be aware of the way in which they are saying it. This is not to say you should try to examine the candidates' responses in a psychoanalytical way. But you do need to ensure you are hearing what is really being said to you.

The brain plays tricks with us all of the time in a number of different ways. We learn to talk and hear what is said to us very early in our lives. You would think therefore that by the time we reach adulthood, providing we have no disability in hearing or speech, we would be good at both these key aspects of human development. Yet breakdown in communication is a major reason for the failure of relationships, both at work and at home. Why should this be the case?

  We hear what we expect to hear. Sometimes, we hear what we want to hear. This happens because we anticipate what the candidate is likely to tell us. We use all available sources of information, choose which aspects best fit the mental model we are developing of the individual and then seek to prove this is correct. We actively discount any evidence that damages this image. This means that we do not hear (or register) parts of an answer to a question that does not fit our developing image of the person speaking.

For example:

Q   Tell me what you enjoyed most about college.

A   I was not that good academically but I did enjoy project work. I also found that the social life was really good. I was captain of the football team in my second year and we won the league.

The interviewer could have heard the candidate say they were only interested in having a good time, that the course was secondary. This would confirm an initial impression of a weak academic performer created by the candidate not specifying the grades of the exams they had passed. What the candidate may have been trying to say was that they did not do very well in exams but were ok in the course work. They may be very strong in motivating and leading other people. This is the perfect case for using follow-up, probing questions instead of taking things at face value.

▮ We also misinterpret what is being said. The English language is very rich. Some of this richness comes from our use of nuances and innuendoes. We tend to understate things and conceal our involvement in events. This is a very culture-bound approach – the British tendency to hide one's talents in self-effacement. (But others disprove this by engaging in trumpeting their talents!) The use of 'we' is also commonplace. We are taught not to promote ourselves and to limit the use of 'I'. As a result we tend to talk in the plural rather than take responsibility for our own actions. It is also well known that more women than men tend to describe their experience in a way that conceals their responsibility for success. They can attribute achievement to luck or the efforts of the team. Men, on the other hand, tend to claim responsibility for the intervention of fate or take credit for collective achievements.

This can be seen in the following examples:

Q   Tell me how you went about introducing the new database software, please.

A   The first job I had to do was to put together a project plan which identified a critical path. My manager helped me do this, as I had never done anything like this before. We worked through the likely pitfalls and planned how we would deal with them.

Is the candidate telling you that the manager did all the work? Or are they saying that as this was a new piece of learning the manager acted as a coach?

A   We then identified what help I would need. All the customer advisers would have to use the new database and there was a lot of muttering about having to change. We managed to allay many of their fears by arranging a demonstration from the suppliers and promising they would all be given training.

Who is the 'we'? Is the candidate telling you that they persuaded other team members and suggested the demo and training? Or did the manager tell the candidate to get on with it?

▌ We confuse humour and sarcasm. Candidates often make wry comments in interviews but these can come out wrongly, especially if the candidate is nervous. For example, what do you think is meant by the following?

Q   How did you feel about the project once the database was up and running?

A   It was a really good experience for me. I learnt a lot.

What is the candidate implying by using the word 'really'? Was the experience a positive or negative one? Was the learning the product of adversity or success?

It is dangerous to guess and of course we use other clues to help us interpret what a speaker means. These include tone of voice, facial expression and movement of the hands.

▌ We do not hear all of what is being said. We may hear the beginning of the answer, but as we start to prepare for our next question, we tend to stop listening. Or rather our mind starts to plan how to phrase what we are about to say and our brain is busy on this task. This level of mental activity can overtake the bit of the brain that should be focusing on listening to what the candidate is saying. Thus we no longer hear what is being said. Watch yourself when you are in a meeting or talking to a colleague. You can test your ability to listen and practise to improve your skill by using the following very simple exercise: Ask someone to tell you something. Then repeat back to them what they have just told you. How accurately and completely can you relay the original message?

Watching

We can learn a lot from watching how the candidates are answering the questions. Again, you are not expected to analyse every aspect of the candidate's behaviour. In fact, there are great dangers in doing so. Behaviour can be controlled and it is easy to misinterpret what is happening if you try to guess what is going on in a candidate's mind. However, there are some signs which, if you watch carefully, will give you some hints of areas needing further exploration.

You do need to learn how to do this and, certainly at the start, you will need to make a concentrated effort. When we are engaged in a discussion with other people, our mind starts to think about what we are going to say next. As well as getting in the way of hearing, this tendency can blind us and prevent us from seeing what is going on in front of our eyes. This is a good reason for working with at least one other interviewer. While you are engaged on the questioning, the other person can be watching. Even so, you need to be alert and watching carefully, for the candidate's reaction can inform your use of a probing question or a closed question to follow up.

For example, suppose you ask the candidates to explain why they want to leave their current job. The sorts of response you are likely to get might include:

▌ I am ready for more responsibility.

▌ I want to develop my career and your job appears to give me the opportunity to move into a new area.

▌ I want to be able to earn more money.

If, however, a candidate goes red and hesitates, then gives you the answer, 'I'm just ready for a move', you might wish to probe a little more. The candidate could be concealing a pending disciplinary case, a breakdown in relationship with their colleagues or manager, the imminent closedown of their current employer, or some other problem at work they would prefer you not to know about.

Foot-tapping, finger-twiddling, flushing and shaking of the hands are typical signs of nervousness and should be taken as nothing more, certainly at the start of the interview. But, if a candidate starts to reveal such behaviours again in the middle, you can reasonably assume that you are getting into sensitive areas. Similarly, if the candidate waffles, starts to tap their feet or tries to take the subject off in a direction other than the one you want to explore, you can conclude that they would prefer to avoid that particular area. It is your job to satisfy yourself that they are not concealing anything from you.

Taking notes

Trying to make detailed notes while you are asking questions can be one task too many for your brain to manage in one go. Your attempts to make notes can occupy your brain and get in the way of your ability to listen to what the candidate is and is not telling you. It can also stop you seeing what is going on.

Yet keeping a good record of the interview is important. Again, this is a good reason for having more than one interviewer. One can be asking questions, the other watching and making notes of the salient points – both the answers to the questions and the way the candidate reacts.

There is no need to make a voluminous record. The notes should, however, provide you with sufficient evidence to enable you to make your decision without having to rely totally on your memory. They should also demonstrate that you have treated all candidates equitably and that the reasons for your decision can be justified.

You can adapt the matrix developed to short-list the candidates as a pro-forma for your notes. Figure 4.1 gives an example of an interview record for the Customer Supporter post.

Post – Customer Supporter	Candidate...............
	Notes
Abilities	
Customer service skills	
Communication and interpersonal skills	
Organizational skills	
Attainments	
Achieved formal qualifications at post-16 level	
Conducted customer surveys and investigations into their needs and wants	
Achievements	
Experience of customer service and complaints handling	
Use of common office IT applications to an advanced level	
Introduction of new ways of working	
Aptitude	
Strong team worker	
Able to challenge others tactfully and influence their approaches	

Figure 4.1 Interview record form

It is possible to develop a rating scale and give weightings to each of the criteria, as discussed in Chapter 3.

It is very unlikely that you will have to make your notes available for external scrutiny, but if you are challenged in a tribunal you will be expected to reveal any contemporary records. If you have not made or kept these, you will be asked to explain why. You do not have to keep your records forever, but they should be kept just long enough so you can be sure you are not going to face a complaint.

Six months is a reasonable time to keep recruitment, selection and interview records.

ASKING THE QUESTIONS

We are now at the stage when the questions can be planned in detail. All the interviews you have ever attended will provide a useful source of guidance. You will remember what you found enjoyable about being interviewed (yes, some people do find the experience enjoyable as they relish the chance to discuss their experience, particularly if they are enthusiastic about their work). You will also remember what you found difficult and challenging. Other people, if asked, will also provide you with stories about interviews they have attended and conducted. We all go through the experience of being interviewed, so listening to what people remember will enrich your thinking.

Examples of both bad and good experiences will help you develop your practice.

Why ask the question?

The most important thing to remember at the outset and throughout is why you are asking any questions at all. The simple reason is that you want to find out whether the candidate in front of you will be the right person for the job you are seeking to fill. No more and no less.

Each question should have a purpose. An interview gives you a very short period of time to gather the evidence you need to make this judgement so each question must earn its place. All the questions should work together to give the interview a flow. They should complement each other so you are able to assess all the criteria in your person specification. Again, the use of a matrix can be useful in helping you plan the questions to make sure your coverage is comprehensive. The example given in Figure 4.2, again using the Customer Supporter job, shows how this tool can help you plan the areas to be explored. You will then need to decide the order in which you ask them.

What answers do you want?

Having identified the questions to be asked, you should give some thought to the answers you would like to receive. It is not always necessary to go as far as deciding model answers but, at the very least, you need to give some thought to what would be an acceptable response. You will not be able to predict exactly what the candidates will say back to you. This is one of the joys of interviewing; you always stand the chance of being surprised. People's experience is so

Post – Customer Supporter	
Criteria	**Question areas**
Customer service skills Experience of customer service and complaints handling	Ask the candidates about their experience and perhaps a difficult situation they have had to deal with in the past. If they are not able to give an example (which may be the case for a person with only limited experience) you could ask a hypothetical question in which you ask them to describe how they would deal with a scenario you create for them. Alternatively, you could ask them to draw from their own experience of making a complaint. You ask them to describe what was done well, what could have been improved (how) and what was not good about the way in which their complaint was handled. This will provide you with information about the importance the candidate places on various aspects of customer service and complaint handling.
Communication and interpersonal skills	Use the interview process and how the candidates relate to you and your fellow interviewers to provide you with evidence of skills in these areas.
Organizational skills	Another opportunity for a hypothetical question to explore how the candidates approach a situation. Alternatively, you could ask the candidate to give you an example of an event or project they have organized in the past. This could be drawn from any aspect of their life so that all candidates, including those seeking their first job or returning to work after a break, have the same opportunity to demonstrate their skills in this area.
Achieved formal qualifications at post-16 level	This is an area for closed questions as you want to check facts. You tell the candidates that you need to go over their CV to confirm the details they have already given you. This may seem like duplication but given the number of applicants known to tell lies or conceal gaps, it is worth obliging the candidates to give you the facts, face to face. This gives you the opportunity to ask very specific and searching questions if you are not convinced by what you are being told.

Figure 4.2 Question planning form

Conducted customer surveys and investigations into their needs and wants	This is an area that demands a very specific closed and leading question such as 'Have you ever conducted a customer survey?' If the answer is 'Yes' you can follow up with a leading question such as 'What did the survey cover?' and follow up with an open question such as 'What would you do differently if you were to do it again?' If the answer is 'No' you will need to probe a little, for example by asking 'Have you ever done anything similar?' Again, if the answer is 'No' you can follow up by asking 'Can you tell me what you think are the important features of a customer survey?'
Use of common office IT applications to an advanced level	You can ask the candidates to give examples of their experience by asking closed questions such as 'Have you ever used Microsoft Access or a similar database package?', or a leading question, for example 'Tell me which office applications you have used and describe the use you made of them.'
Introduction of new ways of working	This topic again requires the use of a leading question to open the discussion. For example, you might say 'We are looking for someone able to help us introduce new ways of working. Have you ever done anything like this before?' The answer will be either 'Yes. When I worked as a senior secretary, my boss, the finance director, asked me to test a new diary manager. Once we were satisfied, I was asked to persuade the other secretaries to use it.' You may get the answer 'No', in which case you can either accept this as the end of the matter or ask a hypothetical question, along the lines of 'Well, imagine you were asked to do so, tell us how you would go about it.'
Strong team worker	This is a difficult area to explore by questioning alone for it almost invites the candidates to give you the sort of answer they think you are looking for rather than tell you what they are like. In any case, in exploring this area you are, in effect, asking the candidates to describe how others see them. How well do any of us know ourselves? The best that can be done in an interview is to ask the candidate to outline the qualities of a

Figure 4.2 Question planning form (cont.)

	strong team worker and then compare their views with your own.
Able to challenge others tactfully and influence their approaches	This area can be explored by setting up a situation in the interview where you 'invite' the candidates to challenge you. You can do this, for example, by making a slightly controversial statement such as 'Some would say the best workers are the most committed. The people who are prepared to work long hours, take work home and give up their weekends. Would you agree with this?' Many candidates would think that you held this view and would be inclined to agree with you. The candidate you are seeking may be the one who might answer 'Some may say that, but others think that overworking to such a degree can be damaging. It's all about balance. For sure, when going the extra mile is necessary then the hours need to be worked, but if it is all the time then perhaps that is the time to review workload, priorities and working practice.'

Figure 4.2 Question planning form (cont.)

varied, their views wide-ranging and the way they express themselves can be wonderfully different from what you expect they will say. Sometimes people can be funny in what they say and how they say it. Sometimes there is sadness and bad luck; other times they can make you think. In an interview, however, you do need to control your reactions and have some framework against which you can assess the candidates' abilities to do the job you are seeking to fill.

This is particularly important if you are seeking qualities such as customer service experience. What kind of customer service experience are you looking for? Would serving behind a bar count, or a corner shop? Or are you wanting someone with experience, for example, of working in an environment such as an insurance broker, bank or building society? Perhaps you need experience of working on a help line or in a call centre. All of these are examples of customer service environments but they are very different. Does it matter so long as the candidate has had the experience of dealing directly with customers and is able to tell you the important features of a good standard of customer care?

There are some topics where it would be reasonable to have model answers. These would include:

▮ technical areas, such as choosing the right equipment or software application for a particular job (you would not expect, for example, someone to use a spreadsheet to create a letter);

▮ areas with clearly right and wrong approaches (for example, dealing with an abusive customer);

▮ legal matters or those covered by regulation (such as the use of dangerous chemicals or the right and fair way to dismiss an employee).

What answers do you not want?

As well as considering the responses you want the candidates to give to your questions, you are advised to think about the answers you do not want to receive. The latter are more than simply wrong answers; they are the ones that indicate that the candidate would not fit into the team or with your organization. They tell you that the candidate has different values and standards. There may be nothing wrong with the answers. The approaches being outlined by the candidate may be perfectly alright for some organizations or situations. They are just not the ones you are looking for right now.

The different styles of leadership illustrate this point very well. These fall between two poles. On one end lies the command and control model in which the leader knows best and issues instructions to subordinates. On the other sits the model in which the leader is highly facilitative and inclusive, drawing on the experience and views of all team members. The first approach works really well when deadlines are tight, the risks of failure are high, employees are not particularly experienced and the team is comparatively new. The strengths of the second approach can be found when the team members are experienced and the levels of trust between them and their leader are high, the objectives to be achieved are familiar and within reach, and the environment comparatively conducive. A competent leader can read different situations and is capable of adapting their style accordingly. They will be able to decide which approach to adopt and move between the two ends of the pole without confusing members of the team.

How do you find out whether the candidate sitting in front of you in the interview is competent or whether their preferred style is confined to one end of the spectrum? You can only do so by finding out how the candidates approached certain types of situations in their past or how they would deal with a given scenario if faced with it in the future.

The behavioural event interview is particularly good for teasing out exactly how candidates tackled a particular incident. Using a combination of leading and open questions, the candidates are asked to describe what role they played in the build-up to a situation, how they behaved and what determined their choice of actions. For example, the candidates may be asked to describe how they have dealt (or would deal) with a team member whose performance was below the standard expected and whose failure to achieve was likely to adversely affect the team's ability to complete an assignment on time and to budget. The responses you receive will indicate the candidates' preferred leadership styles and give you some insight into how they might manage both the individual and the team as a whole.

The same technique can be applied to any aspect of work where you are looking for clear standards or preferred approaches. These can include, for example, attitudes to quality control, safe working practice, standards of customer care, relationships with team members and with other sections, and commitment to improvement and learning. If you know the sort of behaviours that would not be acceptable as well as the ones that you are looking for, you will be able to recognize which of the candidates will be the best person for the job.

What are the answers telling you about the candidate?

The whole purpose of the interview is intended to help you judge and differentiate between candidates. The process is a very simple flow:

You ask a set of questions.
⇨ The candidate answers.
⇨ You assess the way in which the candidate responds.
⇨ You decide whether you like what you hear and see.

Put like this, the interview seems to be a very straightforward process. If only it were so. Unfortunately, the assessment part is not easy. It means you have to interpret what the candidates are saying, assess them against the criteria you are using to help you make your decision and develop a total picture of the candidate. From this picture you need to project the candidates into the real world of work and predict how each one is likely to behave and interact with other people, both those in your organization and external contacts. This is a complex set of mental processes that are, as we have already discussed, prone to containing biases, making errors and using unacceptable shortcuts.

The most dangerous of these is our unwitting desire to fill in gaps in the evidence in front of us. This is most likely to happen if the candidate's reply has been unclear, ambiguous or confused. Our brains do not like not knowing or being uncertain. If there is no evidence, for example, of how the candidate is likely to respond under pressure, we are inclined either to assume or to draw inferences from other evidence. We interpret what we know and massage it to fit the picture we want to see. Even worse is our inclination to use the stereotypes we hold to pre-judge how we think someone, for example, from a particular background or of a certain age, is likely to behave. Being aware of these tendencies can help you avoid falling into the traps. More important, however, are the golden rules.

If the way in which a candidate responds to a question creates some uncertainty or raises doubts in your mind, it is better to spend a little more time during the interview to follow up on that area by asking supplementary questions. If you find that you are still not sure by the end of the interview, by discussing your perceptions with your fellow interviewers you may find that your mind has cleared or that your doubts are shared.

Take the following exchange as an example:

Q   We would like to ask you about how you go about solving problems. Assume you are under pressure to finish a report, it is the end of the day and everyone else has left the office. You are on your own and are about to print out the final draft of your report for one last check before sending it off to your boss, who wants it first thing in the morning. You find the printer has run out of ink and the stationery cupboard is locked. What would you do?

A   This is the sort of situation some people call 'Murphy's Law'. It is impossible to predict when such situations will happen and most of the time they never do. But you can be sure that it will happen in the sort of situation you are talking about. You can never plan for all eventualities but when it happens you wish that you had asked the office manager to make sure the cupboard keys were available all of the time or that a cartridge was kept next to the machine. But then the chances of such a situation happening are so small; would anyone have thought about it? I know we should be more risk aware and carry out assessments so that we are able to predict what sorts of things might prevent the achievement of our objectives. Risk assessment tends to be seen as being more relevant to healthy and safe working practice. I know the approach can be used with any aspect of work but how many people would apply it to the sort of situation you are asking about? I would think very few as the chances of it happening are so small, I doubt anyone would think about it or even consider it important unless it had happened to them before. Even then, what would be the chances of it happening a second time? Very unlikely I would guess, unless the individual is particularly unfortunate.

What has this told you about the candidate's ability to resolve problems under pressure? It tells you that they know a little about risk assessment and that they are able to waffle. Having received such an answer you have two choices: accept it as it is or probe some more. If you decide to accept the response without doing any follow-up, you can choose whether to disregard the evidence given by the answer or use it to form a conclusion. You could conclude that the candidate did not know how to answer you and so waffled in an attempt to avoid answering the question. Alternatively, they may have faced just that situation and had responded inappropriately, for example by ringing in sick the next day. Your question may have revived an embarrassing memory and the waffle was an attempt to cover this up. Who knows? If you try to guess, you are likely to be wrong. The only way to be sure, if you need to know, is to ask and follow up by probing.

Questions to open the interview

Starting the interview with a series of detailed, probing questions is not the best way to relax the candidates so they are able to display their potential. Your initial aim should be to welcome the candidates and enable them to settle in quickly, so they are as comfortable as possible given the inherent stresses of the interview process and ready to be open with you. You do not want the candidates to be suspicious of you or crippled by nerves. Getting the opening stage wrong will only create a tense and difficult situation which will leave you with little evidence on which to base your final decision. You need the candidates to talk openly about their experience and abilities so that you are able to assess their fit with your job and organization on the basis of good quality information. If they are tense and stilted because you have created an inhospitable environment for them, they will not demonstrate their abilities to the full and you will find it harder to distinguish between the candidates. Moreover, you will not be able to detect whether a candidate is failing to be open with you because they want to conceal some aspect of their past or whether it is simply because they are uncomfortable and on their guard.

Constructing a welcoming setting designed to establish a rapport will help the candidates over their initial nervousness. Therefore, the opening stage of the interview should contain questions that will allow the candidates to get their mind into gear and tune in to the situation about to unroll before them. A possible sequence of opening statements and questions could include:

▌ Thank you for coming. (Shaking hands is a widely accepted welcoming gesture.)

▌ May I take your coat?

▌ It's been a lovely day / it is getting colder now / has it stopped raining?

▌ Please take a seat. Would you like some water?

▌ I am .... May I introduce the other interviewers ....

▌ We will each ask you a series of questions and then give you some time to ask any questions you want to put to us.

▌ If you are ready, I would like to start by asking you some questions about your CV.

This gentle build-up is taking the candidate from the door of the interview room to a state of readiness. Your simple conversational questions will give the candidate the time to take in the room and have a look at you and your fellow interviewers. They will have a chance to form their first impressions, just as you and the other interviewers are doing the same. Now the real work of the interview can begin.

Questions for the main part of the interview

This is the section of the interview when you explore, probe and challenge the candidate. Your aim now is to gather sufficient evidence from each candidate directly and in detail so you can assess their abilities against the job requirements and the criteria set out in the person specification. This is the final chance you will have to find out which of the candidates is going to be best for you, the job and your organization. It is a responsible task, so do not be surprised if you feel a little bit nervous. Important decisions will rest on the quality of your judgement. Therefore, planning and thinking carefully about how you are going to run this part of the interview can only help you do your job well.

The main body of the interview can be broken into several sub-stages which allow you to:

▌ examine the facts given in the CV to ensure that any gaps, ambiguities or contradictory statements are clarified;

▌ check the candidate has the required level of knowledge;

▌ explore the candidate's experience to assess the truth of their claims and determine the extent of their abilities;

▌ assess their attitude to work and other people;

▌ investigate how the candidate would approach particular situations and the job, in general;

▌ find out what they want from work and what they want to achieve in their career;

▌ find out what they are seeking from you as an employer, what provides them with a sense of satisfaction and achievement so you can consider whether you will be able to match their expectations.

Opening questions

One of the questions most frequently asked at the start of an interview is *'Why do you want this job?'*

What answer are you expecting to receive from the candidates? They will probably tell you that your job offers:

▌ an exciting challenge;

▌ more responsibility;

▌ the possibility of career development and advancement they do not have with their current employer;

▌ the opportunity to move to another part of the country;

▌ more money.

What do these answers tell you about the candidate? How likely are they to tell you that their reason for applying is one of the ones given in the following list?

▌ My boss is incompetent.

▌ My colleagues prefer to play rather than work.

▌ My current job is boring.

▌ My employer does not believe in training.

▌ There are no opportunities for promotion.

▌ The pay is dreadful.

These will, undoubtedly, be the real reasons for some candidates but very few will feel able to be that honest with you at the start of the interview. The accepted wisdom is for candidates not to be critical of their present employer as it is seen as being disloyal and reflects badly on them as employees.

Even though you may receive a superficial answer to the question, it is one worth asking as it may give you some clues which can be pursued, perhaps at a later point in the interview when the candidate is more likely to disclose further information about their current situation.

Another commonly used question to start an interview is to ask the candidate what skills and experience they have developed so far in their career that will equip them for the job for which they are applying. This may seem a tough one to start with but, in fact, it is so predictable that if the candidate has not prepared for it, there may be little point in prolonging the interview. The candidate should be able to summarize their work experience and tell you where their particular strengths lie. For them the question should be a gift; it is their chance to sell themselves. Asking it as an opening question should allow them to get off to a good start. It is an area with which they should be comfortable and know about (if they have prepared), so it should enable them to take you onto ground that is safe for them. If the candidate is not able to give a reasonable response to this question, either they are paralysed by nerves or not a serious candidate.

Checking facts

Another way of starting the interview is to ask questions that will enable you to check the facts the candidates have given you. Again, this should be a comfortable, familiar area for them as your questions will be based on information the candidates have given you. Asking them to confirm the details of their history may be important, given that up to 25 per cent of people are known to lie or cover up gaps or aspects of their history they would prefer you not to know about. If you suspect any attempt to conceal gaps, you should ask the candidate some direct questions. This checking can be particularly important if the job requires the occupants to have specific qualifications or experience. It can also be vital if the references you have obtained contain information that is at odds with that given in the candidate's application.

For people who have recently completed full-time education, you may start the interview by asking them about their school, college or university experience. For example:

Q   You finished your studies in (July) and I see you obtained (results). You
    also attended X college and Y school and you have A, B and C
    qualifications. Is this right?

For those who have been in work, you can summarize their employment history along similar lines:

Q   I see you worked for Bloggs and Co from 1995 until 1998 and then for the
    Traffic Corporation until 2001. When did you start with the Traffic
    Corporation?

    You say you moved to DDX Ltd in 2002. Is this right? You left DDX in
    2004, when you moved to your present job. What happened between the
    Traffic Corporation and DDX?

This initial and simple check gives the candidate the opportunity to correct any mistakes they have made; it also gives you a chance to watch for any signs of cover-up. If you suspect that a candidate has provided untrue information, if you find out at the beginning, you can assess how serious a matter it is for you. If it is serious, you have the option of ending the interview at its beginning and saving yourself the time and energy. If the matter is not serious, you can clarify the information while making it clear to the candidate that you are not prepared to be misled.

Checking knowledge

Some jobs demand that the occupant has certain knowledge. These jobs include those with technical or professional content. Sometimes, it is good enough to ensure that the candidates hold relevant qualifications or have received appropriate training. At other times, you will need to satisfy yourself that they actually know what they claim to know. More importantly, you will need to make sure that they understand what their knowledge means in practice so they are able to apply their knowledge in a variety of situations and appreciate the implications.

It may be worth having a separate interview or a test if the job requires a high level of knowledge. Alternatively, you can dedicate part of the full interview to exploring this aspect of the criteria. If you do not have sufficient in-depth knowledge of the area you may find it useful to ask a technical or professional expert to join you on the panel. For some jobs, such as those for medical consultant appointments where the Royal Colleges need to be satisfied that the applicant has had sufficient training and experience, this is done as a matter of course. Most other occupational groups are less regulated, but nevertheless there will be times where you need to appoint someone to a job that demands expertise in an area other than your own. Examples can include:

I Health and Safety expert;

I Head of Finance;

I Head of HR;

I Marketing Consultant.

It may be appropriate to ask a colleague from a partner organization to act as an adviser and join you as an interviewer. Alternatively, the professional body, if one exists for the occupation in question, may be able to help. The person joining you will need to be briefed about the job and your organization so they do not import their own agenda and preconceived ideas. They will be able to ask the in-depth questions required to find out whether the candidate's seemingly knowledgeable answers are in fact superficial reiterations of the textbook or whether they show that the candidates know their stuff.

Checking experience

The next stage is perhaps the most important as this is when you will concentrate on the candidates' experience gained from their education or work. This exploration will help you assess their skills and abilities as well as provide you with the opportunity of finding out what the candidates have achieved. For those recently completing their studies you might ask:

Q   What was the most enjoyable aspect of your course?

The reply will give you information about the content and the areas the candidate found most satisfying. Generally, the areas people find enjoyable tend to be the ones they are good at and the ones in which they have the most interest. As well as the content of the course, the candidate may tell you about the social aspects of their experience. This will give you some clues about how they relate to other people.

Q   Which areas were less enjoyable?

This will tell you about the aspects of the course the candidate found difficult, challenging or boring. If the answer relates to important aspects of the job, you may start looking for other warning signs. Take, for example, the job of a human resource adviser where the main aspect of the work is drawing up contracts of employment and writing procedures. If a candidate tells you that employment law was boring so they dropped it in their final year, you may wonder how they would cope with this important component of the job.

Q   Would you return to studying?

The answer might tell you whether the candidate valued their experience. It may tell you that they found the course hard work. Alternatively, their response could indicate that they were ready to move on to a new challenge and are looking forward to learning in a different way. What will it tell you about their ability to do the job? You may wish to explore their learning styles by following up with:

Q   You will find the world of work very different to that of study. For a start, the bulk of your learning will be done on the job, learning from experience. It will give you the chance to find out about how theory works in practice. How do you think you will cope with this change?

The way in which the candidates react to this question will give you some clues about the amount of support they will require and what initial training they may need. For example, if they say something like 'I have been looking forward to this. Sometimes the things we were taught about at college seemed ideal and unreal. I wasn't always sure that they would actually work in practice.' This would suggest a fairly pragmatic approach. If, however, the candidate were to say, 'I would need to think through the implications and work out where the differences were between the theory and the situations I was facing', you may find that their learning style tended more towards the reflective and the individual would benefit from some one-to-one coaching.

You can also explore how the course has equipped the candidate to do the job for which they are applying by asking:

Q   In what ways has your course prepared you for this job?

The candidate should be able to relate the course content and the processes of learning to work. Even if the course was academic, for example a degree in ancient history, the candidate should be able to find features that are relevant. Examples could include:

I   the way in which they were asked to work in a group on assignments has helped the candidate to develop team-working skills;

I   the research carried out for the final year project developed their analytical abilities;

I   the encouragement to question and draw logical conclusions developed problem-solving abilities;

I   writing assignments and making presentations contributed to the improvement of their communication skills.

For those candidates who come with experience of another job, you may wish to start by exploring the work history they have outlined on their CV. It is normal to start with the current or most recent job. A question similar to the one used to explore the candidates' experiences of education would work equally well here as a starting point:

Q   Tell us about your present job. You say you are responsible for (eg providing financial information to line managers). Which aspects do you find most enjoyable?

As with the answers given to the question about the most enjoyable aspects of the course a candidate has recently completed, this question should elicit information about the candidate's views of their current job, revealing the areas of work in which their strengths or sources of satisfaction can be found. Asking about the converse will indicate potential areas of weakness:

Q   Which aspects are less enjoyable?

If the aspects outlined in the reply are critical to the vacancy, you may wish to probe some more to find out why. For example, if the reply was along the lines of 'The managers find it really difficult to understand why we have to allocate overheads to their budgets. We have explained it countless times but they still don't get it. I find it really frustrating having to go over the same thing time after time', you may wish to find out some more by asking:

Q   Why do you think the managers have so much difficulty understanding?

Now the answers are likely to get interesting. They will tell you about the relationship the individual has with the managers, how much patience they have and how they relate to their role in relation to clients. However, you need to exercise some care. There is a chance that such interesting topics arising early in the interview will throw you away from your overall structure. You need to log such interesting answers and get back on track by suggesting that you might return to this topic later. Once you have satisfied yourself of the veracity of the facts, you can start the exploration of the candidate's skills and experience in some depth.

Another common way of opening an interview is to ask the candidate to outline the skills they will bring to the job and organization. This question, being common, is highly predictable but can be challenging to candidates, particularly those who have not prepared very well. In essence, you are asking them to relate their CV to your person specification. The question can take the form of a simple, open one; the answer should be longer. For example:

Q   How will your previous experience help you do the job (for example, of a Finance Controller)?

A   When I worked for ABC Ltd, I was responsible for reconciling invoices and payments. You would be surprised how many companies send in cheques for the wrong amount. I was also responsible for chasing outstanding invoices. I found this enjoyable as it brought me into contact with suppliers and I had the satisfaction of seeing the money coming in. I understand that this is a major part of your job. The other areas of experience that have prepared me to move into this post include....

The follow-up question to this would be:

Q   What particular skills have you developed from your experience so far? How would you describe your strengths?

The answer should enable you to compare the candidate's response to the information given on their CV. If there is a difference, you may wish to discuss this with the candidate. This could easily happen if the candidate is using a generic CV possibly produced with the help of an adviser. This often results in the CV being treated as a 'sales' document, rather than one prepared for a particular job.

Their answer to the question about skills will also provide you with some indication of their insight into their own strengths and weaknesses and their understanding of your job. For example, if you are interviewing for a Finance Controller, you will expect to hear something about methodical approaches, the need for accuracy, keeping up to date and helping internal clients and budget holders understand what is happening to their money. You would not necessarily expect to hear about their ability to give presentations to customers or their talent for thinking up ideas for new product lines.

It is the sort of question that encourages poorly prepared candidates to waffle and avoid giving you the sort of answer you are seeking. On the other hand, for those who have done their homework, it should be straightforward. You can also use this type of question as a building block for later in the interview when you may wish to explore the candidate's development needs, should they be appointed to the job.

Another way of asking this question is to be more direct. Sometimes asking short, to the point questions can surprise candidates. Using a form of words such as *'What makes you think you can do this job?'* may produce an interesting response. Its very directness is challenging, even if the way in which you ask it is not. The kind of response you are likely to get should include a summary of the candidate's strengths and the main components of their experience. Often CVs contain such a list. If you have used a supplementary questionnaire along with an application form, this is the sort of question you could include at that preliminary stage to help with short-listing. If you have done so, you should be able to cross-reference what the candidates tell you face to face with what they wrote in their application.

Having started down the road of exploring the candidates' skills and experiences you will be able to probe in greater detail. Even candidates new to the job market should be able to cope with the following set of questions. For example:

Q   What is your greatest achievement?

The answer should give you some insight into the candidates' level of self-awareness and it will be interesting to compare what they say about themselves with what their referees think about their abilities. The sort of answer you might expect to receive could include:

A   I am very good at art. During my last year at school, we put on an
     exhibition. It was a major project and everyone was expected to be
     involved. I was asked to design the display for the main entrance hall with
     three other students. I was the leader of the team and we worked on this
     for about a month. We won an award given out by the local newspaper.

This can be followed up by a question that would enable the candidate to relate that experience to the needs of the job by asking:

Q   You must have been very pleased with your success. What did you learn from the experience and how will it help you do the job as Sales Adviser?

A   I learnt a lot about getting people to work together. We had one or two arguments but I had checked carefully with the art teacher to make sure I knew what we were meant to be doing. This gave me the confidence to step in and finish the arguments.

Q   How do you think this learning will help you in the job?

A   It will help me work better as a member of a team. I've also learnt that having clear objectives can make life easier as it means that the things that are most important are obvious. The other people in the display team weren't certain about what we were meant to be doing and one of the problems we had was caused by a couple of them doing their own thing.

For those candidates coming to the interview from a previous job, you should expect to hear about more directly related experiences, such as occasions when they were involved in a special project, resolved a difficult situation or received praise for making an extra effort. For example, answers could include:

▌ We were launching a new product and I was asked to be part of the team putting together the mail shot. We were asked to design a flier, draft the covering letter for the MD and pull together the mailing list. In all, we sent out 5,000 letters, so just getting them into the post was a logistical challenge. We had a really tight timescale and a very limited budget but we achieved a response rate of over 12 per cent. This was double what was expected and the MD was delighted.

▌ We had a major client who had a bad run with us. For some perverse reason everything to do with her account went wrong. It was almost as if she was cursed. No matter who dealt with her business, some mistake or other was made. Sometimes, it was only a trivial matter but there had been a couple of incidents that were really quite serious. She complained and threatened to take away her business. I was asked to investigate what was going wrong and to see what safeguards could be put in place to prevent anything happening to her again. I looked into each transaction and found that her surname had been entered into the database incorrectly. No one had spotted it. Her name was Woolliscroft and one of the l's had been missed out. It was really hard to see this on the screen. I only noticed as I had printed out her records. As a result, I recommended that a screen dump be printed every time a new client was entered so it could be checked by a second person. The client was really pleased we had found a reason for the mistakes and the Operations Manager was so relieved.

▌ For some reason, I hit a period of really good luck. Everything seemed to go well for me. I obtained top marks on the project management course. The project I was working on ran incredibly smoothly and I achieved all my targets with two weeks to spare. My boss was so pleased with me that she gave me the maximum bonus for that six-month period.

While these answers may be interesting, they do not necessarily tell you what the person has learnt from the experience and how they will be able to transfer that learning to your job. You will need to follow up by asking the candidates to reflect on the experience and say how they would apply their learning in the context of your organization. You need to know how it will help them perform the duties you need doing.

Moreover, and the last example shows the point, what credit should the individual take for their success? Sometimes luck is responsible, other times it does not play a part. On occasions, other people create the conditions that allow an individual to be successful and sometimes it is down to the person's ability alone. You need to find out which is the case for the candidate you are interviewing. For example:

▌ The school leaver may have been appointed as team leader by the art teacher and given clear instructions. In which case, the individual would have been expected to sort out the highly predictable arguments between the other students. This could have been a deliberate tactic to find out whether the individual had leadership potential and to help them develop these skills.

▌ The achievement of the product launch could be due to other team members. You would need to explore what contribution the individual made to the team's overall success by asking *'What part did you play and how did it help the launch go so well?'*

▌ In the case of the investigation, the individual's role has been clearly spelt out in the answer given by the candidate. Even so, you would still need to explore the learning that has been accrued from the experience and how that will help the candidate do well in the job for which they are applying. A follow-up question could be *'What have you learnt from the investigation?'* You may also like to explore how the other members of the team reacted to the outcome and the recommended solution. Other follow-up questions could be along the lines of *'What did the other members of your team think about your findings? Were they happy with the solution you suggested? Did you have to sell it to them? If so, how did you do it?'*

Why should some people get all the luck and others none of it? Is it purely down to fortune or does the individual have some part to play in creating their own luck? How you view the answers to these questions will depend partly on your own philosophy of life and possibly be informed by your own experience. There is no doubt that individuals do have a part in determining their own fate but the situation and other people can play a major role as well. In the case of the last example, perhaps the project management course had been only introductory and well within the individual's level of capability. Possibly the targets had not been particularly stretching and the other members of the team had not performed very well.

Attainments and successes need to be seen in the context in which they were attained and you need to be very clear about the candidate's role. This area presents one of the biggest challenges for the interviewer. Of course, the candidates will want to reflect in the glory of achievement. All employers want to employ a new person who has a record of success behind them. It is great when you can appoint someone who is able to 'hit the ground running'. However, asking candidates to outline their achievements is so predictable that it would be really surprising if the candidate had not prepared some answers. You therefore need to phrase your questions so that you are able to satisfy yourself that the candidate was responsible for the successes claimed, that some personal learning resulted from the experience and that the individual will be able to transfer that learning into another context.

Exploring attitudes

Attitudes, it can be argued, are personal matters; they are not an employer's concern. To a degree this is true. Does it really matter if one candidate supports a particular football team while another loathes the beautiful game with a passion? Probably not, but there are some areas where attitudes do matter to an employer. These are the attitudes that affect how an individual approaches their work, the ways they relate to colleagues and how they behave towards customers. These attitudes will affect the individual's ability to fit with the team and their performance in general.

Attitudes influence behaviour; they also affect the topics of conversation and the way relationships develop. For example, if one person believes that the reason for going to work is primarily to engage in social interaction, they will be interested in talking to colleagues about all manner of things and engaging in activities in and out of work. They will be the people who organize the Christmas party, run the tea club and organize the lottery club. If the culture of your organization does not encourage this sort of fringe behaviour, that individual may find themselves becoming frustrated and unhappy. If, on the other hand, your organization is highly social and you appoint an individual who does not wish to participate and believes that these types of activity get in the way of developing a highly efficient and productive workforce, you may find yourself recruiting problems of fit. Attitudes to customers are vitally important.

Clearly, you will need to recruit someone who shares similar values. You can explore attitudes by asking general questions such as:

Q   What are the important features of a happy and productive workplace?

Q   What are the important elements of good customer service?

The answers you receive may be 'textbook'. You will have no way of assessing whether the candidates really believe what they are telling you and will translate those beliefs into practice. You will have to judge from what they say and the way they say it.

Other attitudes can influence an individual's performance. These affect their diligence, levels of care and accuracy, and deeper social attitudes. The former may determine, for example, the individual's time keeping, the effort they make to come to work when feeling a little ill, whether they have a tidy desk or have piles of paper scattered around. The latter may affect their relationship to other members of the team. Sometimes differences in attitudes can get in the way of developing good working relationships; for example, the passionate fan who festoons their workspace with pictures of their heroes and memorabilia may be the cause of considerable irritation to their colleagues.

As a prospective employer, you will find it very hard to explore the latter type of attitude during an interview. You may find some clues from what the candidate says to you but, generally speaking, these are the risks you take when bringing a new person into your organization. Rather than go too deeply into these matters during an interview, you are advised to have clear employment policies that enable you to tackle problems such as these at their very early stages.

Exploring skills

Assessing a candidate's skills is also very difficult in an interview. Skills are patterns of behaviour that are learnt, often as a result of experience. They can be developed in an educational setting but usually we expect this learning to be applied in real life. Thus, assessing the work-related skills of someone new to the labour market is more about assessing potential. In other words, you need to work out the chances of a particular candidate, educated to a certain level, being able to perform a task or set of tasks to the standard expected.

The most usual way of assessing skills is by observing or testing. For example, driving skills are assessed in a driving test by an examiner sitting next to the learner driver, watching how they behave and react in typical, given situations. This is accompanied by an examination of required knowledge and understanding. Many work-related tests are practical to the same extent. A test of customer service skills may involve a role-play. Candidates' abilities to prioritize can be explored in an in-tray exercise. Decision-making skills can be examined in a case study. Interpersonal and leadership skills can be assessed by asking candidates to participate in a group exercise designed to elicit evidence of the individuals' abilities. Your opportunities for assessing skills in an interview are limited by its very form. You may therefore decide to add supplementary selection activities.

The only skills you will genuinely be able to assess in an interview are those you are able to witness. The evidence of other skills can only be deduced from other information gathered from elsewhere. The skills that can be examined during the interview, nevertheless, may be very relevant and can include:

▌ interpersonal skills and the ability to build rapport;

▌ communication skills;

▌ influencing and persuasiveness;

▌ the ability to respond to a challenge and answer difficult questions in what may be a somewhat pressurized and stressful setting.

The interview is an artificial situation for many people. It is not the sort of event that occurs to most people in most jobs on most days. Nevertheless, the interview can be taken to represent other similar sorts of situation such as difficult business meetings with important clients or suppliers to discuss contractual breaches, presentations to formal committee meetings or meeting a customer who is known to be awkward. Being able to explain why a particular project is falling behind schedule can feel as challenging as going to a job interview for the person concerned.

The interview is a particularly good form for assessing a candidate's communication skills. You will experience them at first hand. You will be able to find out whether the candidates are able to provide clear concise answers to your questions or whether they waffle, avoid the question or confuse you.

Assessing the level of candidates' interpersonal skills is also valid in an interview. The candidates will interact with you and your fellow interviewers, albeit in a forced and structured social setting. Nevertheless, you will still be able to observe and assess how they relate to you, how they respond to your greeting and the ways in which they variously react to you and the other interviewers. Similarly, the way in which you react to them is also worth monitoring, providing you can attribute the cause to the candidate's behaviour, not to your own particular set of prejudices.

For example, if the candidate avoids making eye contact, rejects your greeting and counters your expressions of interest in their comfort with grunts and brush-offs, you may wonder legitimately whether their interpersonal skills are developed to the standard you require. If the candidate reacts to your probing questions in an excessively hostile and defensive way, you may wonder how they would respond to a customer lodging a complaint.

You will also be able to tell whether the candidate has the ability to influence you and convince you with their ability to develop a line of argument. The interview as a forum for assessing skills has one considerable weakness. It is very difficult to distinguish between those who are very good at talking about what they would do and can paint a picture of previous success but are not very good at putting those plans into action and those who may not be able to artic-ulate their thought processes and behaviours very well but are excellent at making things happen. This is why it is a good idea to use other modes of assessment to complement the interview.

Anticipating the future

Once you have explored the candidate's educational history and previous expe-rience, and done your best to determine the levels of their abilities, you will be ready to move on to assessing their potential for performing your job to the standard you want in the future. This is the main purpose of the interview and should therefore take most of the available time and certainly should be the part the candidates find the most testing.

In terms of time allowance, assuming you have set aside 45 minutes for each interview, the opening should last between 5 and 10 minutes. You will need to allow at least 5 minutes for the candidate's questions and 5 minutes for closing and leaving the room. This leaves you with 25 minutes for the main part of the interview. You should therefore plan to spend, say, 10 minutes on exploring the candidate's past and 15 minutes on assessing their future potential.

The candidates should have settled into the interview process by this time. They will have answered your questions concerning the areas with which they are familiar using questions they should have expected. Having covered such safe ground, you should thus be able to move into more challenging and testing areas of questioning without disconcerting them over much. Remember, your aim is to find out whether the candidate is likely to be able to do your job, not give them a hard time. If you need to assess whether they are able to withstand pressure and deal with situations that include facing aggressive people, there are other, more effective ways of doing this. We will come to these later.

Meanwhile, you will want to start by assessing whether the candidate will be able to respond positively to the main parts of the job. This is where the situa-tional questions come into their own. However, you will need to find ways of grounding the questions, as there is a danger of getting back the sort of 'perfect' answers we discussed above. If your questions are too obvious, too predictable, the candidates will have been able to do the interview equivalent of exam ques-tion spotting. If, on the other hand, your questions are too hypothetical or too fanciful, you may find that the candidates respond by giving you blank looks or making up the sort of answer they think you are wanting to hear. Either way, you will not obtain the evidence you need to help you assess how the candidates are likely to respond when faced with real situations.

As this is the very purpose of the situational interview, you need to plan the questions with considerable care. The following set are fairly obvious but they can obtain a lot of information that will tell you how much research the candidate has done into your organization before the interview and whether they have thought themselves into the job. You should not expect the candidates to have access to information available to insiders only, but it is reasonable for them to have looked for material that is publicly available and certainly to have read through anything you have sent out prior to the interview.

Q   If you were appointed to the position of Client Account Manager, what would you want to achieve in your first 6 to 12 months in post?

A   I would like to increase the client base by perhaps 10 per cent and to increase the spend from each client by the same amount. I would also like to encourage them to move from one- to two-year contracts. This would save a lot of time each year negotiating new contracts and would give us a better feel for future income projections.

Q   What difficulties do you foresee?

A   The main one, I think, would be encouraging existing clients to spend more with us.

Q   Why do you think that would be the case? (and so on)

Q   How would you go about building your working relationship with other team members?

A   I would first meet with everyone individually and ask them to tell me about their role, what they liked and where they felt improvements could be made. I would then organize an away day so we could look at our priorities and agree how we are going to make the improvements people want to see.

Q   Do you think, as a new manager, they would be totally open with you?

A   It would be naïve to say yes. Inevitably people will be a little suspicious of a 'new broom'. I will have to earn their trust. I will also have to be careful about people's agendas. I have been in situations before where existing staff have resented a new manager and have tried to undermine their authority. I am not suggesting any of your people would behave like that, but I would need to be wary until I was sure of everyone's agendas.

What does this answer tell you about the candidate? Are they worldly wise or have they had a bad experience? Could it be that this experience contained useful learning and suggests that you may have a mature and skilful manager in front of you? It may be worth carrying out some further exploration. On the other hand, you may find that the candidate is paranoid or their previous experience was caused by their lack of decision and clarity. If this was the case, the team members may have simply been exploiting a weak manager. You need to know.

Q   What are the greatest challenges facing this organization?

The answers will tell you how well the candidate has researched your organization. If you have told all the candidates the answer to this question in the recruitment pack, or have set out your challenges on your website, the responses you receive will tell you how well the candidates prepared themselves and how well they understand your situation.

   If the answers are bland and highly typical, such as 'dealing with competition, keeping up with technology or responding to customers' changing demands', you could discern that the candidate has not gone into much depth. You may wish to find out which sources of information they have accessed before the interview. If the answers suggest that the candidate has done their homework and understands the organization's situation, you will be able to continue by asking:

Q   How would you overcome them?

This will give you some ideas about the pragmatism of the candidates. If their plans are grandiose or unrealistic, you might conclude that they are better at talking than doing. If the answers are pragmatic and realistic, at the very least, you can be reassured that they have thought about the issues and how they might be tackled in practice. You will not be certain that they will actually do what they say, but at least you will know that they are aware of what needs to be done.

Q   What are the greatest opportunities facing this organization?

Again, this question examines the candidates' understanding of your situation. By taking a more positive stance than the previous version of this question, you may surprise the candidates. We often look at the worst-case scenarios and take a negative perspective. Asking them to be optimistic may actually require more thought from the candidate. You will be able to use a follow up-question, such as:

Q   How would you maximize them?

This will explore further the candidates' understanding of the broader context as well as their capacity to build on strengths. We often know how we would improve on perceived weaknesses and some people are aware that maintaining a strong position can be challenging but building on excellence year after year is far less easy.

All of your questions in this main part of the interview should have been designed to make sure that the candidates tell you what they would do in certain relevant situations. Your probing should challenge the candidates sufficiently to enable you to assess what they themselves are likely to do. You do not want to hear what actions other people should take or generalized theories. You want to know, with some measure of certainty, what actions they would take if appointed.

You have every right to be robust in your questioning as you need to get beyond the surface. Some candidates will have had more experience of attending interviews than you and so will have developed well-honed skills. They will have thought about the questions you are most likely to ask and will have probably rehearsed their answers. Moreover, we know that some people tell lies and exaggerate their claims in their applications. You therefore face considerable risks of appointing the wrong person, so it is only proper that you subject the candidates to thorough testing.

This responsibility does not give you the right to be rude or aggressive. You can be challenging and thoroughly explore the candidates' abilities without placing them under excessive pressure. We will discuss the use of the stress interview technique later as some people think that this is an acceptable approach. In most cases, however, resorting to this is excessive and unnecessary. In some cases this approach may be legitimate if the job requires the ability to withstand this degree of pressure. For most normal jobs, the interview in itself is stressful enough; ordinary questions which seem straightforward to the interviewers can be difficult for the candidates to answer. The following questions are highly predictable as they are frequently used. Nevertheless, providing the right answer can present the candidates with some difficulty.

Q   If you were to be appointed to this post, describe the value you would add to the role and the organization.

If you were asked this question about your current role, how would you answer? For sure, you could draw on your previous experience and the skills you have developed over the years, but which would you describe first? If you were applying for a new job, how would you outline your talents and abilities without sounding arrogant? Interestingly, research shows that men, in general, are more willing than women, in general, to sell themselves in this way. Women have a tendency to apologize for their success and put it down to luck or the efforts of others. Men, on the other hand, tend to claim success as being the results of their singular efforts and abilities. Knowing about this tendency allows you to use appropriate probes to find out why a candidate thinks their contribution will add value and in what ways.

Another testing but highly predictable question is:

Q   What development needs do you have?

A candidate who gives the answer 'None' is unlikely to be appointed. Not only do they appear as arrogant and self-satisfied, it is probable they are not being honest, with you and possibly themselves. No matter how skilled and experienced, anyone moving into a new job will have to undergo some learning. This may only involve learning new systems and procedures but these are still development needs. Most candidates should be able to predict that this question will be asked and because it is so predictable they should be able to prepare a convincing answer. The sort of reply you might expect to receive could include:

- I know my budgeting skills are a little rusty. I try to keep them up to date by using a spreadsheet to manage my own money but I should imagine the job would be more complex. I think I could do with some refresher training.

- I would need to learn how your internal systems work. I appreciate each organization has its own way of doing things and I would need to understand how yours works before making any recommendations for change.

- The job includes some areas of work that are new for me. That is what attracted me to it. I know it is time for me to move on, so I would welcome the opportunity to learn some new skills.

- I want to advance in my career. Your job would open new doors and I am interested in obtaining more qualifications. I am prepared to study from home in the evenings but I will need some work experience to get the qualification.

The last reply can provide the opener for you to follow up with another line of questioning.

Finding out what the candidate is seeking

The employment contract contains two components: the formal contract that sets out the terms and conditions of employment, and the informal contract. The latter is not written down anywhere but contains the understandings and expectations the parties have of each other. Sometimes this is called the psychological contract. These understandings and expectations are highly influenced by what is discussed during the interview. This is the first time the candidates and their prospective employer meet each other and the first time they can discuss the content and nature of the employment contract.

This is another reason why the interview is so important. Making sure that these understandings are the same and that the impressions being formed are accurate and shared is vital. There are as many tales of candidates being made promises during an interview that do not materialize as there are cases of candidates falsifying their application. The sorts of misleading impressions given to candidates include:

▌ suggesting that development opportunities (including funded training courses) are available;

▌ promising the chance to work on exciting projects;

▌ indicating that bonus and commission payments are likely to be higher than they really are;

▌ creating the impression of greater autonomy and ability to make independent decisions.

The most common result of misleading candidates during the interview and making unrealistic promises is high turnover and a heavy recruitment workload. This can be avoided by spending a little amount of time during the interview making sure both parties have a common understanding of the benefits and opportunities that are likely to be available. For example:

Q We are a highly devolved organization and we see the Customer Manager's role as being pivotal in ensuring the communication flow between the office and the sales staff on the road is effective. What systems and mechanisms would you put in place to achieve this?

A I would ensure that I met with each staff's representative on a monthly basis.

Q How would you do this?

A I would go out to see them on their patch. I think this is important so that I get and maintain a good understanding of their situation.

Q Would you do this every month?

A Yes. I think it would be important.

Q There are 12 sales representatives spread across the country. How would you manage your other duties if you spent so much time travelling around? Just dealing with customer queries creates a heavy workload for the manager. Do you really think that so much travelling could be justified? Can you think of some other ways of ensuring good communication?

This line of questioning, in this case, arose opportunistically. If you do not get the chance as part of the interview flow, you should include some time to ask direct questions such as:

Q   What are you looking for from this job?

The answers could include career development, greater responsibility, the chance to work flexibly, a move into new areas of work, or moving to a larger, more progressive organization.

Q   How do you see your career developing from here?

The reply may give you some indication of how long you could expect the candidate to remain in the job. If they were to tell you that the job was a way into your organization or part of their career plan so they could progress into other areas, you may reasonably conclude they would not stay long.

Q   What are the most attractive features of this job for you?

You may be surprised by some of the replies. They are likely to include some highly predictable answers (such as career development opportunities, working directly with customers, moving into new areas of work); they may also include some aspects of working for your organization of which you were not aware. These could include working for an organization with a good reputation or known to be a leader in a certain area of work, or the chance to work with a particular individual who had a good reputation.

A skilful interviewer, having done his or her homework, may use this as an opportunity to receive some positive and complimentary feedback. We all like to receive praise and hear good things from other people. If you create this opening, be prepared to receive this sort of response. However, do not be seduced by warm words. Differentiating between the flatterer and those giving you honest feedback is down to your skills as an interviewer!

Q   What are you expecting in terms of pay/benefits/compensation/reward
    from us?

You will need to phrase this in the language of your organization. There is no point in discussing health insurance, car loans or a cafeteria type of benefits package if they are not on offer. Do not be surprised if the answers seem a little mercenary. People do go to work for the money and the rewards on offer are intended to motivate and attract people. Therefore, it is not unreasonable for candidates to be up front about what they expect in terms of compensation. Traditionally, men tend to be better at stating their requirements than women, so you may need to make sure that you offer the same package regardless of gender and be prepared to withstand the pressure from the candidates with the well-developed negotiating skills.

Q   Do you expect us to contribute to your course fees?

Q   If we were to offer you the job, would you need to move home? Would you expect us to contribute to your relocation costs?

Q   You mentioned that your current employer pays for your health insurance premium/gym membership/professional body fees. Would you expect us to continue to fund these?

Depending on their relevance, once you had the answer to any of these questions, your follow-up will depend on your organization's rewards policy. If, as a matter of course, your organization does not pay such fees or removal expenses, you should be honest with the candidate as your reply may affect their willingness to accept an offer of employment. However, if your organization does make these sorts of payment, there may be scope for negotiation providing you have some flexibility, after the decisions to offer and accept employment have been made.

Q   This job is a junior manager's position. What sorts of decision do you think you will be able to make alone and which would you need to refer to your manager?

The sort of answer you could reasonably expect would indicate some recognition of the need to learn the job. For example, the candidate could tell you: 'I think, at first, I would want to discuss most matters with my manager but then, as I became more familiar with the job, I would expect to make routine decisions myself and only refer the out of the ordinary to my manager.' If you received the sort of reply that indicated the candidate would decide everything alone, you may have cause for concern.

UNUSUAL QUESTIONS

There are some situations and types of job that make the use of some unusual, almost off-the-wall types of question appropriate. We will now look at some examples of these and discuss how they may be used to best effect.

These questions are most useful when you need to explore cognitive skills and the candidate's ability to respond to the unusual. You should only test these features if they are a genuine requirement of the job and have been included in the selection criteria. If you just want to see how candidates react, you should perhaps reflect on what you are trying to achieve. Playing games with candidates can be good fun, if you are the type of person who enjoys doing this. However, you should ask yourself how such an approach will add to the selection process, how it will predict which candidate will perform well in the job and what it does to your reputation. On the other hand, if you are the type of interviewer who enjoys the 'cat and mouse' technique of interviewing, perhaps you should find out how candidates view you!

You should not ask 'off-the-wall' questions simply because you like the entertainment caused by surprising your candidates and playing with them. The way in which candidates react and respond to these questions can be revealing, but they should be used only when they are related to the needs of the job. Remember the overall aim of the interview is to find out whether both parties are likely to be able to form good working relationships with each other. If you create the impression in the minds of the candidates of you as an employer who plays games with staff and tries to trick them, are they likely to want to accept your offer of employment should you decide to make it?

There is a valid place for asking candidates the 'off-the-wall' type of question as some jobs do demand the sort of qualities they are good at exploring. Generally, situational, hypothetical or behavioural questions are the most appropriate as you will want to know what actions an individual would take in a given situation. You do not necessarily want to know what they know or what they think about an issue. The sorts of criteria this type of questioning can help explore can include:

▌ using one's initiative;

▌ problem solving;

▌ general level of interest in the area of work;

▌ ability to focus;

▌ creativity.

Used in the right circumstances for the right type of job, this type of question can be very useful in helping you assess the candidate's mental processes and the chances of them fitting in your organization. For example, for a job that demands high levels of creative problem solving, such as a Conference Organizer, the following line of questioning may be appropriate:

Q   Imagine a client told you that they needed a live snake as part of their presentation; could you obtain one for them? How would you react?

Possible responses could include:

▌ I would tell them it was against health and safety regulations and they would have to use a plastic one.

▌ I would ask them why it had to be a live snake then, depending on the answer, try to persuade them to use an imitation snake.

▌ I would ask them how big a snake they needed, then ring the nearest zoo.

▌ I would ask them to tell me more about the presentation, what part the snake would play, and then gently explore with them the issues such as the size of snake, how it would be housed before and after the presentation, whether they had considered any regulations that would have to be followed.

If you were the manager of the conference venue and needed to keep your clients happy, which type of response would you prefer to hear?

If you were interviewing for a researcher, you may wish to use some of the following questions to explore the candidate's ability to clarify the question and to find the answers:

Q   How many people do you think are playing golf at the moment?

Q   How many clocks are there in the UK?

The first answer to both questions you would expect from candidates should be intended to clarify your question. In the first case, the candidate that responds by asking you 'Do you mean in this town, in England, the UK or the world' is on the right track. Similarly, for the second question, you would hope to hear the candidate ask 'What do you mean by clock? Do you exclude clocks that are built into other things, such as radios and mobile phones and the little ones that are sold as desk ornaments?' You would then expect to hear how the candidate would start their investigation, what sources they would and would not use and whom they would ask for help.

The candidates who reply by saying '359' or 'I haven't a clue' are heading along the wrong track. They are missing the point of the question. The question is not intended to produce the answer, it is designed to explore the processes the candidates would use to resolve the question.

Off-the-wall questions can also help you detect a candidate's passion for their area of work. This can be important in certain occupations where you will need some evidence of the candidate's willingness to go the extra mile, to be focused and dedicated to their subject. For example, in the case of computer systems designers, you could reasonably expect the candidates to be passionate about IT; in other words, to be a bit of a geek or an anorak. A question such as 'Tell me, if you had unlimited funds, which gadget would you buy yourself?' will tell you a lot about the candidate. Most computer nerds have a long shopping list. If this is the sort of person you want to employ, this area of questioning will provide an indication of the level of their passion. If a candidate tells you about the sports car they would buy, or the latest kitchen accessory, do you think they are likely to have the sort of dedication and approach you are wanting?

Another way of exploring a candidate's level of interest in their work is to ask about how they use IT in their personal lives. Candidates who tell you they would not touch a computer outside work have a limited view of the value of IT. For non-computer-related jobs, you can ask candidates to consider how their professional skills can help in their personal lives. You may find that people with strong leadership tendencies and high social skills are involved in community ventures such as local sports or other types of club, organizing activities for their children and their friends or getting involved in local affairs or professional bodies.

DEALING WITH DIFFICULT CANDIDATES

The interview process is a sophisticated social interaction elaborately designed to carry out an important function – helping people obtain employment and helping you find people able to carry out the work you need to be done. It is a lot more than finding people to do the job; it is also about finding people who will help you build and maintain the sort of organization you want to create. From the individual's standpoint, having a job is about being able to earn sufficient money so they can have the sort of lifestyle they seek. It is also about status and social standing.

Role and social image are important elements of our well-being as they affect our self-esteem. We have all heard of people who, on being made redundant, have not been able to tell their friends and family. They continue to go out of the door at the same time each morning and return at the expected time at night. They are unable to face up to the change in their circumstance or deal with the perceived loss of face. These are sad and extreme cases but they illustrate how important a job can be to someone's self-image. It is not surprising to learn, therefore, that some people will go to extraordinary lengths to get the sort of job to which they aspire. These are the people who acquire rather than attain qualifications, claim successes achieved by others and add a bit to their current salary package.

There are other interview 'types' who can cause considerable difficulties, especially for the novice interviewer. The high levels of unemployment seen in the 1990s led to a growth in the job search industry. Most recruitment agencies provide guidance to job hunters on how best to present their application and themselves at interview. There is also a plethora of books and internet-based guides produced to help interviewees win at the interview game. The end product of this is a population of jobseekers, well informed and trained in the art of attending interviews. In fact, at first, you will find yourself facing candidates who will have attended far more interviews than you have conducted. In these cases, the test you may have to pass is that of maintaining control.

Other types of difficult interviewee you may meet include those whose personality and preferred way of behaving may cause you some problems. Examples will include the candidates who are expert in avoiding the question. They will give you the answers they want you to have, not necessarily the answers to the questions you have asked. You may call this type of candidate 'the politician' as this is an area of skill often attributed to Members of Parliament. Such candidates' success depends on them identifying the points they want to convey before the interview and their adeptness at manoeuvring the situation to enable them to make those points.

Other difficult candidates include those who talk and talk and talk. Keeping rabbits to the point can be difficult. They have no intention of misleading you or avoiding giving you an answer. To the contrary, all they want is for you to ask a question so they can answer it at length. It doesn't really matter if you have some other questions to ask. You can get to these later, a lot later.

The opposite type can also present you with considerable difficulty. The strong silent types are those who take your gift of an open question and discard it with a monosyllabic response. This may leave you gasping in surprise as you are forced desperately to seek a follow-up question while your fellow interviewers are still in the midst of making their notes. This type of candidate could be called 'the robot', only now robots can be programmed to give you answers. After trying to get replies from the strong silent type, you may find yourself wishing that one of these machines had applied for your vacancy!

Do not give up hope. We will discuss ways you can manage each of the difficult types of candidate below.

Telling lies and covering up

If 25 per cent of applicants tell lies on their CVs, you can be sure a similar proportion of candidates will have some topics they would prefer not to discuss. They probably have aspects of their work or educational experience they would rather you did not explore.

A recent court case exposed a senior manager in the health service for telling lies and fabricating qualifications. As he progressed through the managerial ranks, he added qualifications to his CV. These were not attained through additional study, but by the judicious use of his pen (or keyboard). When asked why, in his own defence, he claimed that he had been under pressure to augment his track record in the job with academic attainment. His peers all had degrees and he felt that he needed to be their equal academically as well as in terms of ability. He was found out when, unfortunately for him, his employer decided to tidy up the personnel database and asked all employees for proof of their qualifications. The outcome for him was catastrophic. At the age of 42, he lost his job, was fined £5,000 and given a suspended jail sentence. However, no comment was made in the press about his employers' responsibilities for checking the truth of his application when he had applied for jobs on his way up the hierarchy.

Telling lies in an application can constitute a breach of trust and can be a sackable offence. However, if you do not find out until after the employee has gained employment protection rights and has performed satisfactorily, and if you had not checked facts during the appointment process, you can be in a weak position. Even though the case cited above demonstrates that an employer can resolve the situation, this was done at a considerable cost, which included acquiring bad publicity by all concerned. It is far better to make sure of the facts before any employment contract has been formed.

One area where candidates may be sensitive is the reason for leaving their previous jobs. We discussed earlier the difference between the real reason and those most often given on application forms. Unless you ask, it is unlikely that a candidate will cite the reasons for leaving previous posts on their CV. Most often, all you get are the dates of starting and leaving the various jobs. Research carried out by the Good Boss Company showed that nearly one in four employees has a poor opinion of their boss and nearly half of all employees look elsewhere for a new job because of their boss. Applicants are not going to tell you they want another job because they are not getting on with their boss. They are more likely to give positive and acceptable reasons, such as career development. If it is unlikely they will tell you the real reason for leaving is their poor relationship with their boss, is it likely they will tell you they want to go because it has been suggested they leave rather than face the sack? They may tell you they are going to be made redundant but will they let you know that they are going to be dismissed for deception or bullying colleagues?

Candidates who have something like this to conceal will have well-prepared answers ready to mislead you and throw you off the track. The same will be true for those candidates who have gaps in their employment history. There is nothing wrong with having had a spell of unemployment these days. There have been times in the past when finding jobs, particularly in some areas of the country, has been really difficult. Not being able to obtain alternative employment, for example after an employer closed down, need not be anything to do with a candidate's abilities. Nevertheless, the candidate may be ashamed and would prefer to conceal the break. Other people have gaps due to family circumstances, such as having a career break to bring up young children or to act as a carer. Other people may have suffered periods of illness from which they have totally recovered.

Some people may have spent a period of time in prison or in hospital. The former may be covered by the Rehabilitation of Offenders legislation (we will come back to this in Chapter 5). If the offence is deemed to be spent, the candidate would have every right to expect it to be disregarded. Applicants are encouraged, in the books on how to apply for jobs, to find positive ways of justifying gaps in their employment history. A positive reason may be understandable and acceptable, but one intending to mislead, cover up or fill the gap with an untruth is not.

Another area where candidates may prefer not to tell the truth or the whole truth concerns their existing salary. Many employers have a policy of improving on existing salary as a means of attracting good quality applicants. You will see jobs advertised with the salary as, for example, 'c£25K' or 'in the range of £25,000–35,000'. Sometime you will just see 'Salary negotiable'. This encourages candidates to, shall we say, exaggerate their current earnings potential. They can do this in a number of ways, for example by rounding up, including the possibility of bonuses not yet agreed, or simply lying. This is an area where you need to exercise considerable caution. Responding to pressure to match and improve on the existing salary, without checking with the candidate's current employer, unless you are sure of the justification to do so, you may find yourself in difficulties with your existing employees.

Research has shown that men are more likely to negotiate higher starting salaries than women. They can negotiate harder and are prone to using tactics such as those outlined above. Women tend to undervalue themselves and accept what is on offer. This can lead you to inflate the starting salaries for men and could lead you into a situation where new male employees are paid more than existing female employees in the same job. If you fall into this trap you may find yourself facing an equal pay case. Claiming market pressures is not going to provide you with a defence. If you wish to pay market supplements to occupations in hard-to-recruit groups you need to pay the plusage to all employees, not just a favoured few. Therefore, checking for precise information about existing salary rates or obtaining confirmation from the current employer in a reference check is a sensible way of safeguarding yourself.

As an interviewer, it is your job to be sure you have the answers to the questions you really need answering before you offer employment. You need to remember that a verbal offer is legally binding, so you should be sure before you ask your preferred candidate if they would like the job. The only way you can carry out checks into some aspects of employment history is to ask. You can ask for sight of qualification certificates and seek references to confirm employment and educational history. However, if you do not ask the candidate to explain gaps in their employment history or outline how certain achievements were attained, they may never have to disclose that the claims made in their application were fabricated. Moreover, if you did not raise the question during the interview, you may be placed in a weak position if you find out later that the person you have appointed has misled you.

The expert

The expert candidate will know what to expect. We mentioned above that some jobseekers are trained whilst others have learnt from experience. Groups of employers tend to develop similar approaches to interviewing. For example, NHS organizations frequently have an external assessor on the interview panel. Some sectors favour commonly used psychometric tests in the selection process. Others would expect the candidates to make presentations. Candidates who have applied for several jobs will know what to expect and will be able to make their preparations accordingly, despite what you say in the letter inviting them to the interview.

You will have already given the candidates a lot of information about what you are looking for. This will have been included in the job description, person specification, advertisement and any other information you have given them. Candidates are encouraged to think about how they can make their experience and qualifications fit your requirement. This means that if they have a shortfall in one area, they can compensate by offering you talents and experience in others.

Expert candidates will be able to predict, from the information you have given them, the areas you are most likely to ask about. We have already noted some questions that are totally predictable. The only surprise would be if you did not ask the candidates why they wanted the job and what skills and experience they will be able to offer you. The other area of questioning will also be fairly obvious. If the job is for an IT expert, it is almost inevitable that you will ask about experience of programming and using different types of operating or networking systems. For an accountant, there are bound to be technical questions on accounting conventions and ensuring managers understand the meaning of accounts and budget statements. Using the type of off-the-wall questions outlined above can provide the sort of surprise you may need to unsettle the expert candidate.

Employers want to reduce (or if possible avoid all together) the risk of making a poor appointment decision. The wily, experienced candidate will know that it is their job to prove to you that by appointing them, you will not be taking any risk at all. They will work hard at demonstrating, beyond all doubt, that their experience (even if it is a little different from what you thought you wanted) is exactly what you need in a successful job holder.

Expert candidates will know how to moderate and alter their responses. They will be able to detect from your reaction whether they have given the answer you are seeking. If you indicate, by facial expression or gesture, that you are not satisfied with an answer, the expert candidate will be able to adapt their response until you communicate that you have heard what you wanted to hear.

You will have to work hard to ensure that you maintain control of the interview. Expert candidates will be highly skilful at taking the interview in the direction they want it to follow. This may be different from the one you want. Having several interviewers can help you maintain control, as can thorough preparation. Your interview plan and assessment of candidates against the person specification is the strongest tool in your armoury to help you withstand the dominance of the expert candidate.

The use of closed questions can also stop the expert in their tracks. If you start to ask specific and highly detailed questions that do not allow the expert to distract you, you will prevent them taking the line of questioning in their preferred direction. For example, instead of saying:

Q   Tell us about the most successful project in which you were involved. What led to its success and what did you learn from the experience?

try:

Q   We are looking for someone with experience of leading projects? Have you ever been in that position?

This should give you something approaching a yes or no answer. Depending on the reply you can go on to ask:

Q   If you think about the most successful project in which you were involved, please identify the aspects that went well. Why do you think they went well?

This can be followed by:

Q   Now, please think about the aspects that did not go so well. Can you tell us why you think this happened?

The learning accrued from the candidate's experience can then be explored by asking:

Q   If you were to undertake a similar project, which aspects would you repeat and which would you change? Please give us the reasons for both.

The difference between the two approaches is that in the first, by asking a wide open question, you are giving the candidate the chance to take the question in whichever way they choose. In the second, by asking a sequence of very specific questions you maintain control and can bring the wayward candidate back on track very quickly. The tightness of the structure also means that, if the candidate is aiming to distract you, you can tell fairly quickly that they are flannelling and again you are in a stronger position to probe and test out what is being said.

The politician

A similar approach can work for the politician. However, unlike the expert candidate, whose skills lie in their ability to control an interview and give you the answers they want you to have rather than the ones you are seeking, the politician does not necessarily want to give you an answer at all. They will want to make their points and influence the way you think. They are trying to persuade you rather than control you.

They do this by taking your question as a gift and skilfully turn it so they can introduce their preferred topic of conversation. They will adapt your question skilfully to create the opportunity they seek to make their point. If they are very good, you will not notice that your question has not been answered. You will have heard something very interesting and your mind will have been so well occupied that you will have lost track of the direction of the interview. The politician will have engaged you in a fascinating topic of conversation that will have left you impressed by their wit, quality of insight and their ability to build rapport so quickly with you and the other interviewers.

Such a chain of exchanges might comprise:

Q   I would like to explore your experience of managing projects. On your CV, you say you were responsible for putting in a new accounts package. Can you tell me what features were critical to the success of the project?

A   Whilst I had responsibility overall, we were very dependent on the contractor. This was a renowned IT firm so we expected that they would have well-practised implementation plans. As it turned out, they were chaotic and we were sadly disappointed in the quality of the staff they brought on site.

Q   What did you do about it?

A   We had a well-written contract specification and as soon as it was clear things were not going in accordance with the agreement, we brought in the lawyers. We were then engaged in months of legal wrangling.

Q   What were you doing whilst all this was going on?

A   I was involved in the meetings. It was fascinating to watch the lawyers at work. The IT company had obviously been down this road before and they were able to field a set of legal advisers who were really good at their job. I have to say they knocked spots off our solicitor. We were very nearly taken to the cleaners.

Q   What was your main learning from this? What would you do differently next time?

A   I would ensure the project plan and specification were legally watertight.

Has this exchange told you anything at all about the candidate's abilities to manage a project?

Stopping the rabbit from rabbiting on

The above example gave the interviewers some opportunities to interject and ask supplementary questions. Even if they did not advance the interviewer's exploration of the candidate's abilities, at least they were able to speak. A rabbit will not give you that opening. You will be amazed by their ability to speak without pause or needing to take breath. They excel at the art of being able to use a lot of words yet say nothing. You may have heard such people on trains and buses, in restaurants and shops. You would have been drawn by the glazed look on their companion's face. Following such a person's track can be exhausting as the listener has to work hard at understanding the outpouring. The logic and rational thought patterns may be heavily concealed beneath the weight of the rhetoric.

As an interviewer, you will need to develop a set of techniques to help you wrestle control of the dialogue back from the candidate. Otherwise you will be left as a passive observer of a time-wasting monologue. There are several techniques you can use to help you manage the talkative candidate.

The first is the broken record technique. This is often taught as a technique for developing assertiveness. It simply requires you to repeat a single point. For use with a rabbiting candidate, you will need to develop a set of phrases such as:

I   You were telling me about your supervisory experience.

I   Can we get back to the time you supervised staff?

I   Am I right in thinking that when you were a supervisor, you were responsible for...?

At first you will need to find breaks in the candidate's outpourings to ask your question but as time goes on and this gets more difficult, you may find yourself having to interrupt or speak over the candidate. Normally, this would not be accepted behaviour from an interviewer but if the situation starts to become desperate, it may be the only way in which you are able to get the candidate back on track.

Another way of dealing with someone who is waffling is to use visual clues. If you have been making notes, putting down your pen is a good way of signalling that nothing of what is being said is worth recording. After a while, you can pick up your pen and start fiddling with it. To most people, this indicates that you have lost attention and are no longer concentrating on what is being said. Similarly, you could start flicking through the papers in front of you. Or make a noise, such as dropping your pen on the floor. These are tactics of desperation. You also run the risk of the candidate being blinded and deafened by their own words so they miss your clues.

The use of closed questions is a more effective and politer way of regaining some control. The use of 'Am I right in understanding that…' is a good way of drawing the talkative candidate to a halt. Leading questions such as 'Did you say that you were responsible for a budget of £XXX,XXX?' is another way. Sometimes giving the wrong information so the candidate needs to correct you can also make them pause for thought. This is the equivalent of a speed bump in the middle of the road and it can shock the candidate back into tune with the interview. The rabbit will probably have forgotten about the reason for the dialogue in their enjoyment of the opportunity to talk at length.

You will need to apply your questioning skills to make sure you get all the information you need from the candidate so you can assess their abilities against your specification. When faced with someone rabbiting on, you need to remember that excessive verbosity can be a sign of nervousness. Therefore you do have a responsibility to keep the candidate focused and to make sure everything has been adequately covered. If you let yourself be blinded by the torrent of words, you could find that you have not gathered sufficient evidence for your assessment. You may also find that you have rejected a candidate with the qualities you need. Their nerve-inspired tendency to go on at length could be moderated in a less stressful setting and with some coaching.

Getting the silent type to talk

The opposite type of candidate can be equally difficult to deal with. This is the one who sits in front of you in stony silence. Their reluctance to utter more than a 'Good morning', 'yes' and 'no' could be another feature of interview nervousness. We know that rabbits can be paralysed by fear. Is your interview technique and approach the equivalent of a set of car headlights? It could be that the person you are trying to get to speak is not the silent type after all, just an ordinary person who is a mass of quivering nerves, terrified by the prospect of what you might do to them.

In this case, your job is to find ways of relaxing the candidate. You can do this by turning around the interview structure. Thus you would start by telling the candidate more about the job and your organization and then gently drawing them into the conversation. For example:

Q   We are hoping to expand our customer base. One of the key aspects of the new job holder's work will be to identify potential clients. Have you done anything like this before?

A   Yes.

Q   We already have a very good customer relationship management package and have access to databases and mailing lists but we will need to draw these together so we can target likely customers. Have you done anything like this before?

A   Yes.

Q   Can you tell us what you did?

A   I compiled a list of customers.

Q   How did you go about that?

It should become increasingly more difficult for the candidate to limit their replies as they are gradually drawn into the conversation. By allowing them to get away with monosyllabic replies at first, you are not putting them under pressure. Instead you are allowing their voice to be heard. This should help them gain confidence and overcome their nervousness.

You can also use silence. If you wait rather than rushing in with your follow-up question, you may find that the candidate has more to say. They just needed some space in which to think. Generally speaking, we do not like silence and the pressure on interviewers can mean that they are too quick to come in for a second go at questioning the candidate. You may need to resist this temptation as some people need a little more time than others to consider their reply. It does not mean they are slow, just thoughtful. All they need from you is some patience.

On the other hand, if you wait too long, the silence can become a chasm that is difficult for anyone to cross. It can develop into a game similar to the one played by children in which they try to stare each other out. As an interviewer, it is your responsibility to use silence or pauses in the flow constructively. If the wait for the candidate to answer is in danger of becoming a gulf, you will need to fill it. The use of a simple phrase quietly spoken such as 'let's move on' is all that you need to restart the flow.

Some people are naturally concise to the point of brevity. Unless being an outgoing, fluent communicator is an essential feature of the person specification, you may find that behind the wall of silence you are facing a competent, appointable candidate. There again, you might find yourself faced by someone who has nothing to say. You need to find out. This is where the use of the open and leading questions come in, as the following demonstrates:

Q Let's move on to talk about maintenance. You will have seen from the job description that the post of Operations Manager has responsibility for making sure that the machine downtime is minimized. Do you have any thoughts on how this can be achieved?

A Yes.

Q Could you tell us what they are?

A Simple, the answer is planned maintenance.

Q What would that involve?

A Drawing up a programme, not waiting for breakdowns.

Q How would you draw up such a programme?

A Look at the pattern of previous failures then work out an optimum schedule.

Q Won't that be expensive? We would be spending money fixing things before they are broken.

The use of a challenge here should spur the candidate on to say more about their thinking. You can see from the example that, again, the candidate is being drawn into saying more as the line of questioning progresses. The trick for the interviewer is to keep on. Do not give up; instead, keep on probing until you find out what you need to know. Either the candidate has the ability you seek and you will see signs of it or they haven't. In this case, it will be clear that your line of questioning has hit the wall. Either way, you will be able to complete your assessment rather than being unsure.

QUESTIONS OF DUBIOUS VALUE

There are some interview questions that, though often used, have only marginal if any benefit. It is doubtful whether they add any real value to the interview. Their use is possibly one of the reasons why the interview, as a mechanism of exploring potential and performance in the job, has such poor powers of prediction. On the surface, the following questions may appear to be the ones a clever interviewer would ask. However, if you start to think about the likely answers they would receive and how you would react if you were in the candidate's place, you will quickly see that the chances of gaining the evidence you need to carry out your assessment are low. Moreover, they will do little to help build your reputation as an employer of choice. The questions we have already discussed are far more purposeful, focused and beneficial.

Nevertheless, it is worth considering the dubious type of question, if only because they are so widely used.

Q   Tell me about yourself. What makes you tick?

What would you say if you were asked this? The chances are you would use the features in the person specification to be sure you are telling the interviewer what he or she wants to hear. Alternatively, you would come out with something like:

I   I am a highly motivated team player who is focused on achievement.

I   My job satisfaction comes from giving really high-quality services to customers.

I   I am a trouble shooter.

It is difficult to follow up on these or obtain evidence that would support your assessment. Supplementary questions simply provide the candidate with the opening to expand on the aspects of the job they know you are interested in. Can you imagine asking 'Can you give me an example of when you shot trouble?' Asking 'What aspect of teamwork motivates you the most?' will probably elicit a reply such as 'Working with competent colleagues who are focused on achieving common objectives' or 'Being in a mutually supportive environment'. Does that tell you anything you do not already know or anything more about the candidate's ability to work with other people? A serious candidate is not likely to tell you 'I enjoy the opportunity to develop really good friendships at work. Being able to have a drink with my mates at lunchtime and after-work drinks with colleagues is the reason why I go to work. I hear that your organization has a really good social scene.'

A similar question often used to open an interview is:

Q   What kind of a person are you?

How would you expect a candidate to answer this question? Perhaps, they would say something like:

I   An ideas person (but hopeless on implementation).

I   Someone who is interested in other people (I am nosy and like to know what is going on).

I   I like to get the job done (I am a workaholic).

I   I am methodical and accurate (to the point of being pedantic and nit-picking).

I   I prefer to work alone (I am an introvert lacking in social skills).

I   I enjoy team working (I spend all day talking).

It may seem that they are giving you highly acceptable information about their motivation and attitude to the job, but it is very difficult for you to confirm this. You can only guess at what is behind their answer. The answers in the brackets above give a different meaning to the answers. The question is also giving the candidate the opportunity to test what you are looking for. The wily candidate will be able to assess your reaction and adjust their answer if they suspect you did not like their first response. So the candidate who gave the first response could add 'and I know I need to follow through to delivery by working with other people to develop practical implementation plans'. Your reaction to this change of direction will tell the candidate where they need to go next to form a good impression.

Asking about future plans may seem like a reasonable thing to do, but the world of work is changing so much that you need to pick a realistic time horizon. At one time, a candidate with a well-thought-out career plan was seen as someone whose ambitions were more achievable than the person who muddled through. Now, the former could be seen as someone whose well-developed plans could indicate a rigidity that would prove to be a handicap. Employers are seeking flexibility, the willingness to adapt and people who are able to take opportunities as they appear. Therefore asking 'Where do you see yourself in five years' time?' might not be useful. It might be better to ask the candidates to outline how they would plan the development of their career. Focusing on the processes they would use would be more informative than asking them which rungs of which ladder they intend to climb on the way up the hierarchy.

Asking a candidate to describe their weaknesses is perhaps naïve. Candidates know they are going to have to sell themselves and are in competition. They are also encouraged to turn negatives into positives. Thus the lack of experience in one area would be complemented by having strengths in another. For example, not having a required qualification would be balanced by extra experience and on-the-job learning gained instead of engaging in formal study. Therefore, asking 'What are your greatest weaknesses?' is unlikely to provide you with a truthful assessment of skill shortages or gaps in experience.

The candidate will try to anticipate the sort of answer you want to hear. If they have prepared well, they will have some pretty good ideas about what you are looking for and if they have been trained in interview techniques, they will know how to turn a negative on their CV into a positive. They are able to do this by linking a personal training need to an aspect of the work they know you want to develop. For example, if you have said that you wanted to add to your website, they could express an interest in learning more about website design. If you have intimated that you need to strengthen your complaints handling process or relationships with suppliers, they could express an interest in developing negotiating and conflict resolution skills. Some candidates acquire a wish to learn how to speak a foreign language, if they know you do business abroad. Often you will not be aware that you have given out so many hints. Only with hindsight will you realize that the candidate was doing the interview expert's equivalent of borrowing your watch to tell you the time!

Asking candidates to pitch for a salary figure is like asking 'What would you do if you won the lottery?' If you ask anyone 'How much do you want to earn?' the sky would be the limit. But of course it is not. You are almost asking the candidate to gamble with their prospects of employment. If they pitch too high, you might think they are greedy, motivated only by money, or that they overestimate their own abilities. If they pitch too low, you might think they have flaws they are wanting to hide, that they are desperate for a job or they are a shrinking violet not able to stand their ground. Most employers have a salary range they append to the job. Even if this has not been advertised, some sort of pay pegging will have been carried out if only to make the job affordable and to ensure internal consistency and equity. Asking an outsider to have a guess at what this range might be is not particularly helpful. If you are tempted to enter into pay negotiations in this way, you should ask yourself why you are doing it and what you are hoping to get from the candidates that you could not assess in a more meaningful way.

Enquiring into personal motivation and satisfaction could lead you into difficulties of a different order. It is not uncommon to ask about this area and it can be useful to find out why a candidate wants the job you are offering. As part of the exchange of information you need to know what a candidate is seeking to be assured that your organization is able to match their expectations but you do need to be careful about how you phrase such questions. The example below could land you in considerable amounts of hot water:

Q   What gives you greatest satisfaction?

How does the candidate interpret this question? Are you asking about their personal life or the aspects of work that bring them the most pleasure? If you want to know about the sources of job satisfaction, you would be well advised to be more precise in your questioning.

Another question that could cause candidates some difficulty is:

Q   What do you look for from an ideal job or employer?

They have to be wary in their answer in case you follow up with:

Q   Is your present employer like that?

Or

Q   Do you expect us to live up to your standard?

Another question that appears to be setting up a trap is:

Q   What makes you angry?

A candidate who tells the truth by saying something like 'I dislike sloppiness' runs the risk of creating the impression of being the sort of person who is intolerant of others. Saying 'I find intolerance in others intolerable' sounds like a holier than thou type and the candidate who says 'I rarely get cross' can come across as being either a saint or a liar. How would you answer that question in an interview? What do you expect a candidate to say in response and what is it going to tell you about the candidate's ability to do the job you are filling?

The following what-if questions are also unrealistic and verging on the unreasonable. When thinking about asking them, you should consider what you would expect the candidate to say in response and then consider what their replies will tell you about their ability to do the job in question. We often ask questions for the sake of it, thinking that they are the sorts of question that should be asked in an interview. Perhaps they are the questions that stick in your memory from interviews you have attended in the past. If this is the case, you should ask yourself why you remember them. Is it because they were really insightful, probing questions that made you think? Did they give you the opportunity to tell the interviewer how you had managed a particular project, or how you tackled a difficult situation? Did the question enable you to show yourself off to the best of your ability or did it put you on the spot? Were you obliged to blag your way through and waffle because giving a truthful answer was simply not possible?

All jobs have a component of pressure in them. Some are very stressful, some are complex and others contain more work than can be done in the available time. Often the pressure and complexity are due as much to the environment, context and culture of the organization as the content of the job. It is how those tasks are organized, the internal systems and the working relationships that determine how stressful they are. Asking candidates to respond to 'How do you cope under pressure?' almost invites a question in reply. It would not be unreasonable for the candidates to rejoinder with:

Q   What kind of pressure do you mean?

You also need to consider what you are telling the candidates about the nature of the job, the culture of the organization and your approach as a manager. It is now well established that managers have a responsibility to take steps to reduce undue pressure and stress in the workplace. Failure to do so, if it leads to a deterioration of the health of individuals, can be a reason for ill-health retirement, constructive dismissal and other legitimate claims for compensation. It can also be seen, depending on the circumstances, as bullying and harassment.

The following is another example of a question that begs a question in response. What message does the exchange outlined below tell the candidates about your managerial skills and abilities?

Q   What things do you find difficult to manage?

A   In what sense do you mean?

Q   Well, can you think of any type of situation that is hard for you to cope with?

A   Not really, I can manage to deal with most things that normally happen at work. Do you have anything specific in mind?

Q   No, not really. I just wondered whether there was anything in particular you found difficult.

A   You can be assured that if I did, I would discuss the situation with you before it became difficult for me to manage.

In effect, by following this line of questioning, you will have given total control of the interview to the candidate. You will have put yourself into a situation where you have to explain and almost justify why you asked the question in the first place. Is this the image you wish to create in the mind of a potential employee at the beginning of your relationship? If you need to explore candidates' reactions to difficult and demanding situations, you would be better advised to use a situational question, based on a likely scenario, than ask a wide open question that either requires the candidate to fabricate a response or enables them to take control of the interview.

Asking the following can lead to a similar loss of control and would not necessarily portray you in your best light. You may need to know whether the candidate has the ability or potential to take the lead in certain situations. Take, for example, a job whose holder was required to act as duty manager, say as the head of a section in a retail store or public building, with occasional responsibility for the building, staff and safety of customers at weekends and in the evenings. It would therefore be reasonable to know how they would deal with an emergency. You may be tempted to ask the following:

Q   How would you manage in a crisis?

The sorts of predictable reply could include:

▌ What kind of crisis?

▌ Do you expect things to go wrong often?

▌ Would I be given any training?

▌ I don't know. I have never been in a crisis.

▌ I have a cool head. I would take charge with no hesitation.

▌ I would panic and rush around confusing and frightening everyone.

Is it likely the candidate would give you an honest reply to this question? Often our behaviour depends very much on previous experience and the learning accrued from our exposure to situations. If a candidate had never been in a crisis, they may genuinely not know how they would respond. Moreover, how do you define a crisis? Definitions may vary and again be informed by experience just as much as personality. To some, a crisis is leaving their mobile phone at home, or being made late for an important meeting by a traffic jam. For others it is being involved in the accident that caused the traffic jam.

If you need to explore reactions and likely responses to dealing with crises you would be better phrasing the question in a situational way. The following are all legitimate questions depending on the types of situation likely to occur:

▌ What would you do if there was a fire in the store room? (Used for jobs with responsibility for others, for example a shop, public building or set of offices.)

▌ How would you deal with a phone caller telling you there was a bomb in the building? (Used for telephonists, reception or security staff.)

▌ What would you do if a member of the public collapsed? (Used for staff with direct contact with large numbers of people and responsibility for doing something about emergencies.)

▌ What would you do if you were delayed for an important meeting? (Asking about reactions to different sorts of meeting may give you useful information about the candidate's sense of priorities. For example, would they react differently to a routine staff meeting and a meeting with an important client?)

The conclusions to be drawn from this section are very simple. If you are not sure why you are asking the question or cannot show how it will help you assess the candidates' abilities against the selection criteria, either do not ask it or reframe it in a way that will provide relevant information that will contribute to your assessment.

QUESTIONS NOT TO BE ASKED

There are some questions that you really should not ask at all under any circumstances. You may be tempted to find the answer to the questions but before verbalizing your curiosity, you should ask yourself (or your fellow interviewers, if they suggest asking such questions) why you need to know. All the questions discussed in this section could be taken as evidence of your efforts to discriminate unfairly and illegally against one candidate on grounds other than those related to the needs of the job.

The whole of the selection process is intended to enable you to discriminate between candidates. You need to be able to predict which of the group is most likely to perform the best. But you need to do this by using factors that are clearly related to the job and the needs of your organization. You should also treat each candidate in similar ways. This does not mean you need to develop a script that enables you to ask each candidate exactly the same question (though some organizations do this). It does mean, however, that you need to use the same sort of process and explore similar topics. Thus, if you ask one candidate about their career ambitions, you will ask them all. If you explore aspects of the candidate's CV, you ask the others to explain features of their previous work experience. If you need to ask one candidate a specific question not put to the others, your reasons for doing so need to be clear.

The laws relating to unfair and unjustifiable discrimination are becoming more complex and are being augmented on a regular basis. This book does not aim to provide you with a definitive legal position, for it changes not only as a result of the enactment of new statutes but also because judgements in court and at tribunals are expanding the interpretation of UK and EU laws. You should try to keep up to date if you recruit regularly. If you do not or are not sure, you should check on the latest position. You can do this very easily by using the internet to access authoritative sources such as ACAS or the government and its agencies.

Asking any of the following questions is likely to make you vulnerable to accusations of unfair discrimination:

Q   How old are you?

Does it matter? One reason for asking may be to judge how long a candidate is likely to remain in your employment. Are they likely to retire in the next year or so? Are they likely to leave to take care of children? Are they likely to want leave to care for other dependants? Are they likely to leave for a better job? What relevance does age have? And in any case, how long do you expect people to stay with you? Reasons for leaving quickly are not necessarily a product of age. You may have other reasons for asking. Do you think older people are likely to have more sickness? Is this proven by your absence figures and those of other employers or is this a figment of your prejudice? Do you think that youth is a sign of a lack of experience or maturity? If you need experience, what kind of experience are you seeking? Maybe you would be better asking about the candidate's employment history rather than making assumptions about the relationship between a candidate's age and their track record.

Q   Are you a man or a woman?

Admittedly, sometimes it is difficult to tell. Fashion and mode of dress can conceal gender – but does it matter? You can require job holders to be of one sex or the other, providing this is a genuine occupational qualification. The conditions needed to satisfy this requirement are strictly laid down and, in most cases, basing decisions on the sex of an individual is indisputably illegal. Moreover, there are recent judgements concerning individuals who have undergone gender reassignment treatment protecting their rights to fair treatment. Any organizations basing decisions on these grounds have received exceedingly bad publicity as well as having penalties imposed upon them for their discriminatory practices, if the individual pursued a case.

Q   How many children do you have?

You can get away with asking this question if you ask it to all candidates, men and women, those in relationships and those living alone, providing it is relevant to the job. However, what are your reasons for asking? Are you expecting staff to work long and inconvenient hours? Do you require them to be away from home for long periods? If these are reasonable components of the job, you should be able to explore them directly. However, if this is your normal working practice, perhaps you should consider the impact working patterns have on staff in general, not just on their ability to exercise their parenting responsibilities.

Are you worried about school holidays or absence caused by childhood illnesses? Does this matter if a candidate has grown-up children? What about those people whose children live with their other parent? What impact would your question have on those who have lost a child? In any case, people have other sorts of out-of-work commitments that can have similar impacts on their attendance at work. Perhaps you need to explore this by asking:

Q   The demands of the job can vary. This may mean that you could be
     required to work over (or away from the office) on occasions. Is there
     anything that would limit your flexibility to do this?

Asking the following has absolutely no justification, under any circumstances.

Q   Who looks after your children when you are at work?

It is none of your business. Providing the individual is able to honour their contractual requirements to attend work, at the agreed times, how they organize their personal lives and domestic commitments is their concern, not yours.

The next question is another no-no:

Q   Are you planning to have children?

Would you ask this of a man? How would you react if the candidate said 'I want to but am infertile'? All you need to know is what career ambitions the candidates have. You can explore this area by asking far more relevant questions such as those outlined above. Their reproductive ambitions are not for you to know.

If the job does require the holder to be away from home on a regular basis, this should be made clear in the information sent out in advance. It should be no surprise to the candidates and should be compensated for as part of the remuneration package. For example, it should be clear that expenses are covered and that possibly time in lieu or other flexibilities and benefits are provided. If these points have been covered and discussed as part of the information exchange, is there any point in asking:

Q   What would your partner say about you working away?

It is far better to discuss the matter in the following way:

Q   As you know, this job entails a lot of travelling and the person appointed
    will need to be away from home overnight. This is likely to happen several
    times a month. Would this cause you any practical difficulties? (Some
    people may have pets!)

Employers are now expected to have mechanisms in place for informing and consulting their employees about matters that affect them and their work. In the past, this was frequently done through formal industrial relations machinery involving the trade unions. However, union membership has declined significantly in the past 20 years so other ways of encouraging the participation of the workforce in decision making have been developed. Employers have very different views about how much involvement the workforce should have and some hold very entrenched attitudes about those actively pushing for greater levels of participation than they are prepared to grant. Individuals trying to organize their colleagues and promote union involvement are still protected by various pieces of legislation, so asking the following question is ill advised:

Q   Do you belong to a trade union?

Questions about religion or belief could also be seen as being unreasonably intrusive. Asking:

Q   Do you go to church regularly or say prayers during the working day?

is straying into areas that could lead the candidate to ask you why you wanted to know and possibly conclude that you were prejudiced against them for reasons of their religion.

Changes to immigration rules and work permits now require employers to demonstrate their need to offer employment to a candidate who is not a UK citizen. This also extends to candidates who are required to show that they are entitled to work in the UK. This requirement applies to all, regardless of the colour of their skin or place of origin if this falls outside the scope of the legally defined entitlements. To work in the UK you can ask candidates to provide such proof, providing you apply the requirement to all. You should not ask:

Q   Where were you born?

Q   What is your ethnicity?

Q   Where were your parents born?

It is better to ask:

Q   As a result of the Migrant Worker Registration Regulations, we ask all successful candidates to provide proof of their entitlement to work in the UK. Would you be prepared to do this?

Similarly, questions about first or preferred languages can be seen as being discriminatory. The following question could send out negative messages about your reason for asking:

Q   Which language do you speak at home?

If you have a need for staff who can speak several languages, it would be more appropriate to ask:

Q   Can you speak any languages other than English?

There is considerable evidence to show that people tend to follow similar career routes and occupational preferences to those of other family members. There is clear proof that such influences at home and in an individual's early years can have considerable effect on their later choices. However, this is not always the case. How would the following line of questioning help you decide whether the candidate sitting on the other side of the interview table has the skills and abilities you seek?

Q   What does your father do?

▮ My father died before I was born.

▮ My father left home when I was little.

▮ He was a miner (from an applicant applying for work as a lawyer).

▮ He is a high court judge (from some seeking work as a gardener).

Asking about other family members can be equally uninformative:

Q Do you have any brothers or sisters?

▌ No.

▌ Yes, there are 10 of us.

Will you go on to ask about the occupations of all of them?

It may be useful to explore candidates' hobbies and interests. In fact, some application forms have space for details of club membership or pastimes. You need to be clear, however, about how this information will help you make your decision. Will asking the following simple question give you the evidence you need?

Q Are you a member of any sports or social clubs?

▌ No.

▌ Yes. I am a member of the local civic/operatic/allotment/football/table tennis/gym/Harley Davidson owners' club.

What does this tell you? If you need to know how out of work activities could indicate the existence of relevant skills and experiences, you could ask:

Q Do you belong to any clubs or groups that would help you do this job?

Information about candidates' occupancy of roles such as being a secretary or treasurer of a club, or being involved in a professional or community association would help you discuss their learning gained from these activities and how it has helped the development of their skills.

Asking questions about health can lead you into a minefield which you do not need to enter. You can ask candidates to complete a form which asks them to reveal conditions that may affect their ability to do the job for which they are applying. After all, as an employer, you have legal responsibilities to make reasonable adjustments to ensure that those with disabilities are not unfairly disadvantaged. You can require candidates to complete a medical questionnaire and undergo a medical examination but you are not allowed to discriminate against them on grounds relating to their condition unless you can clearly demonstrate that the individual would not be able to carry out the majority of the responsibilities and duties and that the aids and adaptations they would need would not be practical or feasible. For most people with most disabilities, the help they need is neither complex nor expensive. Mostly, all they require is flexibility, simple aids and the chance to demonstrate what they are able to do. Often this is far more than is credited on first appearances. You should not ask:

- Have you ever been tested for HIV or AIDS?
- Do you have a disability?
- How is your health?
- Have you had any recent illness or injury?
- How much do you weigh?
- Do you smoke?

These are not questions related to an individual's ability to do the job. The answers would not give you any information to help you accommodate any special needs required to enable a person with disabilities to perform their duties. They could be construed as being personally intrusive and an indication of a nosy, controlling employer. It is better to say:

Q   We ask everyone to whom we offer a job to complete a medical questionnaire and if needs be attend for an examination. We will send you the form if we decide to offer you the job.

Some employers have very strict rules about the use of controlled and illegal substances. They retain the right to carry out tests and ask employees direct questions about their use of substances, including alcohol. The reasons for doing so are clearly connected with abilities to do the job and often are related to safety requirements. For example, airline pilots and sports competitors are not allowed to drink before work or make use of prescribed drugs. However, for most occupations, this is a matter of personal choice. It is for the individual to decide if they want to take the risk of damaging their own health and being caught. Unless you are appointing to an area of work where drug taking or drinking is prohibited, asking questions about this is very similar to asking:

Q   Do you break the speed limits or park in areas where parking is not allowed?

The Rehabilitation of Offenders Act 1974 is designed to support those wishing to rehabilitate themselves after committing a serious crime and serving their sentence by allowing them to conceal their criminal history. The Act specifies the conditions which, if met, allow the conviction to be treated as spent after a period of time. The length of time depends on the age of the individual at the time the crime was committed and length of sentence given. However, some jobs fall outside the provisions of the law and employers are allowed to ask applicants to disclose any and all convictions. It is normal good practice to make this clear from the outset. If you ask at interview:

Q   Have you been convicted of a crime?

you may find that you are contravening the Act's somewhat complex provisions. If you feel that the job may be exempt (for example, if it involves handling other people's money, dealing with sensitive, confidential information or working with vulnerable adults or children), you should clarify the position before placing the advertisement. If you then need to know whether the applicants have been convicted of a crime, you can include the question in the application or by asking the applicants to complete a pre-interview questionnaire.

Mental illness, perhaps, carries as much stigma as criminal convictions. There are more people claiming Incapacity Benefit because of mental ill health than there are claiming Jobseeker's Allowance. This is a dreadful indictment as many would be capable of working if only they were given the chance. Those whose mental illness has required them to be sectioned under the Mental Health Act face even more problems when trying to obtain work. They will have gaps in their employment history which will need to be explained. Not only do they have to overcome the wide discrimination against those with mental health problems, they have to deal with the misunderstanding of the legislation. Often, those who do not know any better think that being held under the Mental Health Act is the same as being held under other legislation. Often, the provisions of the Act are used to protect the individuals from themselves as much as safeguarding other people. Being held under the Act does not mean the individual has done anything wrong or that they will never recover from their illness. It is often used as a way of dealing with an emergency. If you need to know whether the candidates have been sectioned (and you should be clear why you need this information), the question should be asked on a confidential medical questionnaire, not in an interview.

Some organizations have policies about employing family members or those in close personal relationships in the same section. Some employers are also concerned about employing individuals who are known to senior managers or others in positions of authority, such as non-executive directors or board members. This can be a perverse form of discrimination and could deny the organization capable employees. The fear is as much to do with the perceptions and insecurities of other people as with the reality of nepotism, the leakage of confidential information and the use of relationships to exercise undue influence on decisions. Nevertheless, some organizations find it is best to bring such matters out into the open from the outset rather than take the risk of finding out that, unknowingly, the niece of the managing director has been employed. This can be done in a subtle way by asking:

Q   Do you know anyone who already works for or is involved with this organization?

There are certain jobs and occupations that require job holders to wear protective clothing or uniforms. Often, the reasons for requiring staff to comply with strict dress codes concern:

▎ the need for cleanliness (eg catering workers, health care providers);

▎ to protect the workers (eg construction workers);

▎ to convey a corporate image (eg airline workers);

▎ to make the employees stand out (eg police officers).

Some organizations have dress codes because senior managers have strong views on how workers should appear. This can be found particularly when staff are providing services to members of the public. Examples include shops, banks and building societies, and government offices. Enforcing such dress codes can be problematic, however, especially if the rules are applied differently to men and women or members of different ethnic groups.

   Some classic cases have made the headlines. Examples include requiring Sikhs to wear corporate headgear rather than allowing them to wear turbans, not allowing men to wear earrings but permitting women to do so, forbidding women to wear trousers at work or expecting men to wear ties even when they do not come into contact with the public. If your organization has a strict dress policy you need to be sure that it is related to the needs of the job and can be justified. You should also make sure that new recruits are aware of the requirements before they are offered and accept employment. You can do this by sending out such information before the interview or by asking:

Q   We have a dress policy for all staff who (for example) come into contact with clients, work in the kitchen, in the workshop or on machines. Would complying with this policy cause you any difficulty?

QUESTIONS THAT NEED TO BE ASKED

There are some questions that you might have to ask to ensure that certain facts are checked and requirements met. These mainly concern the need for certain qualifications, registration or licence to practice. These can include:

▌ Clean driving licences for jobs that involve driving. As well as complying with the law, employing non-qualified drivers or those with penalty points might invalidate your insurance coverage.

▌ Evidence of training. This is usually important in areas of work that carry high risks, such as operating dangerous machinery, working with hazardous substances or in a high-risk environment, including working underground or at heights.

▌ Membership of a professional body, eg Law Society, Institute of Civil Engineers or Chartered Accountant, as this provides assurance of the individual's achievement of certain levels of knowledge and ability.

▌ Registration of fitness to practise. This is required for social work and health care professionals, such as physiotherapists, doctors and nurses.

Rather than simply accepting the candidates' assurances of their status and qualifications, it may be so important that you will need to ask for sight of certificates of membership. If a candidate tells you they have lost the original, you should have cause for suspicion. Most people in the sorts of occupation that require such levels of attainment know the importance of being able to prove their status. If the original has been mislaid or damaged, copies can be obtained from the relevant issuing body. If they have not replaced the lost document, you might wonder about their appreciation of the need for such qualifications and the seriousness of their commitment to other important matters such as continuous development and the updating of skills and knowledge.

We have already mentioned the need to check on the entitlement to work in the UK. These measures were introduced to prevent those with no rights to be in the UK from obtaining employment and to address the problem of illegal immigration without unduly inhibiting employers to recruit staff with skills and experience in short supply. The regulations are strict and if you are in any doubt you should ask all candidates to provide proof of their entitlement to work in this country. This evidence can include production of passports or other authoritative forms of proof of identity. Simply asking candidates the question:

Q   Can you work in the UK?

would not provide you with sufficient defence if your employment and scrutiny practices were to be investigated. You would need to demonstrate that you have taken all reasonable steps to ensure that those you employ are only those who are entitled to obtain work in the UK and that you have obtained the necessary permits.

OTHER INDICATORS

In addition to asking candidates questions during the interview and noting their answers and reactions, there are other indicators you can legitimately use to assess their abilities to do the job to the standards you require. However, you need to be particularly aware of your own biases and prejudices when using some of the following modes of assessment. With such insight you can make good use of indicators such as appearance, behaviour, speech patterns and interactions to enable you to predict how well the candidates are likely to perform.

Appearance

We tend to have fairly traditional opinions about what people should wear to work. Some of our attitudes are influenced by fashion but, by and large, we tend to be conservative and do not expect to see the extremes in places of work, particularly amongst staff with direct customer contact. There are some organizations where the breaking of social mores is permissible, almost expected, and the 'anything goes' attitude can be found. These organizations tend to be confined, however, to certain sectors such as the creative industries. For the most part, the mode of dress that people are expected to wear to work is governed by the nature of the occupation, the industrial sector and the position the individual occupies in the organization.

Therefore, how an individual dresses for an interview can be taken as revealing something about their approach to their work. If you are going to take notice of appearance, however, you do need to be careful not to make assumptions about the meaning of certain pieces of apparel, particularly if the item of clothing is associated with religious beliefs or norms of other cultures. Unless the occupation requires the occupants to wear uniform or protective clothing and unless you have a strict dress code, what people wear within certain bounds is their own personal choice. It is not the 'what' that matters most but 'how' the individual presents themselves.

If someone turns up to an interview in clothes that fall into the extremes of fashion, are untidy or even dirty, you could legitimately ask yourself how seriously they are taking the occasion. At the very least, it is reasonable to expect candidates to make an effort to present themselves physically to their best advantage. This means appearing as they would when representing your organization and this means dressing appropriately for the situation.

Behaviour

People can choose how to behave. Most people find going to an interview an intimidating experience and may be very nervous at the outset. For some, their nerves can dominate their behaviour and overcome them. These extreme cases are not that common. Most often candidates will suffer from the normal symptoms we all experience when meeting new people. The flutters in the stomach, flushing, sweating palms and the need to move one's fingers or feet should not be too disabling.

Knowing that you are likely to see these patterns of behaviour with most candidates will leave you free to observe other behaviour patterns. We have already mentioned the importance of watching what the candidates do during the course of the interview. You do need to be careful not to try to guess at motives for behaviour. For if you do, the chances are you will be wrong. However, this should not prevent you from watching and noting what people do.

For example, if you wish to enquire into a particular aspect of the candidates' experience or explore how they would react in a given situation and they start to shuffle their feet, when they had been perfectly relaxed previously, you could legitimately wonder why they had reacted to your question in such a way. Rather than guess at motives, their behaviour should indicate to you that you should probe some more. The exchange could take the following form:

Q Let's talk some more about the building project you managed. You referred to it when we talked about your time at Bloggs and Co. Can you give me some more details about the scope and size of the building project?

A Oh, it was not that important. At the time I was more involved in making sure the contract specifications were comprehensive. (You notice the candidate's face goes red and their eyes start roving around the room.)

Q You know that the Site Manager will be responsible for overseeing the construction of the new warehouse so I would like to hear a little more about your experience of managing building work. You did state on your CV that you had been responsible for a £3 million project and successful completion was a major achievement.

A Yes. I was very pleased that we completed within budget. I think this was down to the detail we put into the specification. (You can see that his/her fingers are twisting.)

Q But with regard to managing the actual project, can you tell me how you approached that?

A Err, well, I did have an excellent deputy who did the day-to-day operational stuff. You know, making sure that the plant and materials were ready on time and talking to the contractors regularly. Their relationships were first class. I had weekly meetings with my deputy so that I could make sure that everything was going smoothly. Being able to trust him/her meant that I could concentrate on getting the contract right.

Q Thank you. Let's move on.

The answer came out eventually. The success of the project was down to the efforts of the deputy. This exchange illustrates how using the behavioural clues can help you recognize that there may be more to the story than the messages conveyed by the words. The clues are there and tell you to probe.

You may find it helpful also to make a note of how candidates behave as well as recording what they say in reply to your questions. This will help your memory when discussing each candidate's performance with your fellow interviewers when you come to make your decision. Your notes together with those of the other interviewers will help to give a more rounded picture of the candidate's suitability for the job.

Speech or communication

As with behaviour, how people speak can be the result of positive decisions on their part. We are not talking about the effects of accent or dialect. These are factors often outside the control of the individual but the tone they use can be adapted to achieve a desired result. For example, candidates can choose to be gruff, defensive, verbose or to mutter.

If a candidate reacts to a question in a hostile or defensive manner, you will have every reason to note the fact or even explore their response with them at the time, especially if their body language suggests to you that something is going on for the candidate:

Q   Can you tell me some more about how you would deal with conflict between members of your team?

A   I would get them in a room, tell them that arguments are not acceptable and make it clear they are to sort it out. (The candidate sits back and folds their arms.)

Q   Can you tell me some more about what you would do to help them resolve their differences?

A   I wouldn't get involved. (The candidate's tone is getting gruff.)

Q   Have you experienced situations like this before?

A   Umm, once or twice.

Q   Would you like to describe what happened?

A   Rather not....

How far you would probe thereafter will depend on how important this area of work is to the overall performance of the job, but clearly something had occurred in this candidate's past that has influenced their willingness to talk about their approach to conflict resolution. You should avoid guessing what this might have been or trying to sort out why the candidate was reluctant to discuss the matter.

You are not trying to psychoanalyse the individual or provide therapy. It is worth noting, however, that there are questions around this aspect of the job. If the person specification includes conflict resolution as a major skill requirement, you may have to decide, if this particular candidate is the best performer in other areas, whether you can reassign this responsibility or help the candidate come up to the standard required through the provision of training or other developmental actions.

Interaction with interviewers

How the candidates interact with you and the other interviewers is a legitimate way of assessing their interpersonal and communication skills. In fact, it can be the only way in which you can really do this, even if you can ask questions that seek examples of what a candidate has done in the past or could do in the future; for example:

Q   Have you ever had to communicate difficult or complex messages to others? Tell me how you went about it.

Q   What would you do if you had to give bad news to the team, for example if the company had lost a major contract or was expecting bad year-end results?

The answers could easily be about the processes the individual would employ, not about their skills. You will only be able to deduct their skill levels from the way they communicate with you.

Assessing influencing and negotiation skills poses similar difficulties. Setting up an exchange in the interview during which you challenge a candidate, for example by disagreeing with a response they give to a question, is a valid mechanism to enable you to discern their ability to convince you and other interviewers of the value of their perspective.

CANDIDATES' QUESTIONS

It is normal to allow time during the course of the interview for the candidates to ask you questions. The modern approach to interviewing is to treat it as a two-way exchange of information. You ask questions to find out whether the candidates are up to the job and meet the criteria you have set down. Equally, the candidates ask questions of you to find out whether you are the sort of manager they could work with and your organization will offer the sorts of rewards and outcomes they are seeking. It is a fact-finding exercise that begins the negotiation of a contract of employment.

Candidates are able to reject your offer just as much as you can turn down their application. Can you estimate how many times the following has been said by candidates to their colleagues after they have attended an interview?

> They offered me the job and I know it looked like a really good opportunity but I wouldn't work there if they paid me in gold. The way the interviewers treated me was awful. They really put me through the mill. They didn't let me finish my answer to one question before they asked the next. They kept interrupting each other so I didn't know who was asking me what. They didn't answer my questions about training. They said it was something that could be discussed after I started. Something told me it wouldn't happen. So, on balance, I think I would be better staying in my present job. Tomorrow I'll talk to my boss and see if I can persuade him/her to let me go on that course.

If you have provided a lot of information about the job and the organization in the run-up to the interview, the candidates will have much of the information they need to help them make up their mind whether to accept the job if offered. They could also be expected to do more research in preparation. You can find out if they have done so, for example asking:

Q   Have you had chance to look at our website? We are always interested in receiving feedback from users. What did you think of it? Has it prompted you to think of any more questions you would like to ask us?

What do the questions asked tell you about the candidate?

The sorts of questions the candidates put to you can be interesting. They will reveal what is of importance to the candidates and what they are interested in. For example, some will want to know about parental leave, some will be concerned to find out about the organization's pension arrangements. Others will want to know about flexibility in working patterns whilst some will want to know about training and development opportunities.

As with assessing behaviour and modes of speech, you need to be wary of trying to guess at the candidates' motives for asking the questions they put to you. The reason for asking may be due to your failure to put sufficient information in the recruitment literature or advertisement. If you did not reveal the salary or holiday entitlement, for example, and fail to mention them in the interview, it would be reasonable for the candidates to ask you how much you are planning to pay or how much leave is given. In the latter case, the candidate could have made holiday or other plans for the weeks just after the date they would start to work for you, if you were to offer them the job. You should not take their questions to mean that they are only interested in time off work; they may simply not want to lose the money they had already paid out for their holiday.

How long do you spend answering?

Dealing with candidates' questions fully during the interview is important. You should allow time for this stage when planning the structure of the interview and should endeavour to give full responses to the matters they raise. However, satisfying one candidate's queries should be balanced with the needs of the others. Therefore you do need to be mindful about how time is passing. Keeping to time is courteous and contributes to the impressions the candidates form about you as an employer. You should not brush off a question but there is no need to go into large amounts of detail, especially if it is a matter for negotiation with the candidate to whom you offer the job. The question of training opportunities, for example, can be dealt with satisfactorily by saying:

A   We do have a policy that ensures that everyone gets the training they need to enable them to do their job. We also have an appraisal process so we can agree development plans. These are all customized to meet the needs of the individual and job so we would discuss training and development needs with the person appointed to the job soon after they start working for us.

Keeping a note of the questions asked by candidates provides a useful reminder of what was discussed when you come to the stage of negotiating the contract. Undertakings made in an interview can set up reasonable expectations in a candidate's mind. If promises are made and you fail to honour them, you could be setting down grounds for future difficulties in the working relationship. The best advice is not to make promises you cannot keep at any stage of the recruitment and selection process, particularly during the interview.

STRESS INTERVIEWS

We know that interviews are challenging and uncomfortable. This is largely because most of us want to give a good account of ourselves when meeting new people. The job interview adds a different dimension. No wonder the occasion is important – the outcome could affect the rest of the candidates' working lives. It should therefore be no surprise to find that most candidates are nervous.

Some interviewers also find the prospect of conducting an interview nerve-racking. They may experience similar anxieties when meeting new people as do the candidates, as they also want to give a good impression. They too have a lot resting on the outcome of the interview. Getting as far as this stage will have involved a lot of work and probably a considerable outlay of money. Moreover, there is always the risk of not finding a suitably qualified person to fill the vacancy. This could endanger operations and any delay in filling the post could place considerable workloads on existing team members. No wonder the manager is nervous!

Interviews are therefore stressful occasions for both the candidates and the interviewers alike. Yet some interviewers seem to revel in the chance of making them more so. They seem to enjoy piling on the pressure and watching candidates squirm as they try to provide the answers to impossible-to-answer questions. Do these interviewers think that this is what effective interviewing is about? Or are they just masochists? Do such interviewers think about the impression they are creating on candidates and the way it might affect their reputation? Are they aware that such behaviour might jeopardize their organization's ability to attract good applicants? Do they care? You might wonder.

Inappropriate approaches

Some jobs undeniably are stressful and, in these circumstances, it is only right that employers explore candidates' abilities to work productively in such conditions. Testing for these abilities in an interview does not absolve the employer of their responsibility for managing stress once the person is in post. This involves taking steps to reduce unnecessary stress and putting in place mechanisms for controlling the remaining stresses. The employer is also expected to provide adequate training and support mechanisms. The task of the interviewer is to design questions that make the exploration of the candidates' inclination to work in such an environment and their abilities to do so possible and appropriate.

Understanding what is inappropriate is a good way of developing good practice. You can do this by reflecting on your own experience. Have you been to an interview when you thought the interviewer was acting over the top? What did the interviewer do to lead you to think that? Did they:

∎ ask you questions that were intended to be embarrassing? (eg what was your greatest mistake?)

∎ ask you personal questions? (eg how much do you weigh?)

∎ ask multiple and confusing questions?

∎ ask trick questions? (eg 'We have employed people from XZY Ltd (the candidate's current employer) before. They didn't work out. Why should you be different?)

▌ interrupt you and not allow you to answer the questions fully?

▌ change tack rapidly?

▌ talk about you in the third person with the other interviewers?

▌ take telephone calls or respond to e-mails in the middle of the interview?

Can you think of other things you have experienced or heard about that meant the candidates felt badly treated or prevented them from giving a good account of themselves? You may like to make a list of examples of interviewer behaviour that you think should not be exhibited. If you write this list in one column, you can have a second column for examples of opposite types of behaviour. This will be the start of a behavioural checklist you could draw up to develop your interview practice.

Using stress interviews well

If the job you are interviewing for really does require the ability to withstand stress, you will need to explore candidates' competency against this criterion. If you use the good practice you have started to develop in your checklist, you should be able to explore resilience and tolerance of stress in ways that will create a good impression instead of the candidates thinking you are a real so-and-so. A series of competency-based questions is the key. The following exchange illustrates how this can be achieved:

Q   What sorts of situation would you say cause people to experience stress at work?

A   Not being clear about what is to be achieved can cause problems. I also think not knowing why certain tasks need to be carried out makes work stressful. The other main difficulty, I think, comes from being overloaded, not being able to say no. I think a lot of the stress in the work environment is due to people simply being tired.

Q   Have you ever been in such situations? If so, how did you handle it?

A   I was once in a job that was not manageable. There was too much work for one person to do alone. My manager kept piling on more and more. I think he was struggling as well. His office was filled with papers and he could never find anything. All members of the team were working long hours and were feeling that we were not getting anywhere. Working relationships were getting strained as we started to quarrel with each other. Going to work was getting so bad that I started to suffer from indigestion. I talked it through with my doctor who was tremendously supportive. On his advice, I discussed the situation with my colleagues and we agreed that we should ask for a team meeting with our manager. We told him straight how we were feeling and made some suggestions about how the situation could be improved. Fortunately for us all, he realized how serious the situation was becoming and agreed to our proposals. These included weekly team meetings. From then on, things started to get better.

Q Can you identify the actions that led to that improvement?

A I think the main thing was us approaching the manager as a team. If I had gone on my own, I doubt if he would have taken the situation so seriously.

Q Anything else?

A Yes, I think having some suggestions. Rather than just presenting the problems, we had some practical ideas about what we wanted to do. This said to the manager that we were prepared to help and share responsibility. We were not just going to dump everything on him. It was clear that he needed help from us as much as we needed him to do something about the situation.

Q Is there anything you could learn from this experience that would help you, as a manager, manage your team's stresses?

A Yes. Have regular team meetings so that team members are able to say how they are feeling. Plan work and make sure it is distributed fairly amongst team members according to current workload and ability rather than just dished out. I would also make sure that people knew why they were doing the particular tasks and how it fitted into our overall objectives. In my previous experience, in the end, none of us knew why we were doing the work or where we were heading. I think having clear and understandable objectives is key to coping with stress and pressure of work.

This sort of exchange is far more revealing than causing the candidates embarrassment or asking them to give examples of situations they found stressful.

You can also ask difficult questions. After all, the interview is intended to be testing. There is no harm in asking questions such as those given below. The replies will give you some good indications of the candidate's attitudes and values and you will need information on these if you are to assess the candidate's fit with your organization:

▌ What do you think are the qualities of an effective manager?

▌ All jobs have their good and bad points. What are the worst aspects of your current job?

▌ What kinds of people do you find it easy to work with and what kinds cause you the most difficulty?

▌ What kinds of situations do you find hard to handle?

If you decide to ask these sorts of questions, you have to be sure why you are doing so and what the answers will tell you about the candidate. This information should then be related to the criteria contained in the person specification so you can separate out your personal preferences and concentrate on the features that will add to or detract from the prediction of effective performance in the job.

OTHER SOURCES OF INFORMATION

The interview is frequently the only method used to explore candidates' abilities directly before employment. There are other methods that can be easily combined with the interview that will strengthen the process. Combining two or more methods will produce a process that will have greater predictive power than the interview alone. However, if you choose to do this you need to ensure that the methods you select are designed to explore the specific requirements contained in the person specification and will actually add value.

Some employers are known to throw together methods because they like the idea of them rather than because they are complementary. The use of psychometric tests is particularly prone to this danger. Organizations make use of other selection methods simply because they are seen as the latest must-do. Examples of this can include versions of assessment centres and informal visits. As well as costing a lot and taking time, these methods, if badly used, can increase the possibility of introducing unfair and discriminatory bias. This is not an argument for not using them. On the contrary, these methods can be extremely valuable – providing they are used properly and are clearly related to the needs of the job.

Best practice suggests that the whole selection process should be designed to ensure that all the criteria are explored and sufficient evidence is obtained to differentiate between the candidates so that the one who fits most closely can be identified. If the person specification contains criteria that cannot be explored in an interview setting, then some other means of assessing them needs to be found. Examples of these sorts of criteria can include:

▌ cognitive abilities (such as reasoning and deduction, problem solving, analytical abilities, numeracy);

▌ personality traits (such as preferences relating to working relationship, thinking styles, feelings and emotions);

▌ practical skills (such as planning and ordering work, customer relation skills, mechanical and IT abilities).

Discussing these other selection methods is beyond the scope of this book but further information about them and how they can be used to good effect can be found in my *A Manager's Guide to Recruitment and Selection* (Kogan Page, 2003).

CLOSING THE INTERVIEW

Once you have covered all the questions you need to ask and have answered the candidate's questions, you need to bring the interview to its close. There are some golden rules which, if followed, will leave the candidate with a good impression of you and your organization. This is important because the final impression may influence the successful candidate's decision and inform what the others will say about you elsewhere. This could impact on your ability to attract high calibre candidates in future. If your organization has the reputation of conducting harsh, inconsiderate interviews, very few people will put themselves forward for such a negative experience.

If, on the other hand, you have a reputation of being fair and conducting interviews that enable everyone to give a good account of themselves, candidates will not be put off applying for your vacancies. If it is known that candidates, even if not offered the job, leave feeling that they have benefited from the interview, others are likely to want to go through such an experience.

The following checklist can be used to close the interview and make sure that all the necessary factors have been covered:

▌ Ask the candidate if they are still interested in the job. This can save you both a lot of time. If the job and organization, as revealed during the interview, are unlikely to meet the candidate's expectations, it is better to know at the end of the interview rather than go through the assessment of the individual's abilities and then offer a job to someone who does not want it.

▌ Notice period. Knowing how quickly an individual will be able to start the job could influence your choice. If you have two equally able candidates and an urgent need to fill the vacancy, knowing that one would have to give, and work, three months' notice may make the one who is able to start in two weeks more attractive.

▌ Telephone number or contact details. It is only courteous to let the candidates know the outcome of the interview as quickly as possible. However, when making contact you should consider confidentiality and how you are going to get in touch. Some candidates may have taken a day's holiday to attend the interview, not telling their current employer of their intention of moving jobs. If the only phone number you have for them is their work number and you leave a message which says you want to offer them a job, you could do considerable damage. You can do similar damage if you ring to tell someone they have not been successful, just as they are about to give an important presentation. Simply asking how and when to contact all the candidates at the end of the interview can overcome these problems.

▌ Timescale. Many employers have good intentions and tell candidates they will contact them that day or the one following. Then they do not do so. This leaves the candidates hanging on in suspense. When you tell the candidates when you plan to contact them, please allow yourself a realistic timescale and then keep your promise. Even if this means contacting the candidates to tell them that you have not reached a conclusion, at least they will know where they stand.

▌ Who will be in touch with them. It is good practice to tell the candidates who will make contact with them. If they are not able to take the phone call, you will then be able to leave your name and number without breaching confidence.

▌ How to make contact. Using e-mail does not guarantee confidentiality; other people are able to read messages over the individual's shoulder or open messages if the computer is left unattended. E-mail should only be used if the candidate agrees to it. After all, they are the ones who know how secure it is in the layout of their own office. Telephone or letter is the more common way of letting candidates know the results of the interview.

The physical parting should be as warm and welcoming as the opening, despite your impression of the candidate. Candidates will interpret your body language and form conclusions about their success from your behaviour. The last thing you will want to do is to lead the worst candidate to think you are going to offer them the job. Likewise, you will not want the best candidate to think they have no chance. The impression you want to achieve is one of total neutrality. All the candidates should believe they have been given a fair chance and a good hearing but nothing more.

When you have told the candidates what will happen next and when, it is courteous to:

▌ stand up;

▌ help with any coat or jacket and make sure they have collected all their belongings (notepad, bag etc);

▌ shake hands;

▌ walk with them to the door;

▌ thank them for their time and effort and say goodbye.

EXERCISE

Before we move on to look at how to decide which candidate best fits your requirements, you may wish to use the following space to create a checklist to inform the planning and conduct of your own interviews. Think about what is important to you for each of the following matters:

▌ planning the interview flow and content;

▌ preparation of the interview room;

▌ whether you will want to use any other selection method and how it will complement the interview;

▌ who else to involve in the interview;

▌ role and training of the interviewers;

▌ how you will work together;

▌ how you will keep records of the candidates' answers and behaviours;

▌ how to get the candidates into the interview room;

▌ opening the interview;

▌ questions for:

- the opening phase
- the exploration
  - education
  - experience
  - skills
  - knowledge
  - attitudes;

▌ how candidates will react to questions;

▌ which answers you want to receive;

▌ which answers you do not want to hear;

▌ what questions the candidates are likely to ask and what information you will need to answer them;

▌ how to close the interview;

▌ who will inform the candidates of the outcome of the interview;

▌ whether you will provide any feedback and if so who will do it.

5

Choosing the best person

INTRODUCTION

There is only one reason for holding interviews: to enable you to decide which of all the people who applied for your vacancy will be the best person for the job. For all sorts of reasons, this decision needs to be made in a transparent way and be based on the criteria you have set out in the person specification. If your decisions are made in this way, you should be able to justify your selection and be sure in your own mind that you have made the best possible choice.

You can only make your decisions on the information available and so the whole selection process should be designed to provide that information, as its purpose is to help you predict which candidate will be the best performer in the job. However, we need to acknowledge from the outset that at its very best, an interview is a poor predictor. It is possible to improve its performance by using other selection methods (such as tests and activities), making sure the interview is structured and involving several interviewers. You can also improve your chances of picking the right person by making full use of all the information you have obtained.

If you have followed the guidance given in Chapter 4, the interview will have been rigorous and you will have obtained a large quantity of good quality information. This needs to be recorded in a form that enables you to pool the views of the other interviewers and to show that each candidate has been assessed against the selection criteria. You will also need to find a way of combining the information you have obtained from other sources throughout the recruitment and selection process. The application form or CV will have provided you with information supplied directly by the candidates. If you have used other selection methods they too will have given you evidence of some if not all of the criteria. The main part of this chapter will look at how you can draw together information gathered from all these sources. You will need to do this systematically so that you and your fellow interviewers are able to consider all the evidence against the criteria and demonstrate that each candidate has been given due consideration.

Some interviewers fall into the trap at this stage of trying to compare the candidates against each other. This comparison should actually be the last stage of the decision-making process. The first part is to assess each candidate against the criteria. It is only when you have done this and have two or more candidates who fit the criteria that you will be faced with the task of choosing between them. The chances are that if you have carried out a detailed assessment, one candidate will stand out from the rest for reasons that are abundantly clear.

Offering the job to a candidate is not the end of the process. Often, it is the beginning of a negotiation. During this phase, the details of the package you are prepared to offer the candidate will be discussed. When making the offer you should remember that you are forming a legally binding contract. The offer of employment need not be in writing for it to be binding so you must make sure that you set out the details clearly. It can also help you both to get to know each other better and clarify expectations. We will discuss how you can conduct this phase so that the chosen candidate turns up at work on their first day. The ultimate recruitment tragedy occurs when a candidate is offered the job but it is not possible to reach a satisfactory understanding on the details of the job or the terms and conditions of employment. We will look at the common pitfalls so that, fore-armed, all your hard work should result in the agreement of a contract that will form the basis of a productive working relationship.

Before we can do this, however, we will need to look in some detail at the checks you will want (or may need) to carry out before making the offer. These will probably include approaching the referees nominated by the candidates. It is reasonably common practice to take up references before finalizing the decision but there is a wide range of views regarding the usefulness of other people's opinions. We will discuss the pros and cons of relying on references as well as considering the other checks you may need to carry out. In some organizations and for some occupations these may be required.

HOW TO AVOID BEING TAKEN IN WHEN TAKING UP REFERENCES

We know that many candidates falsify their qualifications, embellish their achievements and exaggerate their current salary. The easiest way to avoid being taken in is to carry out checks with previous and existing employers. It is common practice to ask others to give a view on a candidate's suitability for your job. The CIPD advises against this, recommending instead that the use of references is confined to factual matters such as length of employment, nature of the job in which the individual was employed and their reasons for leaving.

It is normal practice to take up references only when the candidates have given their permission for you to do so or after you have made the offer of employment. This is to protect the candidates' position with their current employers. Some employers do not like the idea that their employees may be looking for alternative employment and can look very unfavourably on individuals who decide it is time to move on. Therefore, there is little point in creating upset if the individual's chances of being appointed to another job are low. However, once called to an interview, the chances increase and time off work is usually needed. At this stage, most people tell their employer what is going on. Some will just take leave or a sickie!

It is not feasible to ask for references for all those called to interview, and it is courteous to ask the candidates' permission to do so.

If you ask for references before the interview, you have to decide whether to read them before seeing the candidates or wait until after you have formed an impression. If you obtain the reference beforehand, you will be able to make use of its contents during the interview.

Some organizations wait until the decision to offer employment has been taken but this can cause delay in the process and can introduce another complicating factor. Making an offer of employment subject to satisfactory references on the surface seems a reasonable thing to do but ACAS advises against doing so. The problem arises if: a) you do not receive the references – research shows that sometimes response rates can be as low as 35 per cent; b) the reference is not satisfactory.

You can enhance the value of references if you ask the referees to provide certain types of information. Some organizations send out questionnaires to enable referees to focus their comments. This allows the information to be supplied in a consistent form so it can be compared to the candidates' responses to the questions posed during the interview and used to inform the assessment against the selection criteria. This always supposes the referee is prepared to cooperate with such an approach. Most will write what they want to write rather than take the trouble to fill in a questionnaire or structure their response. This, of course, assumes they are prepared to reply to your request at all. If you make the provision of a reference hard work, you will reduce your chances of getting a reply, as there is no obligation on employers to provide references. There is, however, a reasonable assumption that, as most employers want references, most employers will provide them.

As matters stand, a written reference is a privileged document. This means that its contents can remain confidential between the writer and the recipient. However, if you breach that confidentiality by, for example, telling a candidate about some of the contents of a reference, you lose the whole protection. Similarly, if the candidate suspects that a reference contains incorrect or defamatory material, they could apply for a disclosure order. Therefore, in the interests of all parties it is important that references are accurate, factual and unambiguous.

Some interviewers prefer to talk to referees, believing they are more likely to tell the truth and reveal some aspects of the candidates' performance and personality they would not be prepared to disclose in writing. Whether this is true or not is for you to decide. Whether it is legitimate is also a matter of opinion. Off-the-cuff comments about a candidate's performance are unlikely to have any validity. At best, the referee will remember recent contacts with the candidate and may recall some outstanding aspects. It is unlikely that, without thought and time to consider, the referee will be able to give a balanced view of the candidate's overall performance. Surely, it is the latter that is needed to enable you to make your decisions, not a five-minute chat. The CIPD recommends that you obtain written references as they provide a formal record. Moreover, if the referees have to take the time to write a letter or fill in a form, you can assume that they will have given some thought to the matter.

If time is pressing and you need to be certain of the referee's opinion, it is better to make an appointment for a telephone conversation and fax or e-mail some questions or an outline of the areas you want to discuss. Now we have the technology, written references can be obtained exceedingly quickly. The only worry is the amount of consideration that will have been given by the referee.

When do we use other people's opinions?

If you obtain references before the interview, you may need permission from the candidates to do so, certainly before approaching their current employer. If this is a problem, you could obtain references from previous employers and make do with the information they give. Obtaining references at this pre-interview stage gives you the opportunity to question a candidate about any inconsistencies or areas of doubt. However, if you do so, you must take care not to damage the confidentiality of your source of information.

In the latter case, you need to work out what to do if the reference caused you to withdraw the offer. The chances of this occurring are, in reality, low – so why bother with references at all? You should also ask yourself what sort of information would be in such a reference. When assessing the value and validity of a reference, you need to keep in mind the reason you obtained it in the first place. The best role of references is to confirm or disprove facts. If you use them to confirm your opinion and then allow your judgement to be overturned, you may find yourself being misled by someone you do not know and who has no reason to have your best interests at heart. More importantly, giving undue weight to such evidence could lead you into other difficulties.

If you receive a reference whose contents are so damning you decide to withdraw the offer, the candidate will have the right to ask why. It will be obvious to the candidate that the referee was the cause of the offer being withdrawn. It is not unknown for vendettas and personality clashes to be acted out even when an employment relationship has ended. There have been cases where an ex-employee has been able to claim racial or sexual discrimination after the termination of employment because of comments made in a reference. You would not necessarily wish to be caught in such a maelstrom. It may be wise, therefore, to obtain references and use them before you finally decide to make an offer of employment.

You may find it more effective and safer to make the appointment subject to the completion of a satisfactory probationary period than the receipt of a reference if you have reason to be unsure of your decision. This approach gives you the opportunity to test your own judgement and gives the candidate the opportunity to demonstrate their abilities. It also provides you with a safe and legally defensible exit route if the candidate does not achieve the standard required. You will have incurred some costs but you will have avoided the danger and potential expense of litigation. We will discuss the use of probation again in Chapter 6.

How much weight should we give to the views of referees?

It is unlikely that a candidate will give the name of someone who will give them a poor reference. This means that you may have to read between the lines. Trying to interpret what someone is really meaning when writing about another person is fraught with difficulties and the chances are you will get it wrong. Research has found that the predictive power of a reference is as bad if not worse than that of an unstructured interview, yet we continue to rely on them. Perhaps it is because we are not confident in our own judgement and need reassurance from someone else to prove us right.

There have been several cases regarding the use and content of references. One (Hedley Byrne v Heller, 1964) puts the responsibility on referees to provide truthful, accurate and reliable information and places a duty of care to those to whom they are providing the reference. Another case (Spring v Guardian

Assurance, 1994) also places a duty of care to those providing the reference. Failing to disclose relevant information (such as the individual being the subject of continuing investigation) is as serious as providing misleading or inaccurate information. There is also a view that employers have a duty to provide references for their existing employees if their chances of being able to obtain another job depend on the provision of such information, but this has not yet been set down in case law.

It is exceedingly dangerous to place faith in a reference, for unless you know the referee you are placing a great deal of value on the opinions and motives of an unknown person. You will have no way of knowing if the referee has his/her own agenda or the quality of their judgement. They may be really poor judges of character. Some referees are not very good at seeing potential in other people. In any case, we know research indicates that many people want to move jobs because they are seeking opportunities to develop their skills and widen their experience. We also know that they want to change managers.

Traditionally, referees are asked to provide an opinion of a candidate's suitability for a new post. This makes a number of assumptions:

▮ The referee understands the content and nature of the job for which the person is being considered. Providing a copy of the job description and person specification gives some basic information but it is unlikely that the referee will fully understand your context and culture or even the job.

▮ The referee is in a position to pass an opinion on the individual's performance, abilities and potential. Often references are provided by HR departments or a candidate's manager's manager. How can you be certain the referee has direct, recent and relevant knowledge on which to base their opinion?

▮ The referee is unbiased. Some managers are known to give bad references to excellent performers because they do not wish to lose the individual. Alternatively, and this is far more common, a glowing reference is given to a mediocre performer hoping this will increase their chances of getting another job.

There is nothing wrong at all in using a reference to check facts and confirm your own judgement. However, allowing a referee to sway your opinion could lead you to reject a potentially good candidate. Alternatively, if you allow a reference to convince you that a marginal candidate is better than you thought, you could find yourself appointing someone who is not up to the job. You could seek damages from the referee but only if you can prove that the information given to you was inaccurate and if you have actually suffered a financial loss. Otherwise, you will have to write off the mistake to experience.

Other checks

You may need to check other factual matters before offering the job. The ones most often carried out are set out below.

Qualifications

If the job requires the occupant to possess certain qualifications you should have set this out clearly in either the advertisement or the recruitment literature you send out. It is wise to ask the candidates to bring copies of their certificates with them to the interview and you should remember to ask the candidates to let you see them.

If you have any doubt about the validity of the qualification, you should check before offering employment. Most qualification bodies, schools, colleges and universities maintain records of previous students, but you may find that you will need the permission of the individual to gain access to their files.

SAS has a service called *Text Miner*, which helps employers to explore basic facts given in a CV. These confirm, for example, whether a university was running a course at a particular point in time. If you need to go to such lengths, however, you should consider why you think your applicants are being so untruthful and what this says about you as an employer.

This offer is subject to...

It is not unusual to make an offer of employment conditional on the receipt of the proof or independent evidence of qualifications or ability to do the job. However, you could find yourself in some difficulties if you later obtain information that makes you withdraw the offer. You will have to explain to the candidate why the offer is being withdrawn and by that time, you will have probably told the other candidates that their applications have not been successful.

Individuals can ask to see their references but access can be denied if the author can be identified. Some employers give their employees sight of their references before sending them off, but others wish to say things to a new employer they would not want the individual to know. If the reference contains facts, you may wonder why there is such a need for secrecy. If the reference contains information of a personal nature, you may wonder why the current employer has not made their views known to the employee anyway. The need for such a degree of secrecy may make you wonder again about the validity and usefulness of a reference given under such conditions.

Medical checks

Some organizations with employees in high-risk occupations, exposed to defined hazards such as asbestos, lead and radiation, are required by law to carry out pre-employment checks. Other organizations, as a matter of policy, require all staff, especially those in key posts, such as senior managers, to undergo a medical examination before the offer of employment is finalized.

Usually the candidate completes a medical questionnaire as part of their application, which is scrutinized by an occupational health professional. Based on the information thus supplied, the individual may or may not be asked to undergo a full examination. This will be to ensure that the individual is fit enough to meet the requirements of the job or that any existing condition will not be made worse. Again, the process is totally dependent upon the honesty and openness of the applicant.

Why do you need medical checks? Because there is some doubt about:

▌ the individual's fitness for the job;

▌ the individual's ability to carry out the duties of the job efficiently;

▌ the capability of the individual to attend regularly for work.

You may also require checks to find out whether the individual's state of health is likely to present a danger to themselves or others or whether the individual has a chronic health problem that may adversely affect their future employability.

The Disability Discrimination Act requires that you give equal opportunity to those with disabilities. It also requires that you make reasonable adjustments to accommodate their disabilities. This means that if alterations to, for example, working hours and attendance levels are needed, you, as an employer, should be prepared to be tolerant and allow variations from the norm to accommodate the individual. However, the Act does not require you to endure a poor attendance record caused by factors not related to their disability. This can be a highly technical area and so the advice of a medical or occupational health practitioner or the Disability Employment Service may be useful.

If you receive advice that suggests the state of a candidate's health indicates that you should not make an offer of employment or withdraw the offer already made, you should discuss the matter with the individual concerned. The examination may have revealed a serious condition that was unknown to the candidate. You need to remember that the final decision rests with you as the employer. You also need to remember that your medical or occupational health professional can only give you an opinion.

Criminal history and police records

We discussed in Chapter 4 how the Rehabilitation of Offenders Act is designed to enable those with criminal convictions to move on from their previous misdemeanours. There are, however, certain situations where employers are required to carry out checks into people's offending history. The Criminal Records Bureau (CRB) is the central agency that carries out these checks. Standard disclosures apply to those jobs exempt from the provisions of the Rehabilitation of Offenders Act (eg jobs involving contact with children and vulnerable adults). The information you will receive back from the CRB includes details of spent and unspent convictions, cautions, reprimands and final warnings. Enhanced disclosure applies to those jobs involving a greater degree of contact with vulnerable people, such as providing training, supervising or being in sole charge.

You will only be able to apply for this information if your organization is registered with the Criminal Records Bureau. In other words, you can only obtain it if you have a recognized need for such information. Application for the information has to be made with the express permission of the individuals concerned and you will be expected to comply with a strict code of practice, which sets out how the information may or may not be used.

The need to carry out such checks should be revealed at the outset of the recruitment process. In this way, there will be no surprises for anyone and it leaves an individual free to decide whether to expose themselves to the risk of their past being disclosed to a third party.

If you receive information about your preferred candidate that makes you wonder whether to offer the individual the job, you should discuss the matter with them and assess the degree of risk you would face if the individual were to be employed. However, in certain situations, it is illegal to employ certain types of ex-offender in some occupations. If you find yourself faced with the prospect of offering employment to someone with a criminal history in a sensitive occupation, you should obtain professional advice before making any sort of offer.

Employment permits

The Asylum and Immigration Act 1996 places the onus on employers to make sure they employ only those persons legally entitled to work in the UK. Failure to do so is a criminal offence. Legal entitlement includes the possession of a work permit or being in an occupation where such a permit is not required (eg as an au pair). This piece of legislation may seem to contradict other Acts and, as we discussed in Chapter 4, any question designed to find out if an individual requires a work permit must be phrased with care.

There are sources of help. London Jobs, for example, provides a service that carries out checks into the visa status of candidates and examines the eligibility of an individual to work in the location stated in advertisements placed on its website. Again, it is better to obtain advice if you are not sure, before making any form of offer, as this is a complex and specialist aspect of employment law.

Testing for drugs

Some employers, with the need to take a higher than normal approach to safety, increasingly want to be sure that employees and prospective employees are free from drugs and alcohol as the presence of such substances in the body can impede performance and endanger the individual, other workers and customers. If this is the case in your organization, you should ensure that you have a clearly set out policy, sent to all applicants early in the process, which makes it clear that you may expect candidates to undergo a medical test before an offer of employment is made.

Financial checks

Experian has an online candidate checking service, which explores financial details and credit history. There could be a case for using this service in occupations that present a lot of temptation to those perceived to present such a risk, for example those with a record of debt or defaulting on commitments. Such occupations might include, for example, those involving the handling of cash or carrying out financial transactions. This level of caution makes sweeping assumptions about the honesty of people who have fallen on hard times or who are not very competent when dealing with their own money.

It is reported that some employers are considering using lie detectors as part of their selection process. We know that as many as one in four applicants exaggerate or tell lies in their application and that employers take this degree of deceit seriously. If you are tempted to resort to such a degree of checking, you should ask yourself the following questions:

▌ How serious is the risk presented by candidates misleading you in their applications?

▌ What would be the consequences of employing someone who has not told you the truth?

▌ How much does it cost to carry out the checks?

▌ How long will it take to get the information back?

▌ Can you carry out the checks in any other way?

▌ What will you do if you receive adverse information about your preferred candidate?

The final question for you to answer is: 'Is the likelihood and size of the risk worth the time and cost of the checks?' If you decide not to carry out these checks, you may find that you have been deceived but, on the other hand, you may find that you have appointed one of the one in three who does not tell lies in their applications.

MAKING THE DECISION

The steps outlined below will help you make your decision in ways that can be defended, as they are intended to introduce a degree of transparency to the process. Basing your assessment of each candidate on the person specification criteria will provide this certainty. The process will also give you confidence in your decision.

Once you have carried out all the necessary checks you need to find a way of pooling all the information you have gathered about the candidates so you and your fellow interviewers can identify the best one. Often, this is done immediately after the last interview has been completed. When planning the interview timetable, you should build in the time needed for a thorough appraisal of each candidate. If you are seeing six, you should really allow at least an hour for the wash-up session. That is only 10 minutes for each candidate. Additionally, you will probably want to have a short break before starting to assess the candidates and you may find that you will have to spend longer on some candidates than others. If you have seen a lot of candidates, inevitably you will all be tired. Interviewing demands a lot of concentrated effort and if you are not used to it, you may be surprised at your level of fatigue. Therefore, having a structure and mechanism to support your decision making can help you to maintain focus.

If you think the decision is going to be hard or protracted you may wish to postpone the assessment until the following day. This has the benefit of allowing you and your fellow interviewers to sleep on the matter. Research has shown that letting the brain process information during sleep can improve the quality of decision making and judgement. This is because recently acquired information can be added to that 'filed' in the deep memory store. Delaying decision making can also help you counter some of the errors known to occur in decision making, as the candidates will all be seen in greater perspective.

However, you will be under some pressure to make the decision and memory does fade quite quickly. Therefore, unless you have made good notes, you could find that certain aspects of the candidates' performances during their interviews have slipped away from you.

Pulling the facts together

One of the common errors made in decision making is due our tendency to give greater weight to events witnessed at the start of an episode and to those seen at the end. Thus, the first and last candidates you have interviewed will stand in sharper relief than those you saw in the middle of the process. Similarly, you will remember more clearly those candidates who stood out. The reason for their salience need not have anything to do with the criteria you are using for selection. It could be as silly as knocking over a glass of water or having a sneezing fit. Even though the event may have been trivial and irrelevant, it can serve to position the candidate more clearly in your memory than others.

The tendency to favour recent information also inclines us to focus most strongly on the information gathered during the interview and neglect that obtained from other sources. Thus, we can reduce in value the information provided in the CV or application form. If any tests or other selection activities have been built into the selection process, ways of ensuring that the evidence thus collected is included in the overall evaluation of each candidate need to be found.

A simple way of doing this is to make further use of the matrix developed from the person specification. This device will enable you to pool all the information available to you and stand back from your immediate impression of the candidate. At first, it may seem a bureaucratic approach but in reality, using a decision tool will focus your discussion and prevent you wasting time. Assessment discussions run the danger of becoming circular or going off track, especially if you are tired.

The short-list matrix illustrated in Chapter 3 for the post of Customer Supporter has been modified to support decision making throughout the process. Initially it was used to inform the advertisement and then to help you decide which of the applicants should be short-listed. In Chapter 4, we discussed how it could be used to help you decide which selection methods would best enable you to assess the criteria and to act as the basis for your notes. Now, as seen in Figure 5.1, it can be used to draw together all the information you and the other interviewers have gathered about the candidates and to structure your final decision. It will then go on to act as the formal record and can be used for the induction and appraisal of the person appointed. Such simple devices can be extremely valuable!

Post – Customer Supporter	Candidate...				
	Source of evidence				
Abilities	**CV**	**Ref 1**	**Ref 2**	**Test**	**Interview**
Customer service skills					
Communication and interpersonal skills					
Organizational skills					
Attainments					
Achieved formal qualifications at post-16 level					
Conducted customer surveys and investigations					
Achievements					
Experience of customer service and complaints handling					
Use of common office IT applications to an advanced level					
Introduced new ways of working					
Aptitude					
Strong team worker					
Able to challenge others tactfully and influence their approaches					
Appoint or reject – reasons					

Please use the following symbols to record your assessment of each application against the criteria laid out in the person specification:

✓   Meets criteria   X   Does not meet criteria   O   No evidence

Figure 5.1   Final assessment matrix

Each interviewer completes an assessment form for each candidate, independently, during and at the end of each interview. If other people have been involved, for example in assessing a test or exercise, information can be obtained from them. If the same matrix is completed before the interview, you will be able to draw on the information or lack of information to help you focus on any criteria or aspects of performance that need greater exploration. Alternatively, you could receive the assessment after the interview. This could be provided verbally by those who carried out the assessment or in the form of a written report. The latter is often the outcome of psychometric tests.

Alternatively, the matrix can be used as the 'agenda' to structure the discussion of each candidate. In this case, one of the interviewers would complete a form for each candidate on behalf of all the interviewers.

Decision making

Having pooled all the available information, you will be ready to consider the candidates. You can start the discussion by asking all the other interviewers to write down the name of any candidate they think is not appointable. This approach can be useful if you have seen a lot of candidates, as it will reduce the amount of time needed for the wash-up session. If there is agreement on one or more candidates, you can leave them until the end after you have assessed all the remaining candidates' suitability. In fairness to the candidates you decide at the outset not to appoint, you will need to be clear about the reasons for their lack of suitability against the criteria.

You should also have some feedback ready in case they ask. This will also help you avoid having to say that another candidate was better. This statement can be difficult to defend if challenged. However, if you are able to point to areas where the candidate was assessed as being weak or that the evidence of their abilities was not provided, you will be able to justify your decision if challenged. It will not matter if the candidate claims to have these abilities. If they were given fair and equal chances to display them but they failed to do so on the day, and you can demonstrate they had the opportunities but they did nothing to evidence their abilities in those areas, you should have a fairly strong defence.

You can then consider all of the remaining candidates one at a time, completing the overall assessment matrix to give you a basis for deciding which candidate best meets the criteria. It will also help you to avoid the temptation of comparing candidates with each other until the very end. Assessing the candidates against the criteria is more robust as it provides a degree of transparency and independence to the process. You will be matching your evaluation of their degree of fit against the requirement rather than trying to compare them against each other. This will give the process rigour and place you in a stronger position should your decision be challenged.

The assessment will also provide you with useful information about the candidate you ultimately decide to appoint. This information can be used to help identify their initial training and development needs. It is unlikely that you will find a candidate to match your criteria perfectly. If you do, be suspicious! The person specification describes the ideal person. Very few of these walk the earth. It is more likely that you will find someone who is a good fit against the criteria, but your rigorous assessment will have revealed some gaps and possibly some development needs. An additional value of carrying out such a detailed assessment is that you will have good quality information to help you and the candidate draw up their training plan.

Scoring schemes

The rating scale and weightings shown in Chapter 3 can be used to develop a scoring scheme. This apparently introduces a degree of objectivity into the process. However, it can be argued that all judgements made by one person about another are always subjective as we rely on our personal preferences and experience. Nevertheless, having criteria supported by a scoring scheme bounds those judgements by providing a factual, evidence-based foundation.

The matrix shown in Figure 5.2 illustrates how the scoring scheme uses numbers to assess the evidence against the criteria and develops a score that positions each candidate in relation to the others.

The numbers should not be allowed to take away your responsibility for deciding which candidate to appoint. The scoring scheme is used to bound your judgement, in other words to provide a structure and reduce the impact of erroneous factors. However, this approach is only quasi-science. Human judgement is not objective or scientific. You can control the degree of subjectivity but it cannot be replaced entirely. Therefore, the matrix and resultant scores should be used to inform your decision, not make it. In any case, there are some qualitative aspects to take into account when deciding which candidate will be the best for your job. This is fine – so long as you can evidence your conclusions against the criteria and relate them to the needs of the job.

NOTIFYING THE UNSUCCESSFUL CANDIDATES

When should you tell a candidate that their application has not been successful and how should you communicate that message?

If you have given the candidates an indication of the time when you will be in touch with them, you should do your best to honour that commitment. All the candidates have invested time and emotion in their application and they deserve some consideration in return. If you promised to contact them at the end of the interviews, you should do so. This is why, perhaps, it is better to say you will contact them the following day. This gives you some breathing space, which may be needed if you are faced with a difficult decision or have a lot of candidates to assess. It also allows you to have a discussion and possibly several discussions with the preferred candidate.

Candidate			
Criteria	**A**	**B**	**C**
	Score	**Weight**	**Total**
Abilities			
Customer service skills		15	
Communication and interpersonal skills		15	
Organizational skills		10	
Attainments			
Achieved formal qualifications at post-16 level		5	
Conducted customer surveys and investigations into their needs and wants		10	
Achievements			
Experience of customer service and complaints handling		15	
Use of common office IT applications to an advanced level		10	
Introduction of new ways of working		5	
Aptitude			
Strong team worker		10	
Able to challenge others tactfully and influence their approaches		5	

Please allocate a score in column A using the following scoring scheme to assess the evidence collected about each candidate against the criteria:

6   Meets criteria fully
5   Meets the criteria but has some inconsequential gaps
4   Meets the criteria but has some gaps that require further consideration
3   It is not clear whether the criteria are met. More information required
2   Significant gaps
1   Does not meet criteria
0   No evidence

Then multiply the raw score by the criteria's weight, given in column B, entering the answer in column C.

Then add up all the numbers in column C.

Figure 5.2 Scoring matrix

MAKING THE OFFER

The person to whom you wish to offer the job should be the first person you contact. If he or she should then decide to reject your offer, you would at least have the chance of offering the job to another candidate. There can be some danger in going to the second best and these dangers are increased if the person knows they were not your first choice. However, if you have not told them their application has not been successful, you will not be placed in the embarrassing position of having to tell them that you have changed your mind.

When you offer your preferred candidate the job and they accept, you will have entered into a legally binding contract. Many people are under the mistaken impression that an offer has to be made in writing before it becomes enforceable. This is not the case. This is why you need to be sure of your decision and certain about what is on offer. Careless and generous words can cost you dear.

If your preferred candidate wants time to think about your offer, as many do, you will have to decide whether to notify the unsuccessful candidates regardless of the process not being completed.

It is usual these days to notify the candidates by telephone. Sending rejection letters takes time and is cold. Using e-mail is faster and the medium lends itself to being less formal but, as a form, it is still cold. You may like to ask the candidates how and when they would prefer contact to be made.

Some employers offer the unsuccessful candidates feedback. Others do not. If you decide to make this offer, it is wise to tell the candidates that it is available when you tell them their application has not been successful but then to give them a chance to reflect and decide whether they want it or not. Giving them this option provides them with some control over the process. Forcing feedback on someone who is not ready to receive it can convert a disappointed candidate into a resentful or angry one. These are the people more likely to challenge your decision.

FEEDBACK

Some employers are of the view that, after the interview, the less said to unsuccessful candidates the better. The reason often given to these people is that another candidate was better. This approach has gained currency with the growth of claims for unfair treatment during recruitment and selection. However, the lack of information or bland platitudes, it can be argued, will encourage a candidate who suspects the process to be a fix, thinks the decision was made before the interview or believes they have been discriminated against unfairly, to lodge a claim. In the end, providing feedback is a matter of opinion. There are merits and risks either way.

If you have analysed the content and needs of the job and have made use of the job description, person specification and any other relevant selection criteria throughout the process, you should have nothing to fear. Your records will demonstrate that your decision making has been fair and, by being based on explicit criteria, open.

Having assessed each of the candidates' application and performance against the criteria, you will be in a position to provide factual and useful feedback. The purpose for giving such feedback is twofold. First, it will help candidates understand why their application was not successful. Second, it should help them identify ways of improving their application and behaviour during interview. Many candidates, especially those new to job seeking, benefit hugely from the post-interview help. The only thing it costs you is time.

The main benefit you will accrue from giving helpful feedback to unsuccessful candidates is the way in which it will enhance your reputation as a good employer. This will come from treating people with respect and recognizing that they deserve something in return for all the work they have done in preparing their application and attending the interview. One reason why interviewers are reluctant to give feedback is the dislike of giving out bad news. Giving feedback requires the transmission of personal information and many managers recoil from this task, even with their own staff. Post-interview feedback can be eased in the following ways:

▎ You do not need to see the unsuccessful candidates. You can give the feedback by telephone but doing so by e-mail may increase the risk of an individual misunderstanding your meaning. Careless words or phrases that are ambiguous, even if you intend to be helpful, can be taken to mean something different from what you actually meant. This can inadvertently increase the risk of the candidate claiming unfair treatment. Telephone conversations give you the chance to check that the candidate has received the message you intended to transmit.

▎ Ask the candidates to tell you how they think they performed during the interview. Most people have reasonably good insight and are able to identify the weaker aspects of their application and performance during the interview. If these coincide with your assessment, all you need do is to confirm their assessments.

▎ Limit the amount of information you give to two or three main points, relate them closely to the criteria, and do not forget to include some positive feedback. Overloading unsuccessful candidates with a long list of things they have done wrong or badly could amplify any negative feelings they may have and fuel resentment. By concentrating on the points that matter, you will be able to move on to ask the candidates to think about ways in which they could improve their performance for their next application. When giving positive feedback, do not be over-generous with your praise. Otherwise, the candidate will wonder why you did not appoint them.

MAKING SURE THE BEST CANDIDATE ACCEPTS YOUR OFFER

As we noted above, making a verbal offer of employment is a legally binding contract but only if:

▌ the offer is made and accepted;

▌ both parties intend the contract to be binding on them both;

▌ there is sufficient certainty of terms;

▌ there is something of value attached to the contract (such as wages).

You would therefore be well advised to think about what you are going to say to the successful candidate before you pick up the phone. If it is the first time you have offered employment to anyone, you might like to prepare a script of bullet points. This will help you to be clear about what is on offer as well as provide a record of what you said, in case there is any dispute. Some recommend that the offer should be made in writing, so the terms are clearly set out. If you choose this option, you should be prepared for the exchange of correspondence to take at least a week.

Let us hope that your preferred candidate will say 'Yes, thank you' immediately. However, sometimes candidates need time or have second thoughts. Changing jobs can represent a big step, especially if moving home is involved. The candidate's decision may also affect other people so it would not be surprising if the person says 'Thank you. I need time to think and to discuss it with my partner and other members of the family.'

Once an offer is made, it changes the balance of power. As soon as you tell the candidate that you want to offer him or her the job, he or she is the one to make the final decision. Some candidates will use this position of strength as a basis for negotiating a package better than the one initially offered. You need to be careful at this point, as you could find yourself creating imbalance between existing employees and the new recruit, which could lead to claims for equal pay for work of equal value or set up a cause for resentment.

Conducting the negotiations

Not all the power need transfer to the candidate once you have made the offer. You do have some choices. The first of these will concern the identity of who will make the offer and discuss terms with the individual. If you have used recruitment consultants, you may find that as part of their services, they will support you in this and act, in essence, as an intermediary between you. This can be useful if the package on offer is complex and the candidate is a serious negotiator. This can happen in some senior jobs where there is a lot at stake for both parties.

Large organizations often have Human Resources departments so it is possible for the internal professional resource to take over the negotiation or act on behalf of the manager making the appointment. Really, the manager should make the final decision regarding the content of the package.

If you are conducting the negotiations, you should be clear about the limits of your authority and the content of the package. The latter should have been decided before the interviews were held but there may be exceptional cases when something extra is needed or when the package needs to be adjusted to suit the needs of a candidate. Similarly, if others are acting on your behalf, they should be aware of how far they can go.

What's on offer

The offer should set out clearly:

I the job title;

I any relevant conditions that apply to the offer such as the need for proof of qualification, satisfactory references, medical examination or completion of a probationary period;

I conditions of employment such as place of work or working hours.

The offer letter need not be part of the contract. The contract is the understanding formed between the parties. You are required by law, however, to issue a statement of terms and conditions within two months of the person starting work. This written document is often called the explicit terms of the contract. The understanding you reach during the recruitment process and any subsequent negotiations conclude the implicit terms or the psychological contract.

Starting salary is the term most frequently negotiated after the offer of employment has been made. It is common practice to offer a sum higher than the candidate's current earning levels as an inducement. If the salary has been published in the advertisement or recruitment literature as, for example, c£25,000 or as a range, such as £25,000–35,000, you will have given yourself some flexibility and scope to match the candidate's current earnings level. Using bands can also protect you from inadvertently introducing unequal pay. Recruitment supplements can be paid should the needs of the market justify such payments, but you should be sure that this need is demonstrable. It should also be paid to all employees in the same job, not just the individual who argues the case.

You also need to be aware that, generally, men are better at negotiating higher salaries than women and that, if you use existing salary as the basis, unless you have checked with the current employer, you cannot be sure the individual is telling you the truth. Exaggerating current earnings is one of the most common untruths contained in applications and is an easy negotiating ploy.

Having a clear policy set out before you enter the negotiating phase gives you some protection and provides you with limits. If the candidate is making demands you are not able to meet, you will have grounds for wondering whether your preferred candidate is in fact the best choice. It is highly likely that this pattern of behaviour will continue into other areas after the person starts to work for you. Is this the kind of person you would want in your team? Perhaps the answer is yes, if well-honed negotiating skills are required. However, if they are not, you may have grounds for reconsidering your decision.

Other benefits

You may be able to offer your preferred candidate a number of other rewards and benefits as part of the overall package to tempt them to accept your offer of employment. Some of these, such as the reimbursement of relocation costs, are, in some organizations, so standard that they are taken as givens. In other organizations, making them available could make the difference between the candidate being able to afford your offer and turning it down. Moving house, especially if other family members are involved, can represent a considerable burden. However, if the candidate does not need to relocate, offering to cover the costs of removal would be a meaningless gesture.

There are other rewards that would apply to all candidates but you must exercise care to ensure that you do not contravene the equal pay for work of equal value legislation. You may find yourself in some difficulties if you offer a reward that is not available to other staff doing like or similar work or whose jobs are assessed as being of the same size. It is not totally clear which rewards in addition to base salary fall within the scope of 'pay' in this sense. Pension entitlement clearly does.

There is a growing realization of the importance of pensions so the inclusion of this benefit may be a determining factor for the individual deciding whether to accept your offer of employment. Other pay-related benefits include holiday entitlement and the provision of rewards, such as transport allowances. At one time, the provision of a company car was seen as a reward worth having, but the HM Revenue & Customs has tightened its grasp and now imposes income tax on such benefits in kind. These can include the provision of computers for use at home and mobile phones as well as cars or travel vouchers.

Health insurance and provision of sickness pay in addition to the statutory minimum can also be included as part of a benefits package designed to tempt people to the organization and to retain experienced employees. Another benefit commonly offered is child-care, though the value of this is reducing as the state has extended the provision of services to help parents return to the workplace.

Some employers have developed what has been called a cafeteria approach to the provision of additional benefits. These can include perks such as the payment of health and leisure club or professional body membership fees, the payment of private school fees, personal loans and mortgages at preferential rates, discounted purchases of products or services, or social events.

In some settings, resourcing an individual's training and development can be seen as a definite perk, especially if this is the individual's motive for changing jobs. Some organizations fully fund the cost of study, especially if this leads to a qualification relevant to the individual's job. This can include the time needed to attend the course, and in some cases, study leave for examination preparation or to complete assignments. Other organizations part-fund courses. Any contribution to help the acquisition of qualifications is a benefit to an individual wishing to pursue a career. As such, this may be a deciding factor for individuals choosing between two or more job offers.

When trying to persuade a candidate to accept your offer of employment you should be clear about why you are including rewards additional to pay in the package and whether they are in fact actually justified. If the candidate needs so much inducement, you could rightly ask yourself just how interested is the individual in working for your organization. There has been considerable research into the factors that motivate people at work. From this, we know that the material rewards matter when things are not going well. The factors that motivate and continue to matter are the intangible components such as the nature of the work, the relationships with colleagues and managers and opportunities for advancement. We also know that people leave their current jobs in search of greater development opportunities, just as much as moving for more money. If you therefore concentrate on these components rather than loading in other rewards and benefits, you may find that you save your organization money, avoid the dangers of introducing inequality and upsetting your existing staff, and concentrate on things that matter most to the person whom you are seeking to recruit.

Start date

You may find that the candidate's availability is a matter that you will have to negotiate with the individual and his or her existing employer. Some organizations have long notice periods. These tend to get longer for senior managers or those in hard-to-fill occupations. The reason for asking for two or even three months' notice is theoretically to give some overlap between the new employee and the person leaving. In reality, this is rarely achieved as it can easily take up to eight weeks to fill a post. It may therefore be possible to agree to a shorter notice period. In any case, an employee who has decided to leave is of dubious value to their current employer, as their interest begins to wane, and it may be better to let the individual to move on to their new job comparatively quickly. Before you can reach sush an agreement you will need to persuade the person to whom you are offering the job that an early start date is needed.

After all of this, hopefully your preferred candidate will say yes and you will be at the starting gate of a productive and happy working relationship. In the next chapter, we will discuss what you need to do, between the offer and its acceptance and the starting date, to make sure that the individual turns up. We will also look at what action you can take in the first few months to ensure that the relationship gets off on the right footing and that the new recruit quickly becomes a valuable member of your team.

SUMMARY

Before moving on, however, you may like to complete the following exercise.

EXERCISE

A References

Think of three ways in which you can improve the quality and usefulness of references.

1.

2.

3.

B Other checks

Should any other checks be carried out before you offer the job to the best candidate?

What information do you need, who is best placed to provide it, and how much will it cost in terms of time, money and effort to obtain it?

What will you do if the information reflects badly on your preferred candidate?

C Making the decision

List five of the most important factors you need to take into account in deciding which of the candidates should be offered the job.

1.

2.

3.

4.

5.

D Informing the candidates of your decision

Write a script outlining what you will say to the unsuccessful candidates.

Will you offer feedback? If so, what do you need to do to ensure that it is as positive as possible for the unsuccessful candidates?

What will you say to the successful candidate?

What will you do if they turn down your offer?

E Negotiating the package

List four guiding principles to guide your discussions with the candidate you wish to appoint.

1.

2.

3.

4.

6

Making sure you keep the best person

By now you will have made an offer of employment to your preferred candidate, concluded the negotiations and agreed mutually acceptable terms and conditions. In other words, the two of you will have formed a contract of employment. You may think it is all over, but this is not the case. There are three further critical stages to be completed before the recruitment and selection process has been finished successfully:

▍ The candidate has to start work.

▍ The team needs to accept the new person.

▍ The induction period needs to be concluded.

In this penultimate chapter, we will look at how you can conclude these final stages and make sure that all the work you have put into conducting a good, effective interview bears fruit. The first few months in a new job are critical to long-term success in the post, so what happens during that time will decide whether the individual stays or leaves quickly and, if they stay, will influence their view of the job and you, their employer. It also affects your view of them as your employee. Just as you have planned the recruitment and selection process with care, you can plan the run-up to the starting date and the induction phase so that the chances of the appointment being a success are increased.

BETWEEN THE INTERVIEW AND STARTING DATE

The period between the formation of the contract and the first day at work can be a time of great uncertainty. The candidate may wonder if they have made a wise decision. You may also have some doubts and concerns about your choice. However, unlike the candidate, you will have plenty of documentary evidence you can refer to so you can allay your fears. Not least of these will be your notes from the interview. It is unlikely that the candidate will have the same quantity of material to help them. They will have to work from memory of the interview.

We discussed earlier how impressions formed during the interview influence the implicit contract of employment. Therefore, any important components, such as access to training, should have been confirmed during the negotiations and set down in the offer letter. If these matters are part of the formal terms, for example the acquisition of formal qualifications, they should be included in the statement of terms and conditions you are legally required to provide to all employees within two months of the starting date. Setting down such matters, clearly and in writing, can help to reduce the potential for misunderstandings, disagreements and disputes.

For some strange reason, there is a common view that says a new employer should not talk to a new employee before he or she actually starts work. There is no good reason for this form of purdah. To the contrary, holding discussions during this stage can be an important part of the induction period. You do need, however, not to place unreasonable pressure or demands on your new recruit. It will probably be a very busy time for them as they finish off projects and get ready to hand their work on. There is no reason why you cannot send them more information and hold less formal discussions with them to help them gain greater understanding of their new job, their new employer and you. Taking advantage of this time can play a major part in establishing a productive relationship and helping to address any concerns or doubts the new recruit may have.

This period can be particularly important if there is a long time between the interview and start date. In some cases, this can extend to a number of weeks. For example, if you have appointed a school, college or university leaver, you may have interviewed before the end of the course. In the case of some senior management, specialist or professional posts, the notice period may be as long as three months. Thus maintaining contact can be essential to ensuring that understandings of the job remain aligned. Things can change and impressions can be distorted with the passage of time. Therefore, regular contact can be important to make sure that your separate understandings remain on the same lines.

Even for those with shorter notice periods, regular contact can help the new recruit feel welcome as well as extend their knowledge and understanding of their new job. You can take this opportunity to send additional information, such as the names of their new colleagues, or additional information about the work the individual will be doing and the organization.

GETTING THE TEAM READY TO ACCEPT THE NEW PERSON

At the same time, you need to do some work with your existing employees so they are ready to welcome their new colleague. Their working pattern and routine will inevitably be disrupted by a new person and the team dynamics will alter. As the manager, you need to be aware of the need to assimilate the new person and the potential for tension and difficulty. Ideally, everyone will be looking forward to the new person starting work but there may be some difficulties. These can arise if:

▌ Work has been reallocated. It is possible that one of the existing team was not happy about giving up a cherished task or that a sought-after area of work has been allocated to the new recruit.

▌ New tasks have been identified to form part of the job the new recruit will hold. These may be seen by existing staff as development opportunities or areas of work that could lead to an increase in earnings. Again, there could be some spoken or unsaid resentments or jealousy.

▌ An existing employee applied for the job but was unsuccessful. You may need to give special consideration to ensure that good quality feedback has been given to that person. Unless you manage the situation sensitively, you could find brooding resentment. You may also have to manage the attitudes of other members of the team. For, even when the person directly involved has been satisfied, other people may still feel aggrieved on their behalf.

▌ The new recruit is known to existing employees. This may or may not be a good thing.

In any case, you will have to decide what you are going to tell your existing staff about their new colleague. Everyone will be curious, even if they pretend disinterest. Finding an appropriate way to introduce the new person may be a good idea, if it is possible to make mutually convenient arrangements. Again, you need to remember that, while the new recruit will also want to get to know their new colleagues quickly, they may have existing work commitments that prevent such a meeting. If they are under considerable pressure to finish tasks and assignments before they leave their current job, you may find that you are putting them under unreasonable pressure. Your new employee will want to please you as well as leave things in good order so you should make sure that any demands you make of them are reasonable.

If it is not possible to arrange an early meeting, you will have to consider carefully what to say about the new person to other members of the team. Anything and everything you say will influence other people's impressions. No matter how much they want to make up their own minds, the information you provide and that you omit to give will begin to create the picture. You will want to create a favourable impression about the new person so they have a good platform from which to start to build their working relationships with their new colleagues but if you 'over-egg' the new recruit's abilities and experience you could inadvertently set off a line of thought that goes in the wrong direction. Building up the new person as a superman or superwoman could lead the less confident members of your team to dread their arrival. Those feeling they have something to prove could start to prepare the ground for competition. Did you really want either of these to occur?

A balance is needed between giving out too much and being secretive. As only you know how your existing team is likely to react, you will be able to gauge how much information to give to whom, when to give it and what impression you want to generate. Providing factual and non-emotive information is probably the safest course of action, if it is not possible to find ways of facilitating an early meeting.

INTRODUCING, INDUCTING AND INCULCATING

The new recruit's first day will arrive soon enough. Will you have had sufficient time to plan it? There is plenty of evidence to show that getting the first few weeks right influences how well the person will perform their new job and whether they will stay beyond the first few months. You can do a lot to make sure this period is a positive experience for the new recruit, their new colleagues and for you, as the manager of all of them.

The preparation needs to have three components:

▌ induction – settling the person into the job and workplace;

▌ acceptance into the team – helping the person become a full and productive colleague;

▌ initial training – filling any skill gaps or areas of needed knowledge.

Induction

A typical induction programme has several stages that last for the first four to six weeks a person is in post. The first day tends to be filled with:

I showing the person around the workplace and sorting out basic essentials such as identity cards, parking permits, passwords;

I explaining safety and fire procedures;

I introducing key individuals, if it has not been possible to arrange pre-appointment meetings;

I providing the necessary equipment and explaining simple things such as how to obtain stationery;

I completing any paperwork outstanding from the appointment.

The rest of the first week is often spent meeting other important people and running through the main components of the job. The new starter will have a lot of information to absorb so will appreciate anything you do to make it easier for them to remember critical tasks and routines. These important *aides-mémoire* can include checklists, manuals setting out processes and procedures, and handbooks. They need not be complicated or comprehensive. Sometimes, a simple list is sufficient to reassure the individual that they do not have to rely on their memory alone.

Acceptance into the team

Absorbing a new person in to an existing team will require everyone to make adjustments and accommodations. The focus is usually on the new person and traditional induction programmes are designed to help them learn about the job and their new organization. They are also intended to help them to fit into the team as they learn the ropes and attain an appreciation of the team's culture and social mores.

Most people, however, start a new job with the wish to contribute from their own experience and make a difference. Unless it is their first job, the new starter will probably have views they will want to share. Teams with open minds will welcome this, recognizing a new person's fresh eyes and different experiences will add value to working practices. Closed teams will want the new person to accept the existing ways without question. They will not want to hear what the new person has to offer. In these cases, expressions such as 'In my last job, we did…' and 'When I was with…' are greeted with raised eyebrows and shrugs. The new person, wanting to make a favourable impression, will understand the signs and learn to keep quiet. If they do not, they will risk being ostracized or rejected by the team – the last thing you want. If you see evidence of this type of reaction, you will need to manage the situation. If you have prepared the ground, it should not arise.

Another way of helping the new person be accepted into the team quickly is to ask an existing member of staff to act as a buddy. The purpose of this is to do more than simply show the new starter around the workplace and introduce them to the other members of the team. The buddy's key function is to help the new person understand the team's culture. A team's culture can be seen at three levels:

1. Behaviour – the way we do things around here. Examples include making sure that coffee cups are not left unwashed in the kitchen, that desks are cleared at the end of the day, or everyone has photos or other personal objects around the workspace.

2. Common attitudes – how we approach our work. Examples include being rude about the Finance Department, not putting up with bad language, or teasing the receptionist about his addiction to his favourite TV soap.

3. Shared values – the standards we all ascribe to but do not often discuss. Examples include always being polite to customers, expecting everyone to take their turn in providing cover for the reception desk over lunchtime and providing support to anyone having a hard time.

Levels 1 and 2 influence behaviour but unless the new person knows what the shared values and common attitude are, they will not be able to appreciate how these matters influence what they do. These vital aspects are not very often included on an induction checklist. A buddy, however, can explain what they are and what they mean in practice in an informal and supportive way.

Initial training

The interview, if it has been well designed and conducted thoroughly, is probably the most rigorous assessment an employee will receive during the course of their employment. Their history, experience and abilities will have been examined in some detail against the criteria needed for effective performance of the job. Conclusions will have been drawn about their strengths and any perceived weaknesses identified. It is extremely unlikely that a perfect fit between the person and the criteria will have been achieved so it is probable that there will be some areas where training or development will enhance the individual's ability to do their new job.

It makes sense, therefore, to make use of this assessment to design an initial training and development programme. There is no reason why the individual should not be involved in this process as they will have ideas about which aspects of their new job are most unfamiliar. They too will have been carrying out their own assessment throughout the selection process. They will have considered their own abilities and experience:

▌ When deciding to apply for the job in the first place, they will have considered whether they match the requirements as outlined in the advertisement and any recruitment literature you might have sent out.

▌ In completing the application form or drawing up their CV, they will have had to think about how best to present their portfolio of experience and abilities in a way that would make them attractive to you. This would have involved working out how best to ensure that any gaps did not detract from their application.

▌ When preparing for the interview, they would have thought about the likely questions and considered what answers to give to present themselves in the best light.

▌ There is always a delay between the interview and the offer of employment. During this period, the candidate will have had the chance to go over what happened. They will have identified areas where they could have done better during the interview with you. They may have found that some aspects of the job were more important than they previously appreciated.

In sum, the person appointed to the job will probably have increased their insight into their own strengths and weaknesses as a result of preparing their application and thus will have gained a better understanding of their own development needs. It makes absolute sense to capitalize on this insight and combine the individual's perception with yours to help form their development plan.

If you have made use of the assessment matrix, as suggested in Chapter 5, this can be used as a source of information to inform the training plan, as it will summarize your perception of the individual's potential and development needs. Figure 6.1 shows what such a document might look like.

As the first days become the first weeks, the new recruit will gradually take on more. The incremental approach will mean that you have not dumped everything on them in one go. Building up gradually is a far better way of helping the new person learn the routines and take on responsibilities. Moreover, a staged approach enables you to ensure that each task is properly learnt and consolidated. Thus if progress in one area is slower than expected you can provide extra training and support.

Post – Customer Supporter			Candidate..		
			Source of evidence		
Abilities	**CV**	**Ref 1**	**Ref 2**	**Test**	**Interview**
Customer service skills	Experience of shop work	Dealt with angry customer	X	Prompt and accurate response to e-mails	Identified correctly the main components of good customer service
Communication and interpersonal skills	Well-presented CV and clear letter	Good customer relations skills	Experience of working in a team	Built rapport with tester	Expressed self clearly and with confidence. Answered questions concisely. Came across as friendly person
Organizational skills	Responsible for a small project	X	Completed project on time and to budget	Approached task in a methodical manner	X
Attainments					
Achieved formal qualifications at post-16 level	HND in business studies	X	X	X	X
Conducted customer surveys and investigations	Carried out limited survey to find out which aspects of the service were most valued by customers	X	Pleased with results of survey and way it had been approached	Identified the need to carry out further investigations and not to take problems at face value	Outlined stages needed to carry out an investigation and when making recommendations
Achievements					
Experience of customer service and complaints handling	Yes	Good standard of service	Comments on project	X	Dealt with individual customers but has not assessed where improvements could be made apart from small survey
Use of common office IT applications to an advanced level	Microsoft (learnt as part of course)	X	X	Used PC adequately	Identified need for further development especially databases
Introduced new ways of working	Acted on results of survey	X	Pleased with results	X	Has some good ideas but may need help to gain greater appreciation of why people resist change

Figure 6.1 Completed assessment matrix

Aptitude					
Strong team worker	Part of customer service team in department store	Comments on team relations	X	Rapport with tester	Identified key features of team working
Able to challenge others tactfully and influence their approaches	X	X	X	X	Responded to interviewer's challenge without becoming defensive and was able to stand their ground
Training needs				Survey techniques; Dealing with resistance; Use of databases	

Figure 6.1   Completed assessment matrix (cont.)

This initial training can be done in a staged way:

Stage 1   Show the new person how to carry out the basic routines of the job. This will include the components that form the core of the job and occur most often. You may ask a colleague or colleagues to carry out this training. Sitting by Nellie or Fred is the most commonly used approach for on-the-job training. One of the main worries about using this technique is that Nellie or Fred may teach bad practice. You can avoid this by making sure the person chosen to act as the on-the-job trainer or coach is an effective performer. Nevertheless, sometimes the best performer is not a good trainer so you may need to provide some training in how to help other people learn.

Stage 2   The number of tasks the new person is asked to carry out is increased and expanded as the person becomes more confident and capable. Their learning can be supported by the provision of feedback and coaching in areas where additional attention is needed. The expansion of the range of tasks and their degree of difficulty can be controlled so they match the individual's progress along the learning curve. There is no point in over-stretching or overloading the new person at this stage as the only effect would be to damage their self-confidence.

Stage 3   This stage is achieved when the new person is consolidated as an effective and accepted member of the team. By this time, they will have taken on the full range of their duties and will be able to perform at an acceptable, albeit basic level. This end-point provides the springboard for the individual's progression into a fully competent performer. It can take several months, depending on the complexity of the job, for this stage to be attained.

During the initial training phase, you will have witnessed the new recruit move along the competency trajectory:

> *ability*   *route*

> **unconscious incompetence** – when the individual is in the state of not knowing what they do not know or cannot do;

> **conscious incompetence** – when the individual becomes aware of weaknesses in their performance;

> **conscious competence** – when the individual is able to perform new tasks or use new knowledge but needs to rely on *aides-mémoire* or refer to others;

> **unconscious competence** – when the individual can do the task or apply their knowledge without having to think about it.

Making use of an initial training and development plan, based on the assessment carried out at the interview and drawn up to enable the new starter to take on the full range of duties in an incremental manner, will provide a solid basis for the first review of their performance in the job.

Performance review

This review, sometimes called appraisal, is used by some organizations as the basis for deciding pay. There are a number of different approaches available to help you carry out this review. The choice of which approach to use will depend on the nature of your organization and, to a certain extent, the type of occupations employed. Some organizations, particularly those operating in sales and target-driven environments, find that performance-related pay is most effective as it provides the rewards sought by employees and reinforces the behaviours required. However, to ensure equity, some clear measures are needed so the allocation of increases in pay is done in a fair and transparent manner. The use of the key objectives taken from the job description can provide these measures.

Other organizations review competency as the basis for performance appraisal and decisions relating to pay. Again, clear and explicit criteria are needed. The person specification, any additional selection criteria and the initial training plan can be used to inform this assessment. They can also be used to inform the development plan for the next period and to enable the new starter to increase their contribution to the organization.

This systematic approach will also help both you and the new starter gain a more detailed understanding of the role requirements. It will also help you develop a close and open working relationship. One of the reasons why it is hard to discuss performance is because it is not always easy to work out where to start. One benefit of having a documented, structured approach is that it provides a starting point. It can also provide a degree of detachment.

The review of performance should also be ongoing, so any problems can be addressed at their very early stages before they become established and deep-seated. This periodic review will then enable both the individual and the manager to stand back. There is always a danger of being stuck on specifics but the use of the relevant criteria taken from the person specification will give you and the job holder a framework from which to see performance of the job in the round. This detached view enables you to identify further development needs and will reveal components of the job that may be impeding performance, thus identifying areas where the job rather than person needs to change.

PROBATIONARY PERIOD

The use of a formal probationary period can complement an initial training and development plan, but using a probationary period, especially if it is a contractual requirement, without a training and development plan is not a good idea.

Probation is not used as widely or as well as it might. One reason for the approach's fall from favour is due to the changes in employment law. At one time, an employee gained the right to claim wrongful or unfair dismissal after only six months in a job. It was therefore essential for employers to be able to demonstrate that reasonable actions had been taken to help the individual learn how to do the job and become effective in it. The length of time after which an employee now gains those rights is one year. This has reduced some of the pressure as an employer has a longer period in which to assess a new starter and dismiss them if the selection decision proves to have been a bad one.

Nevertheless, there is always some cost involved in sacking people, not least the expense of having to repeat the selection process. There is also the loss of face with the rest of the team and within the organization. The team's expectations of having an effective new colleague will be have been dashed, their faith in your ability to make good decisions will have been damaged and they probably will have had to cope with the consequences of having a poor performer in their midst. Moreover, having to deal with poor performance is not an easy or pleasant task for you to have to undertake. The poor appointment may not be caused by your decision-making abilities.

You may have found yourself in an unfortunate position at the end of the interview. If you were under pressure to appoint but your assessment of the best candidate revealed some worrying gaps, you may have concluded that the best way forward would be to appoint the person for a probationary period, with a clearly defined training plan designed to rectify the gaps. Making the appointment conditional in this way means that the person's contract of employment will not be confirmed until the conditions set out have been attained or the probationary period has been completed satisfactorily. Examples of the sorts of conditions that can be agreed include:

▌ Attaining a qualification or completion of a course of study or training. For example, you might offer employment to a final year student subject to them passing their degree course. The individual may be allowed to start work if there is a time lag between sitting the exams and receiving the results.

▌ Achieving a proficiency certificate. Examples can include passing a driving test if the job requires some driving at work or obtaining a proficiency certificate to demonstrate competence in a particular aspect of the job, such as a welding or gas-fitting certificate.

▌ Developing a specific skill or achieving an all-round level of competency. As with the assessments made during the selection process, these should be assessed if you intend to make any judgements about levels of ability against job-relevant criteria, preferably those taken from the job description and person specification. Examples can include the ability to create documents to the standard required or to complete all aspects of a task without having to seek assistance.

Whatever criteria you set down for achievement in the probationary period, you need to make sure that the objectives are:

▌ Specific

▌ Measurable

▌ Achievable

▌ Reasonable

▌ Time limited.

You also need to be clear, for your own as well as the new starter's benefit, about how and when progress is to be assessed. Even though the individual, at this stage, has no recourse to law, unless he or she is the subject of sexual, racist or other similar forms of discrimination, you will want to make sure you are using best practice.

You do this by:

▌ agreeing the initial training and development plan, as outlined above;

▌ making use of it during the probationary period;

▌ carrying out regular appraisals of performance.

These do not have to be formal or elaborate affairs. In fact, holding short discussions at frequent intervals may be a more effective way of monitoring progress and dealing with any concerns either of you may have in the early stages. If you are busy and your diary is full, you need to plan these regular discussions to make sure they actually happen. Sadly, this is one aspect of managerial work that tends to be squeezed out of an over-packed day. You should try to make sure the opposite happens, particularly in the early months. Not only are you making sure the new recruit is learning the ropes, you are establishing the working relationship between you and the new member of your team. The quality of the relationship is known to be one of the reasons why people look for other jobs. If you want to hang on to the staff you have worked so hard to recruit, you need to make sure that the relationship between you is of the highest quality.

How to assess progress

The following schedule contains suggestions about how you can engage in a structured review of progress without making it a rigid process. This approach can be used for those appointed for a probationary period, on a contract with conditions, or, in fact, for any new recruit. You will need flexibility to accommodate the demands on your time and to take account of the individual's speed of learning. This will differ from individual to individual and will vary for any one person depending on the task, their overall aptitude and the complexity of the work they are learning to do. Please do not compromise, though, on your commitment to monitoring progress and supporting development. Remember this is the employment equivalent to putting down the foundations for a new building. If they are well constructed the foundations will make the rest of the building work easy and the end-product durable.

End of Week One

Check that:

▌ introductions have been made;

▌ essential equipment has been supplied;

▌ the new person knows their way around their immediate workplace and the other places they need to go to regularly;

▌ information about employment policies and procedures has been given and is understood;

▌ the job's position in the organization has been explained;

▌ the main components of the work have been outlined and any essential initial training given.

End of Month One

▌ Check understanding of the role and its main purpose.

▌ Assess, jointly, progress against the main components of the job (ie the key objectives) and initial training and development plan.

The purpose of this meeting is to identify any areas where additional training is required and to provide encouragement.

End of Month Two

▌ Focus on each key component of the job.

▌ Review extent of progress against the training and development plan and criteria.

▌ Provide coaching and identify next stages of development.

End of Month Three

This is the time for a more structured review. The main tools for carrying this out are the job description and person specification. The purpose of the meeting will be to make sure that the new person understands the scope and demands of the job and can see where the development plan is taking them.

The meeting can also provide the opportunity for you to explore the quality of the growing working relationships and to check that the new person is being assimilated into the team. You can find out from them how they see their progress and listen to any concerns they have. They will probably have some ideas about what they would like to do next to continue with their learning and increase their contribution to the team.

During the meeting, you will be able to provide structured feedback, giving praise and encouragement, as well as agreeing what action is needed so the person can take on the full range of the job's responsibilities and continue their development.

End of Month Four

If the new recruit is progressing well, this review need only be informal. By now, the new person should no longer be seen as new. If everything is going to plan they should have taken on the full range of duties and be seen by their colleagues as a full part of the team.

The review is important, however, as it provides the opportunity to praise and give encouragement. You may identify the need for more training to stretch the person's abilities further but, by now, it should be 'steady as you go'. However, if there are signs that indicate progress is not satisfactory, now is the time to act. There may be concerns over working relationships or the individual's level of ability in some or all aspects of the work. You will need to give the person feedback. You also need to find out from the individual how they feel things are going.

The feedback should be specific so the individual understands exactly where your concerns lie and recognizes what needs to be done to improve or alter their performance. It may be that you will need to organize extra training if they are not grasping one area of work, coaching if the needs are more general or support if they feel they are struggling generally. If their difficulty concerns the quality of the working relationships, you may need to have discussions with other members of the team. Remember that the creation of good working relationships requires all parties to cooperate, as it is possible that the problems are not totally of the new starter's making.

End of Month Five

Assuming everything is going well, the purpose of this review will be to provide reinforcement and identify where further development or support is needed. This discussion will be the lead-in to the formal six-month review.

If progress is not satisfactory, it will be essential that you instigate formal procedural measures. These can include issuing warnings, which may be informal or formal, depending on severity of the problem. The aim of the warning is to make it clear where improvement or change in behaviour is required. There should be no scope for misunderstandings caused by ambiguity. The warning should also outline the action the individual is expected to take and describe the additional support and assistance that will be provided by the employer. This could involve you directly or be provided by other people.

End of Month Six

If matters are not going well you will need to begin the more formal procedures that will lead to dismissal. This is never a step to take lightly but, sadly, it is better for everyone to bring the contract to its end rather than try to fix something that is beyond repair.

Hopefully, this will not be the case. All the careful actions you have taken in the lead-up to the appointment and during the induction phase will have been designed to ensure that your decisions were based on the needs of the job. Your systematic and thorough assessment of the person's abilities throughout the selection process will have ensured that your final choice was based on good quality information. This position will have also have been achieved by the new recruit. There should be no surprises for either of you as you get to know each other better and the individual understands their new job.

In this situation, carrying out a review at the end of six months may seem unnecessary. However, it will give you and your new team member the chance to reflect on the whole period and, after all, this is the end of the first phase of their employment in your organization. If matters have gone well and the individual has made the sort of progress you had hoped for, together you can take stock of what has worked and discuss what will follow.

The aim will be to provide reward and consolidate their performance. It will be the first real chance for you to give them formal feedback on what they have achieved. If possible, the person should be encouraged to identify for themselves their achievements, as this will contribute to their sense of self-worth. Taking this approach will contribute to the building of trust and understanding between you so that if there are problems in future, the individual will feel able to discuss them with you early. It will also mean that you will be able to broach difficulties with the individual before they become problems, thus enabling you to work out what needs to be done to remedy the situation.

FINAL THOUGHTS

The ultimate aim of the recruitment, selection and initial development process is to equip you with a team of people able and willing to contribute to the achievement of your collective objectives and shared ambitions. Whether you are in a large or tiny organization, it is only possible to achieve these ends if you have a good understanding of what the achievement of these objectives and ambitions will mean in practice. The definition of the skills and abilities required to carry out the actions needed to achieve these objectives and ambitions becomes the cornerstone of the process.

The interview contributes to the process by providing you with a mechanism for assessing whether the candidates have the attributes and skills needed to do the job. It also allows you to judge whether you will be able to form a productive relationship and how well each will fit with the existing team. The interview contains all the weaknesses of human judgement, but these can be reduced if the assessment is carried out against predetermined and explicit criteria, by several interviewers. Once the best candidate has been identified and the offer of employment accepted, your key task is to ensure that the person settles in and learns their job quickly.

The following exercise is therefore designed to help you reflect on the actions you need to take after you have offered the job to the candidate you have selected as the best person for the job.

EXERCISE

Using a real example (eg a job that has recently been filled or one you are about to fill):

▎ Develop an induction checklist to cover the first six months.

▎ Identify the key components of the initial training and development plan the new starter will need to follow so they can take on their duties incrementally.

▎ Identify someone within the team to act as an on-the-job trainer and/or someone willing and able to act as a buddy.

▎ Consider what training needs these people may have.

▎ Think about how to monitor the new starter's progress and identify critical stages when their development can be assessed.

7

Good practice checklist

The final chapter is to provide you with a list of the features that make up good practice. Even though the interview is known to be a poor predictor of performance, taking it out of the recruitment and selection process is not possible. The interview is the centre stone and without it the process would collapse. Similarly, without the beginning and the end, the centre stone would float in mid-air with no context or grounding.

The following checklist therefore places the interview in the wider context. It outlines what you need to do in the lead-up to the interview. It also highlights the steps needed to ensure that it produces the results you want from it – identifying which candidate will be the best performer in the job you are in the process of filling.

1. Analyse the job, identifying its main purpose and key accountabilities.

2. Specify the achievements, abilities, attainments and attitudes the job holder will need to be effective.

3. Design the whole recruitment and selection process from start to end.

4. Advertise the vacancy in media where potential applicants are most likely to see it.

5. Provide additional information so potential applicants have a good understanding of the job and what you are looking for so you do not receive futile applications.

6. Short-list using the job requirements and person specification as criteria.

7. Design a selection process that will test all the essential criteria.

8. Identify who else needs to be involved.

9. Ensure everyone to be involved understands the demands of the job, the selection criteria and their role in the process.

10. Invite the candidates, making sure they have good quality information about what is going to happen to them, where and when.

11. Clarify the components of the employment contract that are open to negotiation.

12. Build the structure of the interview.

13. Prepare the other interviewers and if necessary ensure they receive training.

14. Plan questions for each stage of the interview.

15. Anticipate the questions the candidates are likely to ask and make sure you have the information they may need to hand.

16. Enjoy the experience. Good luck!

Index